THE BUSINESS OF FLIPPING HOMES

Short-Term Real Estate Investing for Long-Term Wealth

WILLIAM BRONCHICK AND ROBERT DAHLSTROM

BenBella Books, Inc.
Dallas, TX

BenBella Books, Inc.
10440 N. Central Expressway, Suite 800
Dallas, TX 75231
www.benbellabooks.com
Send feedback to feedback@benbellabooks.com

Printed in the United States of America
10 9 8 7 6 5 4 3 2 1

978-1-942952-77-0 (print)
978-1-942952-78-7 (e-book)

Library of Congress Cataloging-in-Publication Data is available upon request.
LCCN: 2016037696 (print)
LCCN: 2016051587 (electronic)

Editing by Brian Nicol
Copyediting by Miki Alexandra Caputo
Proofreading by Sarah Vostok and Brittney Martinez
Indexing by Jigsaw Information
Text design by Aaron Edmiston
Text composition by PerfecType
Front cover design by Ty Nowicki
Full cover design by Sarah Dombrowsky
Printed by Lake Book Manufacturing

Distributed by Perseus Distribution
www.perseusdistribution.com

To place orders through Perseus Distribution:
Tel: (800) 343-4499
Fax: (800) 351-5073
E-mail: orderentry@perseusbooks.com

**Special discounts for bulk sales (minimum of 25 copies) are available.
Please contact Aida Herrera at aida@benbellabooks.com.**

Praise for *The Business of Flipping Homes*

"A must-read for anyone who wants to learn how to generate serious wealth in the new economy."
—**Dr. Albert Lowry, PhD,** *New York Times* **bestselling author**

"People who tune in to my radio show, or read my books and blog, often ask me how they can create multiple streams of income, one of my five secrets to a happy and successful retirement. Done right, investing in buying and selling real estate can be a tremendously effective way to add an additional source of income to your portfolio. In *The Business of Flipping Homes*, William Bronchick and Robert Dahlstrom provide you with all you need to know to move properties quickly, legally, and ethically. If you're looking for a way to diversify through real estate, I'm a fan of their work, and this book."
—**Wes Moss, host of Money Matters and author of *You Can Retire Sooner Than You Think: The 5 Money Secrets of the Happiest Retirees***

This book is dedicated to the motivated individuals who want to use real-estate investing as a means to take back their financial future.

CONTENTS

PART III: GETTING TO WORK

PART IV: MINDING YOUR BUSINESS

INTRODUCTION

There's more to flipping than redoing a kitchen or staging a property. The two of us, William Bronchick and Robert Dahlstrom, have more than forty years' combined experience buying and selling investment properties. Credited with introducing the term *flipping* into the common vernacular, our best-selling *Flipping Properties* (2001 and 2007) sold a quarter of a million units and started a revolution. Syndicated real-estate columnist Robert Bruss said this about the book: "Cannot be recommended too highly . . . on my scale of one to 10 this book rates an off-the-chart 12!"[1] We have worked with more than a thousand clients and have helped tens of thousands learn the art and science of real-estate investing. We have taken these experiences and written the new definitive book on flipping—the one you are reading right now.

The Business of Flipping Homes shows readers how to flip properties quickly, legally, and ethically. It goes beyond other attempts to write about flipping houses by not only covering the basics but also the many ways to deal with inevitable challenges. Every deal is different, yet each investor must have a clear business strategy. We have outlined a systematic approach and shared our specific knowledge on how to purchase properties and then sell them for a profit. We delve into the business side—either

---

1. Robert J. Bruss, "Book Has Tips on Flipping Property," *Naples Daily News* (Tribune Media Services), October 14, 2001.

as a career or simply as a part-time venture—of this particular type of real-estate investment and cut through the murky waters of confusing information to give you an A to Z guide to flipping.

Real estate has arguably created more millionaires in the US than any other profession. In a 2014 *Bloomberg* article, a survey conducted by Morgan Stanley reported that "about 77 percent of investors with at least $1 million in assets own real estate."[2] One of the few certainties in real estate is that the market will fluctuate. As seasoned investors, we have learned to be successful in all types of markets, up or down, hot or cold.

The principles we present apply to every market and every city, regardless of current economic trends, giving you practical wisdom to limit risks and make sound investment choices. We realize there is renewed interested in flipping, fueled by how-to television shows, highly promoted seminars, and individuals' desires to find new career paths and strike out on their own.

In these pages, we show both new and seasoned investors alike the step-by-step approach to successfully flipping houses. We fill in many gaps other books do not address and flatten the learning curve in a business that can appear deceptively simple. The book begins by explaining what flipping is—and what it is not. We demonstrate how to find, renovate, and sell properties using tested methods from our own personal experiences. Some of the covered subjects include time lines, working with real-estate brokers, understanding the paperwork, analyzing the numbers, utilizing technology, and finding the money to acquire properties. This book explains how to avoid many of the pitfalls and potential issues that not only add cost but could come back to haunt you later. Lastly, we address long-term planning, including how to find and work with partners, structure a business, and harness your talents, resources, and aspirations in realistic ways. Enjoy the book and find out if flipping is the business for you.

---

2. Margaret Collins and David M. Levitt, "Millionaires See Real Estate as Top Investment for 2014," *Bloomberg*, February 6, 2014, http://bloomberg.com/news/articles/2014-02-06/millionaires-see-real -estate-as-top-investment-for-2014.

PART I

Getting It Going

CHAPTER 1

Flipping Explained

Real estate, like any other commodity, is bought and sold every day. Real-estate brokers (we'll use the terms *agents* and *brokers* interchangeably throughout this book) help facilitate a sale by finding and putting together willing buyers and sellers. They then earn some portion of a commission between 3 and 6 percent of the sales price for making the deal happen. Selling real estate is a lucrative field for many agents and brokers. Still, there are better ways for a real-estate entrepreneur to make a living.

Most small-time real-estate investors purchase single-family homes or condos for rental. And of course there are also developers and people who specialize in commercial projects and long-term ventures. Someone who owns only one rental property, someone who is part of a real-estate investment trust (REIT), and someone who owns many large buildings are all classified as investors—the spectrum is broad.

A flipper is yet another type of investor. Investors who flip houses buy real estate with the intention of immediately reselling for profit. It's that simple. Unlike investing in the stock market, investing in real estate short-term places much control in the investor's hands. A flipper is not just speculating about future trends in the housing market but is also buying at a discount (i.e., instant equity) and adding value by preparing the property for a retail sale (i.e., additional profit potential).

If a deal is marginal (with not much profit in it) and the investor adds no value to the property, the flipper's profit is commensurate to that of a real-estate broker—a single-digit percentage. Unlike an agent, however, the flipper may have only a few hours of time tied up in the deal. Furthermore, the flipper's upside profit potential is much higher than an agent's commission because an occasional bargain purchase can bring a tremendous return. The flipper does not need a license to practice, although there are legal guidelines to follow. The flipper benefits from low overhead and flexible work hours and doesn't have to drive a Mercedes to be taken seriously (although a successful flipper can certainly afford one!).

Successful flippers work to become experts and implement a solid business plan. They can leverage existing knowledge and work experience as they begin flipping—either as a part-time business or full-time venture. Many Americans will buy and sell at least one home in their lifetimes, and most understand the basic principles of buying and selling homes (with help from reality television shows and books such as our best-selling *Flipping Properties*). In order to be successful, the flipper must be creative in finding, purchasing, and selling properties. Not only that, being flexible in approaching deals will lead to wholesalers and other investors who are worth working with.

DIFFERENT TYPES OF FLIPPERS

There are two primary types of flippers:

- The wholesaler
- The retailer

Both are looking for essentially the same thing—a distressed property with upside potential—although their back-end resale strategies are different.

What is a distressed property? It's one that creates emotional or financial distress for its owner. Sometimes the owner lives in the home, but often he or she resides out of state and may be an institutional seller or trustee. Distress may be caused by financial problems, difficult tenants, or the fact that the property is in need of repair. Whatever the cause, the owner is motivated to sell the property quickly at a discounted price.

The Wholesaler

Wholesaler is the commonly used name for what we used to call a dealer. Wholesalers locate and secure deals for other investors. They find a bargain property and sign a binding purchase contract with the owner. Then they close on the property and sell it outright, or just sell their contract to another investor. Wholesalers typically put up earnest money to secure the deal, so they do assume some risk.

Wholesalers often resell the property in its "as is" condition to another investor, who will then fix up the property and rent or resell it to an owner-occupant. Wholesalers can sometimes increase their profits by cleaning up their properties themselves. In fact, a simple cleanup job may increase the wholesaler's profit by several thousand dollars. While investors should be able to see past the mess, a spruced-up property is psychologically more appealing to any buyer, even an experienced one. The wholesaler does not need to perform significant repairs or upgrades but simply cleans up the appearance of the property by removing garbage, cleaning to broom-clean condition, and cutting the lawn. This type of labor can be hired out for a few hundred dollars. There are companies that specialize in eviction cleanups and junk removal. Over time, the process will become as simple as a phone call.

Wholesalers can flip as many deals as they can find. On a full-time basis, a wholesaler can make well over $10,000 a month without ever fixing a property or dealing with a tenant. Some wholesalers have impressive operations with full-time staffs and specialized techniques for consistently finding and reselling many deals a month. These investors send out e-mails to their database of potential buyers when they secure a deal and typically sell their deal within a matter of days or even hours. Even on a part-time basis, a wholesaler could easily make an extra $5,000 a month flipping a property or two. (We'll cover wholesaling in much more detail in chapter 9.)

The Retailer

Retailers usually buy a property from a wholesaler or with the assistance of a real-estate broker or "bird dog." Over time, many retailers cut out the middle man, but others continue to pay finder's fees and focus on the rehab and sales processes. The retailer's goal is to fix up the property and sell it for full retail price to an owner-occupant (i.e., a retail sale). Compared to other flippers, the retailer puts up the most money, takes the most risk, and stands to make the largest profit on each deal. Yet it may take the retailer months to realize a profit.

Before someone can become a successful retailer, that person must have a working knowledge of how to renovate a house, particularly the costs involved in doing so. A good wholesaler should also have a rough idea of the cost of repairs in order to buy properties at the right price and resell them to the retailer. Put simply, overpaying for a property is the biggest mistake a wholesaler or retailer can make.

It may make sense for the new investor to work with a more experienced partner. This arrangement allows the new investor to share the workload and the risk. Equally important, a knowledgeable partner can help determine the property's existing and after-repaired value (ARV) more accurately than a beginning investor. Using an experienced contractor will help new investors avoid underestimating the costs of improvements and getting in over their heads. Veteran investors should know what to fix and what not to fix (based on the expected return) and be knowledgeable about the market and the neighborhood. They should also have the resources to get the work done quickly and at a fair price.

Retailers are limited by their financial resources and the number of properties they can rehab at once. Each deal is unique and should be evaluated separately. In fact, it can be sound business strategy to sometimes approach a deal as a wholesaler (in and out quickly) and other times as a retailer (invest time and money for a bigger payoff later). As you get into the flipping business, you will more confidently know when to wear which hat.

EXIT STRATEGY

Every investor should have a means to sell properties quickly. Don't enter into a real-estate transaction without knowing your exit strategy. Consider these questions:

- Are you going to flip the property to another investor, or are you going to fix it up and sell it retail?
- How much money or labor are you going to put into the property?
- How long do you expect to hold it? How long do you think it will take to sell?
- Can you carry the property for additional months? Can you afford to hold it as a rental property?

These questions must be considered before you make an offer to purchase a property.

When you're still getting started, you can sell your first few deals to investors to generate working capital. Assuming a good purchase price, expect to make between $2,000 and $3,000 on your first few wholesales. Once you have located a potential deal and secured it with a purchase contract, you can sell your deal to another investor for a quick profit.

The existing value of any property you purchase or wholesale is important, and the ARV is the most critical valuation you will need to make.

Let's say you find a property worth about $200,000 in its current condition. It requires $25,000 to renovate the property. In its best condition, the property is worth $250,000. You negotiate a purchase price of $160,000 and sign a purchase contract with the owner. You find another investor who is willing to pay $165,000 for the property and do the necessary repairs. Thus, you can sell your deal to another investor and walk away with a $5,000 profit using no money of your own. The other investor will make a nice profit as well. Assuming renovation costs $25,000 and sales and incidental cost about $25,000, the other investor's profit would be roughly $60,000. Keep in mind that this $60,000 is gross profit, not net profit.

Join an investment group. A real-estate investors' club in your area is an excellent place to meet retailers, wholesalers, and other related contacts. A complete list of local groups can be found at CREOnline.com. If there are no clubs in your area, consider forming one yourself. You can find other local investors by networking with lenders, stopping by projects in nearby neighborhoods, and by checking the local multiple-listing service. Potential flip properties stand out if they are vacant, newly renovated, and, if done correctly, staged. In addition, ask some of the local real-estate agents and landlords or apartment associations for names of investors in your community. Lastly, keep an eye out for special events sponsored by "flipping gurus." These events are excellent places to meet new investors. Make sure to thoroughly investigate the sponsors before you sign on; everyone has an agenda, of course.

In this example, this property was purchased significantly below market value. This discount may vary widely, depending on the property, the neighborhood, the trends in your local real-estate market, and how many repairs the property needs. Based on the ARV of $275,000, your purchase price plus repairs ($190,000) is about 70 percent of ARV. (We will discuss a precise approach to making offers later in chapter 7.)

Keep in mind that the retailer stands to make more money than a wholesaler on most deals. But there should be enough room for everyone to profit.

FINDING BUYERS FOR YOUR WHOLESALE DEAL

If you have a property under contract, finding a retailer should be relatively easy. There are many ways to find that buyer/retailer. You can advertise on Craigslist.org and on real estate–specific websites such as Zillow .com or Redfin.com. Try a few different ads (see sample ads on page 234 in the appendix). Many websites will advertise your property for little or no cost. Log the responses you receive in order to track the effectiveness of the ads. More importantly, keep information about the people who call and the types of properties they like. These contacts will bolster your future buyers list. Don't spend too much time with inexperienced investors; they probably don't have the means to buy properties from you.

Qualify the callers by asking the following questions:

- Do you have your own cash to close, or will you borrow it?
- How many houses do you buy each year? In what areas?
- What type of discount do you usually look for on properties?
- How big a renovation can you handle?
- If I find a bargain, how quickly can you close?

SELLING PROPERTIES RETAIL

Most flippers eventually take on renovation projects and sell homes to owner-occupants. As we've pointed out, there is a large profit potential in taking a deal from start to finish. Assuming you've purchased a good property, completed the necessary repairs and updates, and priced it fairly, you should expect a quick sale. Yet not every property can be resold or flipped quickly. You may get stuck with a property for a few months, but this rarely happens if you do your homework. If you cannot get your property under contract to sell within thirty days, you probably made a mistake—either you paid too much, underestimated repairs, or picked the wrong neighborhood.

Because most properties are sold through the multiple-listing service and the largest pool of qualified buyers work through real-estate brokers, the odds of finding a qualified buyer quickly are greatest when the property is listed on the MLS. Yes, consumers have access to much of the same information as brokers, but for the foreseeable future brokers will continue to be the best way to go.

As your advocate when negotiating offers, your broker will make sure the contracts are in order and are executed according to plan. Brokers allow you to focus your efforts on finding more deals rather than waiting for buyers to show up at your property. We'll talk more about using brokers throughout these pages.

GETTING RID OF DIFFICULT PROPERTIES

Sometimes you may sign up a marginal deal and have a difficult time reselling it. Even though selling retail for quick cash was your initial goal, you can find other ways to make a profit. For example, if you have a property that needs a lot of work, you could partner with another investor. You can offer the property as your share of the partnership, while the second investor takes on the carrying cost, the materials, and the work. When you sell the property, you split the proceeds. It's possible you may have to take less than half the net profit to make the deal work. (In the chapters ahead, you'll learn lots of creative ways to move properties.)

MINIMIZE YOUR LOSS

Even seasoned pros occasionally purchase a "bad" house they are unable to sell for a reasonable profit. The problem may be a combination of paying too much, bad market timing, unforeseen repairs, or plain bad luck. In such cases, contingency plans include selling cheap and moving on to the next deal, providing owner-carry terms to the retail buyer, or holding on to the property as a rental.

Remember that when you make an offer for a property you plan to wholesale, you have to include enough room in the deal for your retail buyer to make a profit. You cannot sell a deal to another investor and make a profit if that investor cannot profit as well. If you seek too much profit and hold on to a property too long, you can lose out in the long run. When you are flipping properties, the goal is to move them fast—don't get greedy! You will learn how to make money in all types of markets. If you do your homework and go into every deal prepared, you will come out ahead.

WRAPPING IT UP

- A flipper buys property with the intent of a quick resale.
- There are two primary types of flippers: wholesalers and retailers.
- You may act as a wholesaler on some transactions and a retailer on others.

CHAPTER 2

The Basics of Real-Estate Transactions

Whether you are a novice or an experienced investor, you must have a working knowledge of the legal aspects of real-estate transactions. Yes, reading legal topics can be like watching paint dry, but it's critical that you understand the paperwork involved in real-estate deals. Your risk of making an expensive mistake or missing an opportunity increases tremendously when you lack knowledge of the basics. In this chapter we are going to discuss the nuts and bolts of the legal documents and processes that are essential to you, the flipper.

THE DEED

A deed is a written instrument used to convey ownership to property. Unlike a car title, deeds are created by the parties to the transaction, not issued by the county. The original deed is generally kept by the owner of the property but has very little significance once it has been recorded with the county. The original paper deed is not relevant for a future transfer of the property, since a new deed is created at that time.

Deeds differ by the type of guarantee or warranty they give. There are four different types of deeds: general warranty, special warranty, bargain and sale, and quitclaim.

General Warranty

The general warranty deed, also referred to simply as a warranty deed, is the most complete guarantee of title. The warranty deed promises that the grantor (seller) has full and complete title and forever warrants against any claims against the title. If anyone makes a claim to the property, no matter how old the claim is, the grantor of a warranty deed must fix the problem. If you are receiving a deed, you must insist on getting a general warranty deed. There are exceptions to this rule, but a general warranty deed is the best deed for the buyer. If a title company is insuring the transaction, it will probably insist on the seller executing a warranty deed. (Almost exclusively in California, the grant deed is used in lieu of a general warranty deed.)

FLIP TIP

What kinds of title claims are typical? Rarely does a person pop up and claim ownership over property because of a fraudulent deed in the past chain of title. Typically, the claim is a lien (such as a mortgage) that wasn't released in a previous transaction, or it may be an unrecorded easement (a right to go onto or through the property) across the property.

Special Warranty

The special warranty deed, on the other hand, warrants only that the grantor has acquired title and did nothing to impair it while he or she held title. Public officials, such as a sheriff, use a special warranty deed after a foreclosure sale, since they have no knowledge of what has transpired before their brief ownership of the property. As a seller, you would prefer to give a special warranty deed over a general warranty if the buyer will accept it.

Bargain and Sale

The bargain and sale deed has no express warranties but usually contains a statement of consideration (money or other value) paid and an implication that the grantor has some title or ownership in the property. A bargain and sale deed can have "covenants" (promises), which make it roughly the equivalent of a general warranty deed. This deed is commonly used with some variations in northeastern states such as New York and New Jersey in lieu of a general warranty deed.

Quitclaim

A quitclaim deed (not "quick-claim") contains no promises or warranties. The grantor simply gives up whatever claim he or she may or may not have. A quitclaim deed is commonly used to transfer an interest between spouses or to clear up a title defect. If the seller has good title, he or she can transfer the property with a quitclaim deed the same as with a warranty deed. However, the grantor makes no guarantee that title is good. As a buyer, of course, you would be accepting risk in taking a quitclaim deed without a warranty of title. (A state-by-state list of commonly used deeds can be found on page 235 in the appendix.)

FLIP TIP

Title insurance? Many people wonder what the purpose of title insurance is in a real-estate transaction. Well, if you were the buyer paying $500,000 for a property, would you take the warranty of title from the seller simply on faith and a handshake? Of course not. So you buy an insurance policy from a title company to insure against any claims that could arise. In most states, the buyer pays for the policy, and the insured under the policy is the buyer.

ELEMENTS OF THE DEED

A deed must contain certain elements to be considered a legal and valid transfer. When you execute a deed or pay someone else for a deed to real estate, make sure that the following elements are present.

Generally speaking, any instrument affecting an interest in real estate must be **in writing** to be enforceable. It does not necessarily need to be typed, but it may not be accepted for public recording if it is not legible.

The deed must state **the giver of the deed (grantor) and the receiver of the deed (grantee)**. The grantor's name must be spelled exactly as it appears on the deed that gave him title, even if that spelling is incorrect. In community-property states (i.e., Arizona, California, Idaho, Louisiana, Nevada, New Mexico, Texas, Washington, and Wisconsin), the law presumes that both spouses own all marital assets, regardless of how they are titled. Thus, you also need a separate quitclaim deed from the grantor's spouse, even if that person's name does not appear on the title. Note that in some non-community-property states, there are legal rights called "dower" and "courtesy," which also require a spouse's approval.

The grantee who takes title individually is described as being "in severalty." That sounds like it may be referring to several people, but it actually means "severed from all others." A limited liability company (LLC) or corporation will also take title in severalty, and it is common practice to mention what state the LLC or corporation was formed in (to assist future title searchers).

The actual words that describe the grantee on a deed determine exactly how title will be held. For example, if you say "A & B," then it is presumed that A and B share fifty-fifty ownership as tenants in common. A and B are not tenants in the sense that they are leasing the property, but the language "tenants in common" means they are co-owners, without a right of survivorship. This means if A dies, his share of the property will vest in his estate and his heirs, not in B.

If you say "A & B, as joint tenants," then each has a right of survivorship. Thus, if A dies, B gets A's share automatically (even if A's will directs otherwise). If you take title as "A & B, married couple," in most states this will create a joint tenancy. In some states, husband and wife can take title as "tenants by the entirety," which gives special protection from creditors who may have a judgment against A or B.

The deed must state that the grantor received **consideration** even though no actual money changed hands. You can insert the purchase price (required in some jurisdictions) or simply the words: "The grantor has received ten dollars in hand and other good and valuable consideration, the sufficiency of which is hereby acknowledged."

The **legal description** of the property must appear exactly as it does in the previous deed. It will usually read something like: "Lot 25, Block 21, Harris Subdivision, County of Barrington, State of Illinois." This designation comes from a plat map that was previously filed in the county records. If the description is more complicated than a simple lot and block or government survey description, simply photocopy the description from the previous deed and insert it into the new deed (or refer to it in an attached exhibit to the deed).

The **words of conveyance** spell out what type of deed is given. The conveyance usually reads something like, "The grantor hereby grants, conveys, and warrants" (warranty deed), or, "The grantor hereby remises, releases, and quitclaims" (quitclaim deed).

The **signature of the grantor** must be written exactly as his or her name appears on the previous transaction as grantee. If the grantor is not available for signature, an authorized agent or attorney-in-fact can sign on the grantor's behalf. This process is accomplished by a power of attorney that authorizes an agent to act for the grantor to sign a deed. The power of attorney should include a legal description of the property and should be recorded in county records with the deed that is signed by the agent. The agent does not sign the grantor's name, but rather signs his or her own name as "attorney-in-fact" for the grantor.

The deed should be acknowledged before a notary public. An **acknowledgment** is a declaration that the person signing is who he or she claims and is signing voluntarily. The notary signs the deed, affirming that the grantor appeared before him or her and either knows the person or was provided with sufficient proof of identity. Although acknowledgment is not required to make a deed valid, it is usually required for recording. The proper form of acknowledgment differs from state to state, so make certain your deed complies with your state's law.

Title does not pass until a deed is **delivered** to the grantee. Thus, a deed signed but held "in escrow" does not convey title until the escrow agent delivers the deed. Many people are under the mistaken impression

FLIP TIP

Have a notary on call. Sometimes you will buy a property with a seller signing a deed over a kitchen table. Because the signature of the seller must be notarized, you need to have a notary on call. Virtually every city has a notary with a cell phone who will show up on thirty minutes' notice. See 123notary.com.

that title passes when a deed is recorded. While recording a deed is common practice, it is not required to convey title to real estate.

Once in a while, a seller may place a **deed restriction** that prevents the buyer from reselling within a certain time period. This restriction is a covenant in the deed, which cannot be circumvented because no title company will insure it. You may find this in new subdivisions, particularly in condominium complexes where the developer is trying to prohibit flippers. Also, Fannie Mae and Freddie Mac (two quasi-governmental agencies that own or insure about 50 percent of all mortgages) often place resale deed restrictions on properties they sell as owner of the foreclosed property. These deed restrictions usually prevent you from reselling a property within ninety days for more than 25 percent markup. If you are going to fix and flip the property to a retail buyer, it may take as long as ninety days anyway from acquisition to resale, so at most it will hold you up a few weeks. If you are going to wholesale the property to another investor, then you won't likely mark up the price anywhere near 25 percent and so won't have to worry about the restriction.

RECORDING DOCUMENTS

The recording system gives constructive notice to the public of the transfer of an interest in property. Recording simply involves bringing the original document to the local county courthouse or county clerk's office. In many counties, there are now online filing options as well (if not, and you record a lot of documents in your business, try Simplifile.com). The original document is scanned into the computer and then returned to the new owner. In addition, the county tax assessor usually requires filing a "transfer declaration" or similar document that contains basic information about the sale. There is a filing fee for recording the deed, which runs around $10–$15 per page. In addition, the county, city, and state may assess a transfer tax based on either the value of the property or the selling price.

What happens if John gives a mortgage to ABC Mortgage Company in order to buy a home but the mortgage is not filed for six months, and John then borrows from another lender who records its mortgage first? Most states follow a "race-notice" rule, which means that the first person to record the document wins, as long as he or she

1. received title in good faith;
2. paid value; and
3. had no notice of a prior transfer.

For example, let's say John buys that home by borrowing $175,000 from ABC. He signs a promissory note and a mortgage pledging his home as collateral. ABC messes up the paperwork and the mortgage does not get recorded for six months. In the interim, John borrows $25,000 from XYZ Mortgage Company, for which he gives a mortgage on the same home as collateral. XYZ Mortgage Company records its mortgage, unaware of John's unrecorded first mortgage to ABC Mortgage Company. As a result, XYZ Mortgage Company will have a first mortgage lien on the property.

NOTES AND MORTGAGES

Most people think of going to a bank to get a mortgage. Actually, people go to the bank to get a loan. Once they are approved for the loan, they sign a promissory note to the lender, which is their promise to pay. They also give (not get) a mortgage as security for repayment of the note. A mortgage is a security agreement under which the borrower pledges the property as collateral for payment. The mortgage document is recorded in the property records, creating a lien on the property in favor of the lender.

If the underlying obligation (promissory note) is paid off, the lender must release the collateral (mortgage), which removes the mortgage lien. A release is accomplished by signing a release of mortgage, which is recorded in the county's property records.

About half of the states use a document called a **deed of trust** rather than a mortgage. A deed of trust is a document in which the grantor (borrower) gives a deed to a neutral third party (trustee) to hold for the beneficiary (lender). A deed of trust is worded almost the same as a mortgage. Thus, the deed of trust and the mortgage are essentially the same, other than in the foreclosure process. Foreclosure is a legal proceeding by which a lender attempts to force the sale of a property to recoup the money that the lender has lent to the homeowner.

PRIORITY OF LIENS

Liens, like deeds, are "first in time, first in line." If a property is owned free and clear, a mortgage recorded will be a first mortgage. A mortgage recorded later in time will be a second mortgage (sometimes called a junior mortgage). Likewise, any judgments or other liens recorded later are also junior liens. Holding a first mortgage is a desirable position because a foreclosure on a mortgage can wipe out all liens that are recorded after it (called junior lien holders). We will discuss foreclosures in detail in chapter 8.

THE BASIC LOAN TRANSACTION

At the closing of a typical real-estate sale, the seller conveys a deed to the buyer. Buyers usually obtain loans from conventional lenders for most of the cash needed for the purchase price. As discussed earlier, the lender gives the buyer cash to pay the seller, and the buyer gives the lender a promissory note. The buyer also gives the lender a security instrument (mortgage or deed of trust) under which the buyer pledges the property as collateral. When the transaction is complete, the buyer has the title recorded in his or her name, and the lender has a lien recorded against the property.

WRAPPING IT UP

- Learn the nuts and bolts of real-estate transactions, such as deeds, mortgages, and recording.
- The priority of liens is important, particularly in foreclosure transactions.
- Ownership of property is complete when the deed is delivered, not when it is recorded.

CHAPTER 3

Finding Deals

In chapter 1 we mentioned the importance of buying distressed properties, which in reality means finding distressed owners. Finding these owners—motivated sellers is a better way to put it—is an art that takes years to master. It requires a planned approach. In order to be successful, investors will need to use multiple marketing strategies outlined in these next few chapters. Over time, wise investors will discover which methods work best for them. In addition, they should establish a referral network, which will allow them to find more deals with less effort.

Investors with limited time but available capital may choose to start with retailing properties. Once they connect with a couple of good wholesalers, or possibly well-networked real-estate brokers, they can focus on preparing properties for sale and becoming comfortable with the actual sale process.

The most common problem new investors face is finding bargain properties. Many who start out in real-estate investing quit without ever buying their first property. They go through the motions of looking for deals for a few weeks or months, then decide it doesn't work. They forget that finding motivated sellers is similar to the salesperson finding that first customer—it takes persistence and hard work.

You cannot put together a deal without a motivated seller who is willing to sell at a discounted price, or at least accept unusual terms. A motivated seller has a pressing reason to sell the property below market price.

FINDING MOTIVATED SELLERS

The concept is simple and bears repeating: find motivated sellers who are willing to sell their properties at a discounted price or favorable terms. Currently, interest rates are low, and the real-estate market in most parts of the country is quite healthy. The market will slow down at some point, however. Many people are complaining that the strength of the market precludes investors from finding deals on properties. The popular misconception is that in a rising market even the most motivated sellers can find buyers for their properties at full market price.

The truth is, you can work the concept of flipping properties in any market. Real-estate legend A. D. Kessler once said, "There are no problem properties, just problem ownerships."[1] The definition of a motivated seller fits squarely within Kessler's idea. A logical person knows that time, money, and effort can solve virtually any real-estate problem.

Issues that motivate people to sell include the following:

- Impending foreclosure and other financial problems
- Divorce or death in the family
- Lack of concern or inability to mentally deal with the situation
- Inexperience with real-estate repairs
- Time constraints
- Job transfer
- Landlording headaches
- Relatives or friends living in the property rent free

In short, if you deal only with motivated sellers, you will be able to negotiate the right price and terms. But don't expect many sellers to show their hand openly. Even someone desperate to sell realizes they can

---

1. A. D. Kessler, *A Fortune at Your Feet: How You Can Get Rich, Stay Rich and Enjoy Being Rich with Creative Real Estate in the '90s*, rev. ed. (Chicago: Probus, 1994), 247.

negotiate better if a buyer believes the seller has multiple options. A critical part of the investor's job is building rapport with the sellers and educating them about how you can help them solve their problems.

SEARCH ONLINE ADS

The obvious place to look for deals is Internet-based classified ads on Craigslist.org, Zillow.com, Redfin.com, or other similar websites. Because finding motivated sellers is a numbers game, be prepared to make a lot of calls. Do not waste much time with each seller; ask basic questions to gather information about the property and the seller's needs (see sample telephone script on page 236 in the appendix). Most people you cold-call will not be responsive to you. Don't take it personally; just keep calling. Remember that each time you hear a "no," you will be one call closer to a "yes," and you will be learning along the way. If you live in a less populated area, call every ad.

There are many online ads to sift through, and you will need to isolate the geographic area you desire. Searching multiple markets at once with SearchTempest.com may be helpful with Craigslist. You will want to look for rental and sale ads. In addition, you can look in the commercial section of Craigslist. Whenever you speak with someone asking tough questions, or a potential deal seems overwhelming to you, specify that you can get back with answers after you speak with your "partner." Getting back to a person is always better than making up an answer that may not even be true.

Sometimes you will need to reply to ads by e-mail or text. This is not the ideal method of communication (as compared to phone or in person), but it is what many people prefer these days. It is well worth your time to respond. Be brief, and give just enough information to intrigue the sellers. Each round of texts or e-mails will begin to build your relationship and their trust. Be honest, and don't be afraid to provide useful information they will appreciate. Encourage them to call or provide a phone number you can call. You want to learn about their situations, build rapport, and make your case.

Make sure to call on the ads that are for sale by owner (they don't all say "for sale by owner," but you will learn which ones are). You will notice that real-estate brokers place many of the ads. Most areas require that brokers identify their licensed status within the ad. Agents often ignore that requirement, however.

If you are not inspired to call on every ad, then, at a minimum, call on the ads with key phrases such as "must sell," "fix-up," "needs work," "handyman special," "vacant," and "motivated." Some ads will include the valuable information that the property is in foreclosure or is a short sale. We'll deal with these specific situations a little later. Unusually long ads listing every detail about the property are probably from inexperienced or motivated sellers, so these ads also warrant a call. Telephone numbers with area codes outside your market can be a dead giveaway the ad is from a motivated seller.

REAL-ESTATE BROKERS' ADS

Believe it or not, many of the ads placed by real-estate agents are teaser ads designed to get you calling about a particular type of house or neighborhood in which the agent works. If the ad is for a property in one of your target neighborhoods, then call the agent for a different reason—to let this agent know what kinds of properties you like. Call on all the ads that advertise fixer properties in your target areas and ask for the broker's e-mail address. E-mail these agents a brief personal message, alerting them that you are an investor, that you are looking for fixer properties, and that you can close quickly if the price is right (see sample e-mail on page 238 in the appendix). Send this e-mail to no fewer than twenty-five real-estate offices in your first month of doing business. This letter will get the agents calling you for properties, rather than the other way around.

PROPERTIES FOR RENT

Another way to find deals is by calling the classified ads offering houses for rent. Most cities have more properties for rent than for sale. One reason is that some people become accidental landlords for one reason or another. They may have inherited the property from their parents, or the owner may be a recently widowed person whose spouse had handled the property. These people rent out their properties because they don't know what else to do with them. To find this type of landlord, look for rental ads that have the words "for rent or sale" or "for lease or sale."

Find a landlord. If you come across a rental property in good shape that doesn't have enough equity or upside potential to wholesale to a retailer, you can still wholesale it to another landlord for a small profit. Thus, look at every property's potential as both a fix-and-flip and a rental property. There are just as many landlords in your market looking for good deals as there are retailers.

Calling rental ads can be lucrative because some landlords are simply tired of dealing with tenant- and property-management issues and may want a way out. Don't be afraid to pick up the phone and say, "I saw your ad in the paper for a property you are renting. I am an investor focusing on this area. Are you interested in selling the property?" If the answer is no, give these landlords your name and telephone number anyway, and ask them to call you if and when they decide to sell. Try to build a relationship, and offer to help with questions they may have, even if the questions are more about helping them rent the property than selling it. Next, ask if they mind if you follow up with them in a few weeks. Also, ask them if they know any other landlords in the area who may be interested in selling.

RUN YOUR OWN CLASSIFIED AD

Run your ad in the real estate–services section of Craigslist to encourage motivated owners to call you. Simple classified ads such as these can get your phone ringing:

I Buy Houses for Cash
Any Condition, Fast Closing
(555) 555-5555

Problem House?
We Can Help
(555) 555-5555

You can also run these ads under the real estate–wanted section in local all-advertisement tabloid newspapers such as the *Thrifty Nickel* or under "money to loan" to attract property owners in foreclosure looking for a solution.

Using Craigslist.org, Zillow.com, Redfin.com, or other such websites is similar though not identical to working online newspaper ads. You will still want to look in both the rental and for-sale-by-owner sections. In addition, you can look in the commercial section for multifamily housing that you can fix and flip or wholesale to another landlord.

THE 800-POUND GORILLA

You may have seen bright-yellow billboards that say "We Buy Ugly Houses" in your town. The company behind those signs, HomeVestors of America Inc., based in Dallas, Texas, is a franchise operation that spends a lot of money advertising on radio, billboards, and even on television. The numbers vary from city to city, but there's an initial buy-in for a potential franchise, which includes real-estate training, and then ongoing monthly expenses. We've been told that some franchisees spend as much as $100,000 per month on advertising in some cities. That's a very large budget for you to compete with, but don't worry—some consumers like dealing with the "big guys," and some will do business with you because you are a "little guy." These franchises are often shared; one territory may have several individuals sharing the advertising cost and the incoming calls. This scenario can bring down buy-in costs substantially for would-be franchisees and make such an approach more realistic to many investors. Like with other franchises, having a proven plan to follow can be a huge benefit, but members are paying a premium for those services. And as with other training or marketing programs—and even more so with a franchise due to the high cost—a curious investor should investigate carefully before jumping in.

CALL OTHER INVESTORS' ADS

As mentioned earlier, wholesalers need to find a pool of retail investors to whom they can sell their properties. The other "I Buy Houses" ads are a great place to find these people.

Unless you already have a business office, set up a separate telephone number to handle incoming calls. If you are not available during the day to answer calls, perhaps due to working full time at another profession, use a voice mail that is professional but not too specific. For example, the message could be: "Thank you for calling Real-Estate Solutions. We are here to help you solve your real-estate problems. Just let us know the best way to reach you, and we'll contact you as soon as possible." If you are getting quite a few calls, you can tailor the greeting to screen out the truly motivated sellers from the marginally motivated sellers who are simply looking to shop their properties. For example: "Thank you for calling the Denver Property Group, LLC. If you are calling about a house for sale, please leave your name, telephone number, the property address, and why you are selling." If you choose not to use these or similar messages, then at least have a professional greeting that includes your own name. Many sole proprietors don't even bother to set up a personalized greeting, which often annoys callers, since there is no way for them to know if they've even dialed the correct number.

FLIP TIP

Call waiting. Services such as Google Voice will give you a unique phone number for people to call that forwards to your mobile phone. If you set it up properly, you will see the caller ID of that number showing up on your cell when people call that number—so make sure you drop what you're doing and answer that call!

When making or receiving calls, it makes sense to develop a script, especially when you are new to the flipping business (see sample script on page 236 in the appendix). Be engaging, and ask nonthreatening questions to build rapport. Be honest with sellers, and let them know you are not a large company. You can explain that you will take a personal interest in their specific needs and circumstances. Also mention that you have the resources to handle cash transactions, while your low overhead allows you to pay a fair price for their property. It is OK to gather information about the property and establish that the seller is motivated. But it is best to minimize the discussion; use the call to set up a personal meeting.

REAL-ESTATE BROKERS

Brokers (or agents) can be a great source of potential deals once you learn how to work with them. They are among the most informed people regarding properties for sale, and they have access to more information than investors. Brokers also have many contacts and may know of potential deals that are not advertised on the MLS. These unadvertised leads are called pocket listings. According to the National Association of Realtors' *2015 Profile of Home Buyers and Sellers*, the share of sellers who used real-estate agents hit a historic high in 2015, rising to 89 percent from 88 percent the previous year.[2]

Much of the information that was once exclusively available to MLS subscribers is now available to anyone via the Internet. Consumer real-estate sites, however, are still not as good as the sites real-estate agents can access. The agents-only sites provide better search engines and more data, and they are usually updated more frequently than consumer sites. Even considering all the data now available to consumers, real-estate agents are better able to keep their finger on the pulse of the market. It's common to see contradictory articles regarding neighborhood trends, building starts, sales prices, days on market, etc. A top agent should have good insights to help you sort through all this information.

Agent vs Broker

As mentioned earlier, we are using the terms *agent* and *broker* interchangeably, but there are differences. Typically a broker has more experience than an agent. In most states, a person must be licensed as a broker to list property for sale. A listing is an agreement between the seller and the broker that permits the broker to sell the property for a fee. An agent, like a broker, must be licensed to sell real estate. Each state has its own regulations for agent licensing and handling of commissions, so make sure you're up to speed about your state's requirements.

Agents can also represent buyers or sellers in different capacities, such as buyers' agents, sellers' agents, dual agents, or transaction agents. It pays to understand the various agency relationships allowed in your area. A few states require attorneys to provide services that are offered by agents in the

2. National Association of Realtors, *2015 Profile of Buyers and Sellers*, http://realtor.org/reports/highlights
-from-the-2015-profile-of-home-buyers-and-sellers.

rest of the country. For example, an attorney may be required to handle the closing, create contracts, or add verbiage to state-approved contracts.

Then, to make things even more confusing, there is the term Realtor, which is actually a trademark reserved for members of the local board of Realtors, an affiliate of the National Association of Realtors. The boards are private, self-regulating agencies that govern rules of conduct for their members. Most agents belong to one or more local boards.

Real-estate agents can earn additional designations. Serious agents will typically undergo continuing education to earn designations from the Graduate REALTOR® Institute (GRI), Council of Residential Specialists (CRS), or many others. When evaluating potential agents, ask about their credentials and why they chose a specific educational track. College degrees and previous work experience are especially important if the person has limited experience as an agent. Of course, formal education is only one way to assess your agent's value and does not guarantee that he or she has the skills you need.

The Buyers' Broker

A buyers' broker represents a buyer looking for properties. Most listing agents will offer a co-op fee to any buyers' broker who procures a buyer to purchase the property.

For example, let's say a property is listed at $100,000 on the MLS. The listing broker's commission is 6 percent, and he or she is offering a 3 percent "co-op" fee. The listing broker's fee will be $6,000—the full 6 percent—if that broker also finds the buyer for the property.

The buyers' broker's loyalty and representation belong to the buyer, although buyers' brokers are paid by the listing broker. Because buyers' brokers usually procure buyers to make the sale, they are often referred to as selling brokers. Remember that regardless of agency relationship, the listing broker's first loyalty is to the seller. If you are a buyer, wouldn't you rather have your own buyers' broker to represent your best interests?

Using a good buyers' broker will help you find a lot of deals. The broker can systematically watch the MLS for new, expired, or stale listings. Also, ask your broker to search through the MLS for motivation buzzwords such as "must sell," "needs work," "estate sale," "foreclosure," "divorce," and "rehab." These descriptions indicate distressed properties.

Remember, distressed properties are those that create emotional or financial distress for their owners. Have the broker watch for Department of Housing and Urban Development (HUD), real-estate owned (REO), and short-sale properties. (These types of properties and all foreclosures will be addressed in detail in chapter 8.)

You may find it hard to believe, but many brokers list properties in need of work at full market price. Most likely, these high-priced properties are not worth pursuing, but you can touch base with the broker to see if the seller is willing to entertain lower offers. A popular strategy in listing properties (especially in a strong sellers' market) is to advertise for a very low price in hope of creating multiple offers. Often the broker will instruct buyers that "all offers will be reviewed on Monday." Of course you can make offers on these properties, but don't get overly excited and offer too much. The winning bid in this auction-type environment may not actually lead to a positive outcome for the buyer. In a competitive market you should make appealing offers that still protect your best interests.

In addition, ask your broker to search the MLS in your target areas by withdrawn status (meaning the property didn't sell), or by expired status (meaning the property is no longer represented by the listing broker). These can also generate bargain leads.

Although a buyers' broker can be an excellent source of leads, don't use the broker as your only source. You will benefit from learning about other approaches as well. Busy brokers do not want to waste their time with a beginning investor making frivolous offers that don't get accepted. In a strong market, there are plenty of qualified conventional homebuyers that brokers can work with. You are looking for a top-notch agent but also one who is willing to work diligently for you. New agents are not too busy with existing clients, so if you find a hardworking rookie agent who will put in extra time to find you deals, you can grow and learn together.

As a new investor, you will get discouraged dealing with a buyers' broker who does not make you a priority, so make sure you approach that broker in the right way:

- Present a professional appearance.
- Be respectful of his or her time—ask the agent to e-mail you the listings you are looking for, and set up access to the client MLS portal.

- Drive by the properties you are interested in before asking the agent to show you the inside of each property.
- Don't wait for the perfect situation to make offers, and plan with the agent regarding how many offers to make (you can make lots of lowball offers if the agent is willing).
- Be open about your experience and resources. Let the agent know you intend to buy more than one property and that he or she will have repeat business. If you intend to sell the property retail, offer the agent the listing (and, of course, ask for a discount on the commission for this listing).

Mortgage Brokers

Mortgage companies spend thousands of dollars on lead-generation marketing. They often receive hundreds of dead leads from people in distress with no equity and no ability to qualify for a new loan. Contact some local brokers and offer to pay them for these names. Many of these borrowers are behind in their loan payments and may be facing foreclosure. This information is invaluable because it is not made public until the lender actually commences the foreclosure. Note that even people in pre-foreclosure, which means the foreclosure has been formally filed but the auction has yet to occur, are protected from predatory practices under state law. You will need to learn about the foreclosure rules in your area. We will go into more detail regarding this status in later chapters.

BANK-OWNED PROPERTIES

Contact your local banks and ask for the REO or distressed-assets department. Large banks and lenders work solely with real-estate agents, so it is also worthwhile to learn who these agents are. Once you connect with an agent who works directly with lenders, get on their e-mail list so you can be notified about their new listings as soon as (or before) they hit the MLS. A good place to find REO listing agents is through social media, such as LinkedIn or Facebook.

FARMING NEIGHBORHOODS

Successful real-estate agents use a technique called farming to increase their business activity. They pick a neighborhood or two and focus their marketing efforts within that area. You should try the same technique. Start with a neighborhood that is relatively convenient and familiar to you. It should contain the types of homes you intend to flip. Typically this will be "starter" homes of approximately 1,200 square feet, with two or three bedrooms and one or two baths. Such homes have the most flipping potential because they are in the greatest demand.

Spend a few weekends driving around the area. At first, your goal is to learn about the area, the style of houses, and the average prices. Over time, you may expand your farm area, but stay within areas that contain the type of homes you plan to purchase. It is not necessary to begin your investment career by learning every square mile of a large metropolitan area; it is important to learn the value of typical homes in your target areas. We go into more detail about valuation in later chapters. This knowledge will enable you to make quick decisions about whether a particular prospect is a bargain.

Visit open houses and for-sale-by-owner (FSBO) properties on weekends. Speak directly with the owners and their agents. Pass out your business cards. Make friends. Word of mouth and referrals are a big part of any business. Take a good look at the property and its physical features, and take notes. After going to a couple of dozen open houses in the neighborhood, take the time to follow up and find out the actual sales price for each property. Soon you will know the value of the properties in your area.

While you are driving around neighborhoods, look for vacant, ugly houses. How can you tell if a house is vacant? First, look for the obvious signs of vacancy: overgrown grass, no window shades, boarded windows, newspapers, garbage, mail piled up, etc. If you are not certain whether the property is vacant, knock on the door. If the owner answers, be polite and respectful and ask if he or she is interested in selling. In many cases, it may be a rental property, so ask the occupants for the name and telephone number of the owner. If there are no indications that the house is occupied, you can peek in a window. Of course, you should use a fair amount of discretion. Obviously, you should not visit these properties alone, especially at night.

If the property is vacant, ask the neighbors if they know the owner. Most neighbors are helpful because they realize ugly houses hurt their own property values. In addition, speak with mail carriers—they know all the empty houses on their routes. Leave a brief Post-it note with instructions to contact you, and write down the property address. When you get back to the office, look up the name and address of the owner on the county tax assessor's website.

Finding and contacting the owner takes a little more digging. Try speaking with the neighbors or asking the post office for a copy of a change-of-address form on file for the property. For about a hundred dollars a year, you can subscribe to an information service that provides phone numbers and addresses on file for your missing owner. These services, such as Intelius.com and TLOxp.com, will search public databases, including the Driver's License Bureau, utility companies, wireless providers, and the Department of Motor Vehicles. Even with this information, there's no guarantee you'll easily reach the owner, but in most cases you'll eventually succeed.

Another way to locate abandoned houses is by going directly to the municipalities themselves. Often cities, towns, and counties will tag houses with code violations, posting an official notice on a front door or window. This is a sign of either a neglected or vacant property. Tax records will also show owners who are in default on their property taxes. Ask your city if you can obtain a list of such properties, or find out where this information is publicly recorded.

IT'S IN THE MAIL

Direct-mail marketers are masters at working the numbers game. They mail postcards, flyers, brochures, and catalogs by the tens of thousands to prospective customers. Believe it or not, direct-mail success is usually less than 1 percent. We define "success" as a positive response to the mail piece. That means there's a 99 percent failure rate! Here's a little secret, though: you can get filthy rich on a 1 percent success rate with direct mail.

Consider that a typical subdivision you're planning to mail to may have more than a thousand homes. If you were able to make $30,000 per deal flipping one to five homes in that subdivision each year, you could operate a nice little business. Expand your efforts into multiple areas, and you have a venture worthy of your full-time attention.

Postcards are the cheapest way to cover a neighborhood while also weeding out bad addresses. You'll be tempted to use a glossy, full-color postcard, but in fact they are not effective for this business. Instead, go to the post office and buy a couple of thousand blank postcards. Take them to a printer and have a simple message printed on the card (see sample ad on page 240 in the appendix). You may want to handwrite a personal message with a Flair pen to give the card a more personal touch. Also worth considering is the postal service's Every Door Direct Mail program, a targeted bulk mail service that is less expensive per piece than a postcard. But remember, bulk mail pieces are more likely to be ignored and discarded.

Don't expect to get all the calls at once; sometimes people respond weeks or even months after receiving your cards. Try mailing to the same people four to six times a year. In these days of advertising and general information overload, it takes time for people to notice you. Over many months, people will become familiar with you and will be more likely to call. A few years ago, for example, we bought a house at a nearly 50 percent discount from a man who called us from a postcard mailing. He had one foot out the door and was moving to another state. When we visited his house, we noticed he had our postcard taped to his refrigerator door. We asked, "How long ago did we send that card to you?" He replied, "I got that postcard a year ago, but I've been waiting for my job transfer to go through." When he finally called, he was desperate to be separated from his house ASAP.

TARGETED DIRECT MAIL

In the section above, we discussed directing a blind mailing to a targeted area. Rather than a blind mailing, try mailing to specific lists:

- Out-of-state owners (often motivated landlords or job transferees)
- Homeowners with poor credit and recent credit-card defaults
- People with federal or state tax liens
- People in foreclosure or bankruptcy within the past year
- Homeowners behind on property taxes or homeowners' association (HOA) dues

- Probates (discussed in more detail below)
- People who are thirty to ninety days behind in mortgage payments but the foreclosure has not yet been filed

The names of these people can be purchased from mailing-list brokers. Google "direct marketing" or "mailing-list companies" to find such brokers. A reasonably priced source of leads can be found on ListSource .com. You should expect to pay ten to thirty cents per name, depending on how much information is provided. Once you have a mailing list, consistently send out regular mailings. Your message should be as personal as possible (see sample letters on page 241 in the appendix).

In addition to providing your phone number, you can also direct people to your website, where they can get additional information about what you do. You can also get lists that contain e-mail addresses. Acquiring phone numbers will also increase your odds of success if you are willing to make lots of calls. There are national guidelines for telemarketing and e-mailing, so become familiar with the rules. In addition, always track vacant houses, people who call on your ads, signs, flyers, and other leads.

Many studies have been conducted by marketing companies to determine the most effective color, size, and wording of marketing pieces. While this information is somewhat useful, don't get too caught up in it. The most important marketing strategy is simple: repetition. Keep mailing until the recipients ask to be taken off your list or a postcard comes back marked "deceased"; then find out who the heirs of the estate are and send a message to them.

MORE MARKETING STRATEGIES

When funds become available, consider more aggressive advertising, such as bus-stop benches and supermarket shopping carts. When homeowners in the area are thinking of selling, they may call you before listing their property with an agent. By working with you, they will save a real-estate commission and a long selling process, and you will have the discount property purchase you wanted. Another win-win.

You might try marketing with "bandit signs"—aptly named since they are usually placed without permission. Such signs are used frequently by builders and investors, in addition to a variety of other people trying to sell their goods and services. The signs are usually 18" × 24" and are inexpensive, brightly colored corrugated plastic. You have undoubtedly seen them at busy intersections and on utility poles around your town. Many investors have had great success using bandit signs as their primary means of advertising.

These signs are also the subject of significant controversy and interesting discussions among investors. On the plus side, they are a relatively inexpensive means of generating investor leads. Using these signs requires little experience and has proven successful for years. On the negative side, there is risk of being fined for posting the signs. Also, placing the signs requires quite a bit of time, especially if you remove them at the end of each weekend. Not everyone is comfortable with using this type of advertising. It is a bit hokey, and some even consider it unethical, since it may not be legal and tends to create waste.

If you do choose to use bandit signs, then you'll need to learn about your area's rules for posting them. Most municipalities do not allow them, although some do if handled according to their rules. Builders tend to put up signs on Friday afternoon then remove them Sunday evening. This practice makes the signs less of a nuisance, and local code-enforcement staff won't necessarily consider the signs as abandoned property or as littering. Also, code-enforcement personnel are less likely to work on weekends. But there are people known as "sign cutters" (self-appointed protectors of their community from this form of advertising). There is even an organized group called Citizens Against Ugly Street Spam (CAUSS.org) that aggressively removes signs and may report those who post them!

How you use the signs can make or break your success. There is no one formula, but investors agree that simple is best. Smaller sizes such as 12" × 18", or even 8½" × 11" can be both effective and less intrusive. It's also generally believed that you shouldn't place too many in a small geographic area. A handful in a one-mile radius makes sense. It takes a lot of signs to generate a few responses, however, so you will need to have at least fifty signs out at a time. A simple "I Buy Houses" with your phone number printed on a bright background is the typical sign. Handwritten signs (or printed signs that look handwritten) are also effective. You can adjust the look and text to see what works best for you. Place the signs at busy intersections, on parkway medians, and in high-traffic areas. After you have figured out your distribution system, you might want to pay someone else to place the signs. Generally, place the signs along the busiest streets that feed into your farm area. Posting on telephone poles is also effective, but it creates another potential source of trouble, this time from utility companies.

Don't block or remove other people's signs. You are asking for trouble if you anger your peers. In fact, calling other investors is a good way to expand your contacts list. If you search online for bandit signs or go to BanditSigns.com, you'll find custom-printed signs available for about $1.50 each at quantities of one hundred or more. You'll also need stakes, which may be easier to source locally.

We have completed deals that originated from our bandit sign and have rarely been challenged by authorities. The first time we heard from an enforcement officer was quite a long time ago, and the conversation went something like this: "Hi, I'm calling about your sign that you buy houses. I'm Officer so-and-so, and I wanted to offer you the choice of paying one hundred dollars per sign that I find, or you can remove them all by tomorrow." Of course we were polite and removed the signs right away. Unfortunately, we hadn't carefully mapped out where the signs were and so had to do a lot of extra driving around to make sure we took down all of them (we hope!). After that, we used the short-term approach and removed the signs each Sunday evening or Monday morning.

Some people use hammer staplers (see SignStapler.com) to attach the signs to wooden stakes and post them high up on phone poles where they are hard to remove. Good idea? It depends on who's trying to remove the sign. Other investors list a forwarded phone number (or website) on their signs, making it difficult for authorities to track the signs back to them. Again, this approach has advantages, but may not please the code-enforcement officer who eventually finds you.

You can, of course, eliminate the word *bandit* in this sign-marketing strategy if you get the permission of property owners to post or you post on your own property. You have exposure to potential sellers without the risk of hassles and fines. We advocate this method, but you will have to do extra legwork (and pay a small amount) to get the owner's permission to place the signs. Have the homeowner or business owner sign a simple form giving you permission in exchange for, say, five dollars per month. Check on your signs regularly, since people may still remove them, but you can easily replace them without fear of reprimand. You can also place similar signs on public bulletin boards in retail stores, Laundromats, or community centers. No matter how you choose to post your signs, you'll need to be consistent and keep the exposure going for months to get solid results. And keep track of your results so you can determine where your efforts are most effective.

FLYERS AND DOOR HANGERS

Simple flyers are yet another way to generate leads. Don't spend your time passing out flyers and door hangers; rather, hire kids to blanket the neighborhood for you. But go back and check to see if the job is done properly before you pay them! Instruct them not to place anything inside a mailbox but to put them inside a screen door or fence. Door hangers are more expensive than flyers, but they are easier to distribute because you can hang them (see sample door hanger on page 243 in the appendix).

Carry flyers in your car when you cruise neighborhoods. Whenever you see people in their yards or a for-sale-by-owner sign, stop and talk with the owners and then hand them a flyer. Another option is to leave a yellow Post-it note on the door with a handwritten message that says something like, "Call me at 555-5555, I need to talk with you about the house—Bill."

And speaking of cruising, you can use your vehicle to promote your business by making it a billboard on wheels. We know several investors who have found property deals using this method. You'll need to decide if it suits your personal style. We believe you should have a nice vehicle when you call on potential sellers, so you might not want them to see you pull up in a rolling billboard. You can get custom magnetic signs or vinyl decals that can be removed when appropriate. We've seen entire vans and trucks painted or wrapped with "I Buy Houses" all over them. These investors often deduct the entire vehicle as a marketing expense on their income taxes!

PROBATE ESTATES

Every year, countless owners of real estate in your community pass away. Oftentimes these properties are in a state of disrepair because the owners neglected them during their final years or because they sat vacant after their deaths. The person or persons responsible for the estate are often motivated to sell the property as quickly as possible. Many times there are family members who disagree about what to do with the property, or there are fiduciaries who see the home as a project to be dealt with sooner rather than later. These people are quite willing to sell, and frequently on your terms. When an owner of real estate dies, the ownership may not automatically vest in the heirs of the deceased's estate. The deceased's will must be processed through a court proceeding known as a probate. The probate proceeding can take a year or more in some areas, depending on the backlog of court cases, the value of the deceased's assets, and infighting between the heirs. The typical heirs to an estate are average people; they have no experience in fixing or selling real estate. If the heirs have no emotional attachment to the property, they will be eager for the administrator of the estate to liquidate it quickly so they can receive their inheritance in cash.

You will need to locate the executor or estate administrator (also known as a personal representative), since they will be the party in position to approve a potential sale. You may also need to track down the heir apparent.

There is not a single "best" resource to locate these properties, but your area may have a company that will provide data for you on a subscription basis. Otherwise, you'll need to see where your area posts estate information—usually in a local newspaper. It's generally found under the legal-notices section, and the ad will start with "Notice to Creditors of the Estate of X."

Working with people in any probate situation requires tact and understanding. You may be reaching out to someone who is grieving, so be respectful and patient. Even though particular situations may not present a deal for you, administrators can keep your name on file in case they are the administrator of other estates.

Another way to find these homes is to buy them directly from the heirs after the property has been through probate. Probate homes are deeded from the estate of the deceased to the heir through a special type of deed called an executor's deed. See if you can search online or at the county clerk's office by type of deed and date range. A good service for buying these leads is USLeadList.com (mention our name for priority service).

GETTING REFERRALS

We can't stress enough the importance of referrals (i.e., having others alert you to potential deals). You need to build a network; you need to become a terrific networker. Yes, it takes time, and it begins immediately. And it never stops. It's the lifeblood of your business whether you've just begun or are a veteran investor. In fact, you will find that after a few years in the real-estate business, your greatest source of deals will be from referrals.

Here are a few pointers to provide insight on how to network with the right people. First of all, get a nice business card. No, not a "nice" business card, but a *professional business card* that really stands out. Don't be cheap and use the basic white ones from Office Depot, and don't even think about making one on your computer. When you are dealing with a $200,000 asset, you must look professional. Don't be shy about spending one hundred dollars or more on your business cards. You may choose to have two separate cards: one to give to potential sellers, another for investors and other real-estate professionals. How you present yourself, starting with your business card (and your physical appearance), is so simple yet so crucial.

Your card should be double-sided with a complete message about what you do (see the sample business cards on page 244 in the appendix). Basically, it's a flashy, compact flyer. "B&B Investments" tells people nothing; "Denver Property Solutions, LLC" tells more but in a more professional way. Then there's the issue of whether to include your picture. Again, there are no absolute right answers, but we suggest you seek out a memorable card. Your card represents your personal brand, a key component of your business. We'll devote more attention to items such as how to organize your business entity and build your brand in later chapters.

Many newbie investors use Vistaprint.com, one of the largest printers in the country, for their cards. While there are thousands of sample real-estate business card templates, most investors get lazy and pick the first one, which is a white card with a row of cartoonish houses. You've probably seen some yourself. Instead, start from the *back* of the template choices and find an original design. If you are truly terrible at this task, try Fiverr.com (a website where people offer services for five dollars and up) to get a business card and logo created just for you.

Pass out your memorable, professional business cards to everyone you know, including business and personal contacts. Tell them you are interested in them, hand them your card, and ask, "Can you think of any-one you know who may have a run-down property?" Social media has become the new way to communicate, and we'll address it in the next chapter. Our so-called smartphones now dominate our communications. If you aren't willing to text, then don't expect to do a lot of business with people born after 1990.

THE CARE AND FEEDING OF BIRD DOGS

Even as a new investor, you should engage the services of a bird dog or two. You can offer people a referral fee for information leading to a prop-erty you end up purchasing. This finder's fee can be anything from $500 to $1,000, depending on how good the deal is. If you are looking for bird dogs to work with on a long-term basis, it may be difficult to keep them motivated if they only get paid when you buy a property. Don't be afraid to approach established local workers, delivery people, mail carriers, cable installers, city building and zoning inspectors, or even appraisers who can always use extra income.

Most beginners at any commission-based job quit after a few weeks because they lack the mental discipline to stick it out until their first check comes. Bird dogs are no different, so you need to offer payments to keep them interested. For example, you can pay twenty dollars for each ugly, vacant house they find (test them first with twenty-five or so verifiable leads, so they don't show up with a thousand bad leads expecting to get paid!). The information should include a photograph of the house, the com-plete address, the owner's name, and information about the owner's distress (such as foreclosure, bankruptcy, and divorce). Explain that you want to be fair, and create a plan that works for both of you. You should give them sev-eral hundred dollars as a bonus after you purchase the property. This cash will ensure they bring you quality prospects with potential to become deals.

WRAPPING IT UP

- Find a motivated seller and you find a bargain property.
- Learn how to farm neighborhoods.
- Employ multiple marketing approaches.
- Network and use your existing contacts to get referral business.

CHAPTER 4

Using Social Media

Social-media marketing is an incredibly powerful tool, and these days it is one of the single best ways to find deals as a real-estate investor. Having a website is good, but if you don't drive any people to it, it's basically no more than an electronic business card.

Social media allows you to interact with your audience, to get feedback, to hear suggestions, and to communicate in a variety of different ways. It lets you build brand visibility, and it lets you drive visitors directly to your site. But unfortunately, despite the proliferation of social-media marketing, many social-media marketers aren't getting anywhere near the increase in profits and brand awareness they could be.

Facebook continues to be the biggie, but Twitter, LinkedIn, and Snapchat are quite popular as well. Nextdoor.com and similar online groups are becoming a popular way to tie neighborhoods together. These groups work much like the traditional neighborhood homeowners' associations and garden clubs. But there are no dues or meetings. They exist simply as channels to connect people, and they could become another resource for your own networking.

WHY USE SOCIAL MEDIA FOR REAL ESTATE?

Simple answer: because it's what society has adapted to. If you don't adapt as well, you will get left out in the cold. According to the National Association of Realtors, while almost 90 percent of people end up using a real-estate broker to buy a home, 87 percent first do some searching online.[1] Thus, if you are not working the Internet, you are missing out on potential leads for buying and selling properties.

THE *WRONG* WAY TO USE SOCIAL MEDIA

A lot of people are under the impression that they can just set up an account and post regularly in the hopes that they will start generating lots of followers and "likes." There is no planning and no attempt to take full advantage of the more advanced features and uses of social-media platforms.

Even worse, many use social-media sites simply as a place to advertise. All they're doing is posting, and all they are posting is self-laudatory things like "Our company is the best in the business!" Be honest, is your business one you would follow and share with others? If not, then you can't really expect your social-media accounts to grow.

Player #1: Facebook

Facebook is the largest player in the social-media realm. Having an account with a few dozen strangers you call "friends" isn't going to be effective, though. You must have a game plan.

First, join "groups" that are in your topic (i.e., real-estate investing). Some groups require permission to get in, which is fine. But don't post blatant ads that say, "I buy houses," or you will get ignored, shamed, or worse, thrown out of the group. Instead, offer advice, ask questions, and chat with other folks in the groups. Make sure your Facebook profile has a professional photo of you and a description of the type of business you are in and your unique angle, the one that makes you different from all the other investors online.

---

1. Brandi Snowden and Amanda Riggs, *Real Estate in a Digital Age* (Washington, DC: National Association of Realtors), http://realtor.org/reports/real-estate-in-a-digital-age.

FLIP TIP

Face-to-face. Before we get into the meat of the matter, keep one thing in mind: nothing is a substitute for a personal connection with a buyer or seller. It's good to use technology to generate leads, but in the end, the whole point is to get a phone appointment, and ultimately, an in-person meeting. People often rely too much on e-mail, text, and social media for communication, which is a bad idea. People do business with people they trust, and you can only build so much trust through technology.

Once you have communicated with some people in these groups, ask them to friend you. This will build your following and make you look like a player. In fact, there are services you can pay to add followers, but only consider using such a service if it can find you friends relevant to your line of business, folks who have a genuine interest in what you do. Fiverr.com and Upwork.com allow you to hire freelance service providers for affordable fees to do this work for you.

Paid advertising on Facebook is another option. You will need to set up a business page separate from your personal page to do this effectively. With Facebook marketing, you can target the exact audience you need—not only based on geography and interests, but also those who frequent your competitors' pages! Facebook ads are not cheap; you're looking at one to two dollars per click on your ad, so make sure your business Facebook page is professional, compelling, and offers an irresistible bonus for signing up or "liking" you (a bonus such as an e-book, real-estate form such as a sample purchase contract, or other valuable resource).

Once you have a following, use your Facebook page as a blog. In other words, don't post news stories, cat videos, and controversial political articles. Instead, post tips, ideas, surveys, and links to relevant real estate–related articles or websites. Also, try to include a nice graphic to help get your post noticed. If you are linking to an article or news website, the image will automatically come up. But if you post a few thoughts or a simple survey, there will just be straight text, which doesn't stand out. Find something pertinent to go with it.

Your aim should be to create posts that will get clicked and shared. Pique people's curiosity and they will click. For example: "You'll never believe what happens at the end of this video. . . . I nearly lost my mind!" In other cases, the article might be purposefully controversial; it might suggest some kind of gossip, or it might make outrageous claims. For example: "This one upgrade almost DOUBLED my profit on a flip." These teaser headlines work because people can't help but be curious. Sure, it's probably nonsense, they think, but what if it's not?

Yet you shouldn't go for the surprises and big hooks all the time. You could damage your reputation if people continue to feel conned or tricked by your posts. They'll come to resent you and avoid anything you recommend.

So what do you do instead of tricks and surprises? You create links that are unique, interesting, and hair-raising—and that actually deliver. And you can best do that by creating original content. Cultivate a following by studying your topic in depth, which involves combining different related subjects and finding scientific research appropriate to your topic. Adding your personality and personal experiences is also a nice touch. Slowly but surely people will come to think that you are something of an expert, that you know what you're talking about, and that you can find answers. And slowly but surely more and more people will be reading your content and recommending it to others. Your page will have more—and better—followers.

Player #2: LinkedIn

People tend to use Facebook for personal relationships rather than business ones. LinkedIn is definitely geared more to businesspeople. Make sure to build up your profile completely. The more relevant information the better. When people search for you, they can find you by your profile's keywords, places, employment, and experiences. Your profile is your online résumé. Hire a graphic artist to make your page more professional and compelling. You can also upload pertinent videos to entice people to stay on your profile and want to connect with you.

Additional features of LinkedIn include "company updates," which allow you to write posts from your business (rather than from yourself personally) and "targeted company updates," which let you make posts that will be seen specifically by particular cross sections of your audience—key company decision makers, for example. There's also an "advanced search" that can aid your real-estate lead generation, notably, the ability to discover background information on current leads and to identify new prospects.

When you stumble upon people of interest, send them a personalized message. The key to earning their trust and not annoying them is to be genuine and honest. Tell them you're always looking to connect with locals who may be in the market. Ask questions about their own business or background; people love talking about themselves.

When asking people if they'd like to be added to your network, it is best to start with those you know. Just like Facebook, LinkedIn is very protective of its members and can cancel your membership if they suspect you are spamming other members.

Player #3: Meetup

Another great website to create relationships and connections for yourself is Meetup. But networking via Meetup isn't limited to online; Meetup is used to promote in-person meetings and events. Once you get a little more experienced, consider starting your own monthly breakfast or lunch club with Meetup.

Player #4: YouTube

YouTube is a collection of videos organized primarily by topic and author. While you can join YouTube author groups, instead think of it as a way to attract motivated sellers or potential partners. For example, if you create a video called "Seven Things You Can Do to Stop Your House from Being Foreclosed," a person in foreclosure might search YouTube and find it. You can place "tags" and a description in your video summary, so you'll attract residents of your city or town, or even of specific neighborhoods. Furthermore, since Google and YouTube are siblings, Google searches on a particular topic will often bring up relevant YouTube video results.

Note that you don't need to be a professional presenter or an amazing editor to benefit from YouTube. You can actually create videos from slideshows and save them as video files. Likewise, you can create whiteboard animations, you can use screen capture software (e.g., Camtasia), or you can create stop-motion animations. Just make sure you're providing valuable information or entertainment.

DON'T FORGET FORUMS

The Web was social long before Facebook was a twinkle in Mark Zuckerberg's eye. When the Web first exploded in popularity, people were already having discussions and debates about their favorite hobbies and interests, but they were doing so in chat rooms and on forums.

And while Facebook has more prominence now, forums are still out there and still offer a lot of opportunities.

A forum is essentially a message board (normally attached to a website) where people can post questions and get answers. Users must first create a profile, and from there they can create or respond to "threads," monitor discussions, and send private messages. Those groups provide discussions focused on specific topics, with only forum members allowed to participate and contribute. Exclusivity is one of the biggest attractions of these forums: they offer a VIP feeling that tends to nurture a much more close-knit community. Many people make friends on forums and even end up working together on joint projects.

So while forums are smaller than social networks, they are also much more targeted, and their users are more committed to and passionate about the particular subject. These forums are ideal tools to gain important, focused exposure for your product, your business, and your website.

The problem is, most people have no idea how to use forums. They simply create accounts, log in, post their link like an advertisement, and then wait to see if anything happens. To succeed on forums, wait to post links until you've established yourself as an active member of that community. To do that, you need to take part by answering questions, contributing to discussions, and even starting discussions of your own. This process can allow you to learn more about your target audience, to demonstrate yourself as an expert on your topic, and to find loyal fans and even friends. Once you manage all that, you're likely to find that those fans and friends will gladly help you to promote your business (and you'll help them promote theirs). In short, forums are communities. (A list of real-estate websites with active forums can be found on page 245 in the appendix.)

MAPPING OUT YOUR SOCIAL NETWORKING GOALS

How do you go about setting goals as a social-media marketer? Let's break it down.

Numbers

One of the simplest and most straightforward ways to look at your success in social media is to measure the number of followers/subscribers you have. Over time, if you are posting content that people enjoy and if you are marketing yourself well, you should find people signing up and getting involved. But numbers, no matter how big, are not what really matters.

Engagement

In fact, it's possible to buy several thousand followers for a relatively low sum, but what you'll find is that this effort doesn't do much for you since most of those followers won't be engaging with your content. Engagement means people are responding to your posts, they are private messaging you, they are liking your comments, etc. And that means they're actually finding what you're sharing interesting, and consequently they'll be much more likely to buy the products you recommend or to share your posts with their own network. You can usually see your engagement data by looking at your stats/analytics. The number of deals you get from your social-media efforts will, of course, be a direct result of your followers' level of engagement.

CREATE A BRAND

Consistent, strong branding is crucial to ensuring that all your social-media accounts appear linked. A brand consists of

- a well-designed logo;
- a catchy name;
- a tagline;
- appropriate cover images;

- a website design that incorporates your logo's design language; and
- a consistent tone and pertinent subject matter.

Link your website to your social-media accounts and each of your social-media accounts to each other. Deliver value. Value is what draws people to any social-media account, just as it's what draws them to a website (and, as always, to a storefront). Value is what keeps them there, and it's what keeps them clicking on your links and sharing your posts.

Moreover, value is what helps you build your reputation as a brand that can deliver. And this is absolutely crucial because there's no point having a big audience if that audience doesn't trust you and isn't interested in what you have to offer.

Respond to comments, ask questions, and contribute to the communities you join. This way people will feel like they know you and they'll go from being friends and leads to being trusted fans and valuable contacts.

WRAPPING IT UP

- Learn the major social-media platforms.
- Tailor your social-media activity to attract sellers, buyers, and potential partners.
- Create goals for your social-media marketing.
- Create a unique brand for yourself and use it consistently.

CHAPTER 5

Analyzing Deals

Assessing a potential deal involves taking the right steps, all of which lead to a successful purchase offer. You must maintain control and as an investor become adept at quickly analyzing properties, first ruling out the flops and then securing promising flips. We will teach you how to establish after-repaired value, and then show you how to work backward to determine the time and costs involved to bring a property to ARV. In other words, you need to begin with the end in mind. As a last step, we will explain in detail the additional costs involved, so that you know how much to offer for a given profit margin.

When evaluating properties, learn to look past what is easily remedied and visualize the finished product. Sounds simple enough, but inexperienced investors walk away from great deals because of properties' lingering smells, filthy and cluttered conditions, or other issues that aren't as significant as they may appear to be. For example, you may be unpleasantly surprised by the contents of the fridge if one of the houses you are visiting has been abandoned or not cleaned recently, so keep the refrigerator door closed during your initial inspection. The point is to focus on deal-breaker repairs; something like a dirty refrigerator is easily remedied.

It takes experience to recognize a profitable deal. Of course, experience usually comes from making lots of mistakes. Needless to say, we've made mistakes, and we want you to use this book to learn from our "experience." By understanding and following the guidelines and techniques in this chapter (and throughout the book), you will be able to make quick, informed decisions when making offers. Later in the book we will also show you the steps to take once you have your target property under contract to ensure wise purchase decisions for the best return.

PICK THE RIGHT NEIGHBORHOODS

You've heard it before: location, location, location. It's the same when you're looking at investment properties. Define your target neighborhood, so you are able to establish your investment comfort zone boundary—your "farm area." Buying properties near your home also encourages you to visit the job site more often after you have made your purchase.

Over time, you can expand your area, as you gain experience and enlist the help of trusted experts in making your purchase decisions. You can flip houses in any neighborhood, but we recommend you start in the low to middle-priced areas that are twenty-five to sixty years old.

If a neighborhood is newer than twenty-five years old, then there won't be much fix-up needed; if it's older than sixty years, then there may be additional problems to complicate your deals. Houses built in the 1950s can be drastically different than houses built in the '30s and '40s because of the different methods of construction. In the 1950s, construction standards became much more uniform throughout the country. Because of such similar construction, middle- and lower-middle class neighborhoods are typically the easiest in which to determine values and find good deals. Since your first trusted expert will likely be your real-estate agent, find one willing to work diligently and who knows the neighborhoods in which you plan to work.

The neighborhood does not need to be in a location where you would choose to live. Needless to say, you should generally avoid high-crime areas, regardless of how great the deals may seem to be. Though tempting, the returns are simply not worth the risk. Believe us—we've lived that nightmare a few times. Buy in working-class suburban areas where housing is affordable and in demand. You can make a profit in other areas and types of houses, but those scenarios require more experience and introduce additional variables into the equation. For example, if the houses are dissimilar and not in proximity to each other, establishing value becomes more difficult. Once you have more experience, you can adjust your methods over time to find your niche.

To learn more about a target area, check the local police departments or websites such as CrimeReports.com for crime statistics. You should also research registered sex offenders living in the neighborhood on FamilyWatchdog.us. Other resources include the local chamber of commerce, planning department, real-estate brokers, and census reports. Subscribe to (and read!) local and regional newspapers and community newsletters. Much of this information is easily accessible online.

PICK THE RIGHT KIND OF HOUSE

We suggest you begin your investment venture by purchasing "starter homes" that are tired but not trashed. Starter homes are the least expensive single-family houses in each area. They will typically be two- or three-bedroom, ranch-style houses. Choose houses that are consistent with the neighborhood and suitable to the greatest number of potential buyers. Avoid houses that are the "odd man out" for the area, such as those built in a different era, in an unusual design, or with a functionally obsolete floor plan.

An ideal candidate would be a 1970s three-bedroom, ranch-style house with two bathrooms and a garage. These houses are in abundant supply, relatively modern in their construction, and appeal to a great number of buyers. They are typically easy to update with minimal expense. The older a house is, the more difficult it can be to bring it up to modern standards. In addition, there is more likelihood of running into environmental hazards (more on this in chapter 11). Keep in mind that houses built before 1978 have the potential for lead-based paint and should be tested if plans include extensive remodeling. Buyers realize they must make compromises in their home purchases and often will accept a less than ideal floor plan if they can get the desired number of bedrooms and bathrooms.

Square footage is important. A ranch is the ideal floor plan, though newer neighborhoods tend to have at least two levels above ground, or a main level and basement. Developers seem to put houses closer and closer together to maximize the value during the neighborhood build-out. All other things being equal, the fewer levels, the better. Of course, a thousand-square-foot, two-bedroom ranch would be more desirable if it had even an unfinished basement. Appraisers add less for basement square footage than for above ground square footage. The basement would allow an additional bed and bathroom for a modest cost. The investor decision regarding finishing the basement is another consideration. In most cases, we do not recommend finishing a basement because of the time and expense involved. It is usually more profitable to get in and out quickly and move on to the next house purchase.

Instead of adding or fixing items that add appraisal value, instead focus on things that add to the visual or emotional appeal to the house. Here are some examples of desired amenities that may increase value but may not be worth adding:

- air conditioning (unless you are in a very warm climate)
- a new garage (unless you are the only house on the block without one)

FLIP TIP

Bargain basement? As a general rule of thumb, basements are worth approximately 30-35 percent of the main floor unfinished and 40-45 percent finished. For example, if you had a thousand-square-foot ranch worth $100,000, an unfinished basement of the same size would be worth an additional $30,000-$35,000. If you finished the basement, it would be worth $40,000-$45,000. As you can see, finishing a basement doesn't get you a lot of "bang for your buck." If the house has two bedrooms, however, and you add conforming bedrooms in the basement (i.e., conforming to local housing code, which usually means having full egress windows), then you increase the demand for the house.

- a sprinkler system
- new windows
- solar panels and other energy-saving features

There are always exceptions, and we usually splurge in one highly visible area—for example, an elegant front door or impressive granite slab countertop. There are also certain features that most buyers will demand, most notably a comfortable living space with at least two bedrooms, a bathroom with a tub, central heating, adequate electric capacity, a nice kitchen with a dishwasher—you get the idea. Use common sense: it is a safer investment to buy the cheapest house in a better neighborhood and doll it up than to buy the highest-priced house in a marginal neighborhood with no room for improvement.

Before purchase, search the Internet to see if there have been any arrests or incidents at that address, and also check the National Clandestine Laboratory Register (http://www.dea.gov/clan-lab/clan-lab.shtml) to see if the house was a recognized "meth house." That research should also show if the house was legally mitigated. Of course, not all meth labs are noted in the public registry, and states differ in their disclosure policies.

Later, when you have access to the house, you can get an inexpensive, basic meth test kit at Home Depot or Lowe's. If the test is positive, hire a professional expert to assess it. If it still tests positive, you've got a major expense on your hands. You must hire a contractor certified by the Occupational Safety and Health Administration (OSHA) to do the work and get your local health department to sign off on the renovation. In some states you must disclose either way, but in other states you don't have to disclose if you did the proper mitigation. Either way, it's not a bad idea to disclose, since that nosy neighbor will undoubtedly welcome the buyer with, "Oh, you bought the meth house." That's when the lawsuit begins.

The goal is to do your due diligence to discover something now that a prospective buyer may uncover down the road. We will be teaching you how to look for hazards like these in later chapters.

BEYOND THE BASIC HOUSE

Over time, you may choose to venture into more expensive houses in upscale areas. Generally speaking, the more expensive the house, the greater the potential profit—and risk. These houses can offer large overall returns on your investment, though usually the profit will be a lower overall percentage of sales price. In other words, the profit margin in dollars should be high, but the profit margin percentage may be tighter. These houses can have extremely high carrying costs and tend to take longer to sell because of the smaller pool of potential buyers.

FUNCTIONAL OBSOLESCENCE

Be wary of poorly designed houses. It is OK to buy a house that needs some work or remodeling, but don't buy houses that have inherent design problems, such as three-bedroom designs where you have to walk through one bedroom to get to another. Those types of houses are nearly impossible to sell. After your renovation, the house should be in good overall condition, with no maintenance needed, and it should appeal to lots of buyers.

When you sell a house, it will typically have new paint, floor coverings, and appliances. If possible, it should have an open floor plan. We encourage you to visit model houses to see the latest trends and learn which aspects of new houses you can incorporate into your investment properties.

Finally, keep in mind that the eventual retail buyer will likely purchase the house with loan financing from the Federal Housing Administration (FHA), which operates under the HUD, or the US Department of Veterans Affairs (VA). The house must conform to strict guidelines for the guarantee of the loan. When it is time to sell, your house should have a roof that can be certified as being in good condition. The house should also be free from all safety concerns such as unfinished living areas and obvious structural issues, and fire egresses and handrails should be installed where needed. You can learn about these guidelines by contacting your local HUD or VA office and by talking to local appraisers.

ESTABLISH VALUE

It is important to establish the value of a property before making an offer. Base your offer on current value, but factor in what the house will sell for after necessary repairs, adjusting for the direction of the local market and seasonal fluctuations (e.g., buying a house in February when you plan on selling it in May). Always take a conservative approach until you gain experience in a particular market. Stay in neighborhoods you know, ones that contain similar houses—which makes price comparisons much easier.

Time lines are critical in real-estate investment and tend to be compressed compared to traditional (owner-occupied) sales. Depending on the seller type and motivation, coupled with the investor's resources, closings can occur within hours or months of the purchase offer. Most flips condense the retail sales process (from offer through closing) from the more typical five weeks down to about two weeks. By setting the closing date two weeks out, the investor will have time for a professional inspection and follow-up by structural engineers or other experts. This practice also leaves time for an appraisal from an investment-oriented lender. Cash deals or those involving seller financing, however, may be closed within twenty-four hours of the offer. As an example, we may give a seller twenty-four hours to respond to our offer, then we take about three to five days to do an inspection. If there is a loan involved, it will be with a preapproved company, which means the lender can typically close in ten days or less, because they use in-house appraisers. These investor loans are typically 70 percent or less of appraised value, so the lenders can move quickly.

Another example of a condensed process is foreclosure auctions. The type of investor who attends these has limited time to do online research, drive by the property, possibly see the inside, get to the sale with cash (or, rather, a cashier's check) in hand, and then bid on the property. While foreclosure sales are excellent opportunities in the right market, they are not for the inexperienced or faint of heart (see chapter 8).

When analyzing deals, it may help to think of the valuation process going from macro (big picture) to micro (details). First, the neighborhood should give you a very rough idea of each house's value. For example, let's say the typical house sells for $200,000; you can research that number by looking at the target property on Zillow.com, Trulia.com, Redfin .com, Realtor.com, or other similar websites. Simply look at the estimated value, and then review the estimated value of the neighboring properties. While they are helpful, be careful when using websites that offer computer-generated valuations. These are called automated valuation models (AVMs), which aggregate sales data from comparable properties to determine an estimated price. If the house or a neighboring property has sold recently or is actively for sale, you will be able to see pictures and read a real-estate broker's description of the property. This additional information is extremely helpful, but remember, the agent is trying to emphasize only the positive aspects of the property.

Also, review the satellite and street-view images of the property. Reviewing these images can save you hours of driving time and can help weed out properties in bad locations. Then you can adjust for amenities, and once you've seen the target property, for needed repairs. This basic information would allow you to come up with a rough estimate of ARV. The websites mentioned above also offer property data from the county tax assessor's office, but the information is less detailed than on the paid sites. For example, the seller's name may be missing, which would be quite relevant if the seller is a bank, as in the case of a foreclosure sale. If it was a foreclosure, it's a poor comparable sale because it was a distressed sale. Also be sure properties you are comparing are in the same school districts; otherwise, you may not garner equitable comparable sales (called comps).

Next, analyze the numbers to calculate your maximum purchase price. But if there is not a line of investors looking at the property, take the time for due diligence before making the offer. Remember, we are using the example of an offer that takes two weeks to close. Visit the property, and with the help of a trusted, professional adviser, make a better assessment of ARV, cost of improvements, and additional costs. Only then will you be prepared to make your offer.

Once under contract, you will need to do a more detailed review of potential ARV. Assuming it is in line with your initial rough estimate, you will need to invest in an inspection. Expect to pay several hundred dollars for a professional inspection, or enlist the help of a reliable contractor. Remember, the contractor may fail to discover major defects and also has different interests than you. We always recommend a professional inspector for new investors (and even seasoned investors) who don't have years of experience and relationships with the right contractors.

Doing Your Own Appraisal

As you evaluate potential purchases, you will need more than cursory familiarity with the neighborhood. You must be able to find and evaluate recently sold properties (comps), properties for sale (active listings), and be aware of relevant sales in the area (market activity).

Until now, much of this information was available only to licensed real-estate brokers. Today, most of this data is available through various channels, such as the county tax assessor, websites, or paid providers. Even if you do not have direct access to the MLS, subscriber websites such as Zillow.com give you detailed information, particularly in areas where online data is scarce. In a few states, sales prices of properties are not available publicly, in which case you will need the help of a real-estate broker with MLS access.

Utilizing an AVM site such as Zillow, you will be able to see an estimate (Zillow refers to it as a "Zestimate"). While helpful, this price estimate can be off by as much as 25 percent. As we said earlier, AVMs gather information from public records and do not accurately account for the condition of the property. Be prepared to develop your own ARV. Also, public records often have inaccurate information about square footage, additions, number of bedrooms and bathrooms, and basement versus above-ground living space. The property may have been improved or expanded after it was built (with or without permits).

Be aware of nearby busy streets, railroad tracks, or commercial developments. Of course, you may also find positive community elements such as parks and shopping districts. Lastly, don't assume that an undeveloped parcel will remain that way. Research in this area can help prevent you from buying next to the proposed chicken-processing plant or train line.

Evaluating comps is a mandatory skill you must develop over time. Only look at houses sold in the area within the past six months. Sometimes a comp will be under contract or in "pending" status. Being under contract is a positive sign, but don't assume that it is under contract for full price. The exception to this rule is that if the house went under contract within a day or two of being listed, it likely was very close to full price. In fact, the seller may have even received an offer greater than asking price.

Even if you start out in a cookie-cutter neighborhood, you will soon realize that each house is different. Houses next door to each other may still need adjustments for location. Issues to consider are views, direction the house faces, size and layout of yard, neighbors, busy street (as opposed to a cul-de-sac), lot livability and drainage (i.e., flat vs hilly), power lines, and water features. Compensate for the size, style, and age of each property. Note the property's overall condition, quality of construction, landscape, general appearance, and whether it has a garage (and, if so, how large it is).

Armed with all this information about your target property and its neighbors, and assuming it all looks good, it will be time to drive by these houses and compare them with the subject property. Take the time to get out of your car and walk around properties, while respecting the home-owners' privacy. If you are willing to knock on a few doors, you can often gather crucial information about the neighborhood and the seller's personal situation.

Enlisting a Real-Estate Broker's Help

You will need to enlist the help of real-estate brokers and may eventually choose to become one yourself. As mentioned earlier, good brokers are invaluable for their experience and for their access to information you would not otherwise have. Agents can help you by preparing a comparative market analysis for your target property. A CMA is a quick and dirty appraisal, and, of course, may not be as accurate (or expensive) as a full-blown appraisal. You may have also heard of a broker's price opinion (BPO), which is somewhere between a CMA and an actual property appraisal. Regardless of what you call it, you are engaging the broker to check your work and get a more accurate valuation than what you may have come up with on your own. Though your goal is to build a long-term relationship with a loyal agent, we remind you that your interests may be different from your broker's. Don't wholly rely on a broker's word or choice of sample properties as comps. You must do your own due diligence.

With the help of your real-estate broker, you should be able to see the most current listing and sales information. This information is not always updated promptly on consumer listing sites, but brokers may be fined if they don't provide timely, accurate information on sales and status changes. The MLS database also shows listing history, including the number of days on market as well as broker comments. In addition, the MLS provides information about the type of financing on the house, along with owner concessions, such as paid closing points. Terms can influence the sales price. For example, in a seller-carry sale, the seller takes all or part of the purchase price in the form of a note. The sale is usually at an inflated price and should be adjusted in your figures. Conversely, a distressed sale, such as a foreclosure short sale (discussed in a later chapter), may result in a deceptively lower price. You should be looking for "clean," arm's-length sales between a seller and buyer who is paying cash or obtaining a new loan to live in the property that is in top-notch condition.

Obtaining a Professional Appraisal

An expensive but accurate way to determine the value of a house is to hire a licensed appraiser. The appraisal will cost you around $400–$500. Some appraisers will offer a drive-by appraisal, which is cheaper than a full one but may still be reasonably accurate.

Understand that even a professional appraisal does not guarantee what you can sell the house for, nor does it dictate how long the house will take to sell. Markets are constantly changing, and the nuances of matching a house with a qualified buyer add a gray area to the equation. Learn to think like an appraiser. Even if you don't hire one in the purchase of your properties, you will have one involved when you go to sell them.

It may be worthwhile (and necessary if you are borrowing funds) to pay an appraiser to look over your first purchases to verify your value assessments. First, place the house under contract, and then complete a home inspection.

Licensed appraisers look at the three most similar houses in the vicinity that have sold recently. They then compare square footage and other attributes (see the sample appraisal form on page 246 in the appendix). Many variables will affect the price, but location and the number of bedrooms and bathrooms are the most important factors. As you might expect, there are exceptions to this rule. For example, the architectural style of house, its location and proximity to main roads, and whether it has a view or beach access will greatly affect the value. Of course, you probably will not be flipping many beachfront properties.

Appraisers typically generally look at comps that are within a 20 percent range in square footage as the target property. Often people think that if a house has a thousand square feet and is worth $100,000, then the 1,100 square-foot house next door would be worth $110,000. Wrong! The extra 10 percent in square footage is only a few percentage points in value. Assuming the two houses offer the same location, style, and number of bedrooms and baths, the additional square footage won't have a great impact on property valuation. Why? Property value is based on the value of the land, cost of construction, sewer, subdivision plans, and other factors. An extra few hundred feet of space involves little incremental cost in labor and materials.

Three-bedroom houses are noticeably more valuable than two-bedroom houses. Four- or five-bedroom houses don't add too much value compared to a three-bedroom if they are roughly the same size in square footage.

When comparing bathrooms, make sure you understand the different types of bathrooms and compare them correctly. It may seem insignificant, but buyers do care. A full bathroom includes a bathtub, toilet, and sink. A three-quarter bath has a shower but no tub. A half bath has only a toilet and sink. A three-quarter or full bathroom creates roughly the same value, assuming one bathroom in the house has a tub. Also, a five-piece bathroom (separate shower and tub) won't add much value over a full bathroom.

If the property was refinanced in the past year or so, take a look at the seller's appraisal. Appraisers do have some flexibility in showing a high or low value depending on the purpose for which they were hired. Sellers want a high appraisal, so their appraisers will use the highest comps. Likewise, an appraisal for a person fighting a high county-property-tax assessment may not be as accurate as an appraisal for a sale.

THE RECIPE FOR PROFITABILITY

Figuring out exactly what you should pay for a flip house comes down to subtracting out your projected costs, starting with the ARV in mind. Know your resale price, seller concessions, broker's fees, closing costs, fix-up costs, holding costs, and loan fees and you can arrive at a purchase price. But what about the profit? If you've been paying attention, you'll note that the preceding analysis omits profit. You have to subtract your profit from that final price. So, how much profit is reasonable? Well, that depends on your business model and the strength of your local market, but generally a retailer should seek a profit of 10–15 percent of the ultimate selling price. So with a $200,000 ARV, that's $20K–$30K net profit. However, on more expensive or riskier deals, you may want to set the bar at 20 percent net profit. And on smaller, less expensive homes, a little less profit may be acceptable, particularly if the rehab on the house is minor and you are in a very competitive market.

Another way of quickly analyzing a deal is by a percentage of ARV. In a normal market, offering 70 percent of ARV minus repairs is a good rule of thumb. This leaves a gross profit of 30 percent, a little more than half of which will go to "soft" costs such as closing costs, loan fees, carrying costs, and broker's commissions, leaving you just under 15 percent net profit. If you are buying a property from a wholesaler, your profit may be closer to 10 percent, which is an acceptable trade-off for the steady supply of deals from the wholesaler.

WRAPPING IT UP

- Learn the right neighborhoods to invest in.
- Pick the right houses that are the lowest risk.
- Figure out the ARV of a house before making an offer.
- Enlist the help of professionals to solidify your numbers.

CHAPTER 6

Funding Deals

Cash is king, so they say, but funding deals does not always require a pile of your own money. Let's explore some ways to fund a flip without using any of your own money. Using other people's money (OPM) is a common practice among investors.

CONVENTIONAL LOANS

A conventional loan from a bank or mortgage company will give you the best interest rate, but may not be the best choice for a flip. First, there are many loan costs involved up front that may not be worth it, considering you only need the funds for a few months. Second, it can take quite a while, which ruins your chance of offering a seller a fast and easy closing. Third, most lenders require a minimum 20 percent down payment for non-owner-occupied loans, and you will have to pay for the repairs out of pocket. On a $200,000 purchase price for a house that requires $50,000 in rehab, you are looking at more than $100,000 by the time you are done when you factor in origination fees and closing costs.

Conventional lenders generally penalize you for negotiating a good deal by basing the loan on the appraised value or the purchase price, whichever is less. Let's take a property with a market value (after repairs) of $200,000. This property will appraise for $100,000 in its present condition. You negotiate a purchase price of $80,000. A conventional lender will lend you up to 80 percent of the purchase price (80 percent of $80,000 is $64,000), not 80 percent of the after-repaired value.

HARD-MONEY LENDERS

When conventional financing takes too long or is not available due to a low FICO score or some other reason, hard money can be a deal saver. If you invest in a lot of property, your FICO score can plummet simply due to the number of mortgages you owe. Alternatively, the properties that can be had for an advantageous price may not meet conventional banking criteria. In either case, hard-money lenders are not restricted in the same way that conventional banks are.

Hard-money lenders can be individuals or companies that specialize in investor loans. These loans are based primarily on the value of the collateral, although there will still be some borrower qualification process. If you buy the property at a substantial discount, you may actually receive 90 to even 100 percent financing for the deal. Conventional lenders typically take anywhere from five weeks to six months to complete investor loans. Hard-money lenders can generally fund in one to two weeks from the time you have all the paperwork in place.

Another great thing about hard-money loans is that they are based on the future after-repair value of the property. So, for example, if the ARV is $200,000 and you can buy the property for $100,000 and it needs $40,000 in repairs, you can borrow funds for the purchase price *plus* the repair costs. A conventional lender will not do this kind of deal, particularly when you come to closing with little or no personal funds of your own.

Hard-money interest rates are quite high—usually three to four times the going rate for conventional loans! Plus, you should expect to pay 3–5 percent of the loan amount as an origination fee up front, in addition to the monthly interest payments. Most hard-money loans have a six-month balloon (early-payoff requirement), although you could negotiate an extension up front in case your property is not resold in six months. And most hard-money loans have a prepayment (early payoff) penalty of three months of interest or more based on the original loan amount.

Wow, that is pretty hard! Yet when you consider the speed and convenience of the funds, you'll see that the terms are perfectly reasonable if you are in a hurry, don't want to (or cannot) come up with the cash for a project, or can't qualify for a conventional loan. Also, if you compare a hard-money loan to bringing on a money partner for half the profits, a hard-money loan is *much* cheaper (and often much less of a headache).

Hard-money loans used to be very easy to get, based solely on the equity in the project versus your personal financial condition. What the late-night-TV and seminar gurus don't reveal is that in recent years, hard-money lenders have become much stricter, requiring a minimum FICO score, references, no recent foreclosures or bankruptcies, and, in many cases, a requirement that you put down some of your own cash in the deal. Still, it's significantly easier to get a hard-money loan than a conventional bank loan.

A checklist of items your hard-money lender will likely want to see can be found on page 247 in the appendix. Some sage advice—don't give the information to the hard-money lender in a piecemeal fashion. Put together all the facts, and send it off in a FedEx package or well-organized PDF by e-mail.

FHA AND FNMA

The federal Department of Housing and Urban Development offers an FHA 203(k) loan. You don't technically borrow from HUD; you borrow from a local lender who has to conform the loan to FHA's standards, so that HUD will guarantee the loan if it goes bad.

Basically, a 203(k) is a home-improvement loan. This program can be used to accomplish rehabilitation and improvement of an existing one- to four-unit dwelling (e.g., houses, condos, small apartments) in one of three ways:

1. To purchase a dwelling and the land on which the dwelling is located and rehabilitate it
2. To purchase a dwelling on another site, move it onto a new foundation on the mortgaged property and rehabilitate it
3. To refinance existing indebtedness and rehabilitate a dwelling

We'll focus on the first and third scenarios. To purchase a dwelling and the land on which the dwelling is located and to refinance existing indebtedness and rehabilitate such a dwelling, the mortgage must be a first mortgage on the property, and the loan proceeds (other than rehabilitation funds) must be available before the rehabilitation begins. The 203(k) loan is similar to a typical FHA 203(b) loan in that you only have to put a small amount down (3.5 percent) and you can borrow the rest. Nice so far, because conventional lenders require 20 percent or more down. Now get this, FHA will also lend you the fix-up money *on top of* almost 97 percent of the purchase price. Talk about a low-money-down deal!

Once your loan is approved, a date will be set for closing. After closing, a repair escrow account is set up, and the repairs must start within thirty days of closing and completed within six months. You cannot do the repairs yourself; you have to hire a certified contractor to do the work.

Now, the bad news . . . To qualify for the loan, you must *live* in the property. For how long? Well, that's a fuzzy one. You promise to live there for at least twelve months. Don't lie, though; they will check shortly after the closing by knocking on the door—no joke! And since it's a federally insured loan, it's a federal offense to lie.

There are a couple of workarounds, however:

1. **Move in and then move out.** Buy the property, live in it after the rehab is done, then sell it a few months later. Kind of an inconvenience, but doable if you are single and have no kids.
2. **Have one of your kids live there.** You can have a child or nephew get the loan and buy the property, with you cosigning the loan as a guarantor. Sometime later, your relative moves out and you sell the property and split the proceeds.

The Federal National Mortgage Association (FNMA, known as Fannie Mae) and the Federal Home Loan Mortgage Corporation (FHLMC, known as Freddie Mac) have similar programs that allow you to buy with only 10 percent down. If the property is in decent condition, it's only a small amount of money out of pocket to rehab the place. Unlike a 203(k) loan, you don't have to live in it. There's a catch, however: the property must be purchased from Fannie or Freddie's inventory of foreclosed homes, which you can find on HomePath.com and HomeSteps.com.

HELOC

A home-equity line of credit can be an excellent financing tool when used properly. A HELOC is basically a credit card secured by a mortgage or deed of trust on your property. You only pay interest on the amounts you borrow on the HELOC. If you don't use the line of credit, you don't have any monthly payments to make. You can access the HELOC by writing checks provided by the lender. In most cases, it will be a second lien on your property.

The HELOC should only be used as a temporary financing source, which can be repaid when you refinance or sell the property. You should generally not use your HELOC as a down payment or any other long-term financing source as you may get yourself into financial trouble. If you don't pay the HELOC, you can lose your home!

Some institutional lenders won't lend you the balance if you borrowed the funds for the down payment. But smaller commercial banks that offer "portfolio" loans have more flexibility and may allow you to use HELOC money as a down payment. Once again, use caution when borrowing money in this manner; only do it if the deal is a steal and you can pay off the HELOC money within a few months.

There are limits on the deductions you can take on your personal tax return for interest paid on your HELOC. Generally speaking, you can only deduct that portion of interest on debt that does not exceed the value of your home and is less than $100,000. But if you do your real-estate investments as a corporate entity, you can always lend the money to that entity and have the entity take the deduction as a business interest expense. This transaction must, of course, be reported on your personal return, and must be an "arm's-length transaction" (i.e., documented in writing and within the realm of a normal business transaction). Consult with your tax adviser before proceeding with this strategy.

CREDIT CARDS AND PERSONAL LINES OF CREDIT

You may already have more available credit than you realize. Credit cards and other existing revolving-debt accounts can be quite useful in real-estate investing. Most major credit cards allow you to take cash advances or write checks to borrow on the account. The transaction fees and interest rates are fairly high, but you can access this money on twenty-four hours' notice. Also, you won't have to pay loan costs that are normally associated with a real-estate transaction, such as title insurance, appraisals, pest inspections, surveys, and so on. Often, you will be better off paying 18 percent interest or more on a credit line for six months than paying 9 percent interest on an institutional loan, which has up-front costs that would take you years to recoup.

Promotional interest rates are frequently available on your credit cards, but again, beware. These rates often skyrocket after several months. Chances are, if you have a good credit history, you will be able to raise your credit limits on your existing cards.

High-interest debt must be approached cautiously, and your personality type may not embrace the idea of tens of thousands of dollars in revolving debt. But avoiding mortgages saves you time and often money for short-term borrowing, so keep credit cards in mind. You can also benefit by using department-store cards with no cash-advance features. These cards are available through all the major lumberyards, hardware-store chains, and home-improvement stores. They will allow you to finance your materials costs that can add up to many thousands of dollars. The interest you pay for the use of this money is tax deductible, so be careful to separate your business from your personal credit card use.

FRIENDS AND FAMILY

Sure, friends and relatives are obvious choices for borrowing money, but they may be as skeptical as an institutional lender, if you have no experience in real estate. They may also try to boss you around and nag you about repaying the money you borrowed, jeopardizing your relationship. Do yourself a favor and wait until you have more experience before approaching friends and relatives. Once they see that you're making money, they will come to you!

SELLER FINANCING

Having the seller finance the sale, even in part, is the ideal way to purchase a property. It does not require bank qualification, credit, personal liability,

> **FLIP TIP**
>
> **Out of your own pocket?** You may be able to raise some or all of the cash on your own because you may have more personal sources than you realize, such as the following:
>
> - Old car or recreational vehicle to sell
> - Collectibles, gold, or jewelry to sell on eBay
> - Annuity you can cash out
> - 401(k) at work you can borrow from
> - Part-time job
>
> We know you don't want to give up that special something of yours, but you can always buy another when you've made your first million!

or garbage fees. Realize that if you don't have loan costs involved in the transaction, you can afford to pay the seller a higher price.

A **seller-carry transaction** occurs whenever the seller takes less than all cash for the purchase price. Keep in mind that all cash does not necessarily mean you paid cash out of your pocket; it can also mean borrowed money. The less of the purchase price you have to pay, the better the deal becomes—even if you flip the property to another investor. The ideal scenario would be if the seller owned the property free and clear, then took a small cash down payment and a note for the balance of the purchase price.

PARTNER

Bringing in partners is a good way to start if you are flat broke and lack experience. But choose your partners carefully. Don't select a partner who contributes the same thing you do (i.e., enthusiasm, but no money). Don't pick a partner on the basis of friendship or because you think it would be fun to be in business together. Instead, choose a partner who has money and experience in real estate and who can fund a deal that you have negotiated. If you want to see the process through to the retail buyer (and want to make more profit than if you wholesale the deal), then using a partner with money and experience can be a worthwhile venture.

How to Split Profits

Every deal will be different, but start the negotiating with a fifty-fifty profit split. The partner putting up the money and doing the work may insist on more of the profit if he or she is doing more, such as supervising workers. Based on the estimated sales price, purchase costs, and repair costs, you can make a reasonable estimate of the total net profit. If your projected percentage is not sufficient, consider flipping the property to the investor and moving on to another deal.

Joint-Venture Agreement

If you choose to take on a partner, you've created a joint venture, which is a limited-purpose partnership. Develop a written joint agreement with your partner that spells out, among other things, the duties of each party and the manner in which money is contributed (see a sample joint-venture agreement on page 248 in the appendix). For a long-term partnership arrangement, consider forming a corporation or limited liability company (LLC).

WRAPPING IT UP

- Sell non-income-producing assets to raise capital for flips.
- Learn conventional and creative ways of borrowing funds to buy real estate.
- Alternative funding techniques might not involve banks or mortgage companies.
- Partnerships and seller financing are good ways to minimize cash requirements.

PART II

Knowing the Details

CHAPTER 7

Contracts and Agreements

Talk is cheap. Without a written agreement, you don't have a deal. At some point after negotiating with a seller (or buyer), you need to get things in writing. A well-written real-estate agreement will save you a lot of headaches, arguments, and legal problems, so it is important to have good legal counsel to review your deals and your business practices. But your lawyer won't always be there, so you should learn how to draft your own contracts. While the sample purchase contract found on page 258 in the appendix of this book is a good start, we advise you to review your contracts and processes with your local attorney.

Real-estate contracts are based on common contract principles, so it is important that you understand the basics of contract law.

OFFER, COUNTEROFFER, AND ACCEPTANCE

The process begins with an offer. A contract is formed when an offer is made and accepted. In most states, standardized contracts drafted in the form of offers are used by real-estate brokers and attorneys. The offer is usually signed by the buyer (offeror) and contains all the material terms of a contract, with the exception of the seller's signature.

The basic building block of a contract is mutual agreement. The contract is not binding until the seller accepts, creating a meeting of the minds. An acceptance is made if the offeree (in this case, the seller) agrees to the exact terms of the offer. If the offer comes back to the offeror with changes, there is no binding contract but, rather, a counteroffer. Thus, if the seller signs the purchase contract but changes the closing date to five days sooner, there is no agreement. Furthermore, if the offer is not accepted in the time frame and manner set forth by the offeror, there is no contract. For example, if the contract specifies that acceptance must be made by facsimile (fax), an acceptance by telephone call or mail will not suffice.

Several basic requirements must be present to make a real-estate contract valid:

Mutual agreement. As stated, there must be a mutual agreement or a meeting of minds.

In writing. With few exceptions, a contract for purchase and sale of real estate must be in writing to be enforceable. Consequently, if a buyer makes an offer in writing and the seller accepts orally and then backs out, the buyer is out of luck.

Identify the parties. The contract must identify the parties. Although not legally required, a contract commonly sets forth full names with middle initials (this helps the title company prepare the title commitment). If one of the parties is a corporation, it should state so (e.g., "North American Land Acquisitions, Inc., a Nevada corporation").

Identify the property. The contract must identify the property. Although not required, a legal description should be included. A vague description such as "my lakefront home" may not be specific enough to create a binding contract.

Purchase price. The contract must state the purchase price of the property or a reasonably ascertainable figure (e.g., "appraised value as determined by ABC Appraisers").

Consideration. A contract must have consideration to be enforceable. Consideration is the benefit, interest, or value that induces a promise; it is the glue that binds a contract. The amount of consideration is not important, but rather whether there is consideration at all. It is common for a

FLIP TIP

Write or wrong? As we mentioned earlier, most contracts state that any changes to it must be in writing. What exactly does "writing" mean? Could an e-mail suffice? The answer is, it depends; if the contract says all changes must be in writing and signed by both parties, an e-mail will not suffice. The lesson is, make sure your contract is clear, and if you're not sure, enlist the help of a qualified attorney to review it.

contract to read something like "ten dollars and other good and valuable consideration has been paid and received." Consideration need not be cash; it can be property, a promissory note, or an agreement to perform services.

Signatures. A contract must be signed to be enforceable. The party signing must be of legal age and sound mind. A notary's signature or witness is not required. A facsimile signature is usually acceptable, as long as the contract states that facsimile signatures are valid. Finally, a contract can be signed at different times or on different physical forms (in "counterparts") if the contract language allows it.

EARNEST MONEY

Buyers will usually put up earnest money to bind a contract and show that they are serious buyers. Most sellers ask for an earnest money deposit because they are afraid of tying up the property and rejecting other potential buyers.

The law requires no specific amount of earnest money. In fact, if the transaction involves the buyer simply taking over a loan and the property has no equity, it may be appropriate for the seller to give the buyer consideration. When you are buying, you want to put down as little money as possible ($500 or less), although it will add credibility to give more. When selling, you should get as much as possible ($1,000 or more). The amount of earnest money needed will depend on the motivation of the parties, seller's representation by real-estate professionals, the purchase price, and the length of time until closing.

If you are dealing with a seller represented by a broker, you won't be taken seriously with an offer that involves only one hundred dollars or so in earnest money. Expect to put down at least 1 percent of the purchase price as earnest money if you are dealing with a real-estate broker. Also, when dealing directly with motivated sellers, the amount of earnest money you offer can be a test of their motivation. Try verbally offering one hundred dollars earnest while negotiating and writing up the contract to see how the seller responds.

Attorneys and real-estate agents often "prefill" the contracts before the parties meet. We think this is a mistake. If you show up with a finalized contract, the seller may get nervous and bail out on the deal. Instead, fill out the contract by hand in front of the seller as you negotiate each item. In sales circles, this is known as the order-form close.

If you are afraid of losing your earnest money as a buyer, you may consider offering a **promissory note** as earnest money. A seller may be reluctant to accept a promissory note rather than cash because, if you default, the seller must sue you to collect on the note. As a compromise, you can structure the contract so the seller receives a promissory note as earnest money that is paid in full after the property is inspected, but before closing.

Who Should Hold the Earnest Money?

A big issue for the parties is who should hold the earnest-money deposit in escrow. Theoretically, the escrow agent (the person holding the earnest money) must release the funds to the seller if the buyer breaches and to the buyer if the contract is canceled. But the escrow agent will not usually release the funds without the permission of both parties, even in the face of a clear breach or cancellation. Furthermore, if the escrow agent is the listing broker, he or she may side with the seller and not release the money (listing brokers have an incentive to keep the earnest money, because their listing agreement usually gives them part of the forfeited earnest-money deposit as a commission). The seller would obviously prefer to have his or her broker hold escrow, while the buyer would want a neutral or buyer-friendly title or escrow company to hold the earnest money.

CONTINGENCIES

As mentioned earlier, a contingency is a clause in a contract that must be satisfied for the contract to be complete. If the contingencies are not satisfied, the contract terminates and the parties go their merry ways. The contract will usually provide that in the event of termination, the buyer is entitled to a return of his or her earnest money.

Most standard real-estate contracts contain an **inspection-clause contingency**, which gives the buyer a certain amount of time to inspect the premises. After the inspection, the buyer should provide the seller with a list of potential problems or defects and give the seller a chance to remedy these problems, adjust the purchase price, or choose to terminate the agreement. Most standard inspection clauses place the burden of inspecting and disapproving on the buyer. Thus, the buyer's failure to inspect and object in a timely fashion will result in a waiver of this contingency. Used properly, the inspection clause will allow a buyer to terminate a contract that turns out to be a bad deal.

Inspection clauses can be written in a variety of ways. As the buyer, of course, you would prefer a more liberal, subjective approach, permitting you to perform the inspection without a licensed professional and disapprove of items in any manner you wish. But you cannot use the inspection clause in an arbitrary fashion to cancel a purchase contract, for there is an implied duty of good faith on your part to deal fairly. For example, if you don't inspect the property or you inspect it briefly and raise minor objections and then walk away from the deal, you could be in breach of your contract.

Virtually every standard real-estate contract gives the buyer a **contingency to obtain a loan** to purchase the property. Once again, there's an implied duty of good faith here, so the buyer cannot simply sit back and say, "Oh well, I couldn't get a loan." The buyer is obligated to make reasonable efforts to apply to various lenders and comply with their demands for proof of employment, copies of tax returns, etc. The loan contingency will usually state a certain date by which the buyer must present the seller with a copy of a written loan commitment from the lender. If the deadline is not met, the seller can extend the deadline or the contract fails.

The contract will usually provide that it is **contingent upon proof of a marketable title** by a certain date. The seller is typically required to provide the buyer a copy of a title report or a title commitment showing that the title is insurable. Even if the title report shows problems with the title, the contract is still in force if the seller can cure the problems before closing and deliver a marketable title. For example, an existing mortgage lien or judgment is not fatal, because it can be satisfied by the seller from the proceeds at the closing.

BREACH OF CONTRACT

What happens when one party breaches the agreement? There are many legal implications of a party breaching a contract, but it is more important that you understand the practical side, because real-estate litigation is usually a costly matter that should be avoided.

Buyer's Remedies for Breach of Contract

If the seller breaches the contract by failing to close the title, the buyer has three legal remedies:

1. Sue for specific performance
2. Sue for damages
3. Sue for return of the earnest money

Sue for Specific Performance

Specific performance is a remedy granted by a court, which forces the seller to sell to the buyer. If the property is unique and you feel like spending $10,000 in legal fees, then you will probably win the lawsuit if the seller refuses to close. If the seller refused to close because he or she got greedy and found another buyer, you can record a copy of your contract or an affidavit (called a memorandum of agreement) in the public records. This will create a cloud on the title, which will alarm other buyers and title companies and may prevent the seller from closing with another buyer. Obviously, recording a contract or memorandum is a much more inexpensive and practical approach. (You will find a sample memorandum of agreement on page 261 in the appendix.)

Be mindful that if you record the memorandum without sufficient legal cause, you can be sued by the seller for "slander of title." We advise you to consider seeking legal counsel before filing such a document.

Sue for Damages

If the property was to be purchased at a discount or was intended to be resold for a profit, you may be able to sue for your loss of potential profit. Of course, loss of profit is difficult to prove; it is not clear exactly what price you could have sold it for, how long it would have taken you, and how much it would have cost you in repairs. Even if you could prove this by expert testimony, the lawsuit could cost you $10,000 in legal fees.

Sue for Return of the Earnest Money

If the seller refuses to close and blames you for the incident, you may have to sue to get back your earnest money. Most local small claims courts can hear these types of cases, as long as the amount of earnest money involved is small (most small claims courts will only hear cases involving controversies of less than $2,000–$3,000). If the earnest money is more (shame on you for giving so much!), you will need to proceed to the next highest court, which usually conducts somewhat informal trials similar to small claims court. You may need a lawyer to assist you with the court procedure.

Seller's Remedies for Buyer's Breach of Contract

As you can see, the seller, who has title, is in a better position than the buyer. The seller also has three legal remedies for the buyer's breach of contract:

1. Keep the buyer's earnest money
2. Sue for damages
3. Sue for specific performance

Keep the Buyer's Earnest Money

The seller's best remedy is to keep the buyer's earnest money. If the contract calls for the seller to keep the earnest money as liquidated damages, then the seller can keep it, even if he or she sells the property to some-one else for full price. In most cases, the buyer will walk away and cut any losses, especially if the earnest money is not significant. If the buyer objects and the money is held in escrow, then the seller and buyer will have to go to court to battle it out.

Even if the buyer is in breach, he or she may be able to argue that it is unjust for the seller to keep the earnest money. This argument is not usu-ally successful, unless the amount of money is large and the buyer's breach was insignificant (e.g., the buyer was one day late in obtaining the loan commitment and the seller declared the contract in default). In the case of a forfeited earnest-money deposit, it may be cheaper for both parties to settle out of court.

Sue for Damages

If the contract does not limit the seller's remedy to the retention of the earnest money, the seller can also sue the buyer for actual damages. For example, if the property is in the Northeast and the seller took the property off the market for the summer, the seller may now be obliged to hold the property through the winter at the seller's expense. If the seller can quan-tify the damages, it may be possible to sue the buyer for failing to close. Of course, this can be an expensive lawsuit, but at least the seller will have leverage if the buyer will not agree to release the earnest-money deposit.

Sue for Specific Performance

The seller can also sue for specific performance to force the buyer to pur-chase the property. This course may be futile, since the buyer may not be financially able to purchase the property.

DRAFTING THE OFFER

The sample contract provided on page 258 in the appendix is fine if you are dealing directly with a seller without a broker. It contains all the neces-sary contingencies you need to protect yourself. If you are making an offer through a real-estate broker, you may have to use the standard contract that brokers use, so learn it backward and forward.

The following is a checklist of items to look for when you are buying. Most of these clauses are present in some form in the standard real-estate contract.

The Right to Assign

As the buyer, you want to have the right to assign your contract to another buyer of your choice. An assignable contract allows you to change the buyer to a partner, a corporate entity, or you intend to wholesale it. By placing your name as buyer with the words, "and/or assigns," you automatically give yourself that right. But if the preprinted portion of the contract contains a provision forbidding assignment without the seller's permission, you must also cross out that provision.

Should you disclose that you intend to assign the contract to a third party? Legally, a purchase agreement is assignable in the absence of any provision that prohibits assignment, as long as the assignment does not unreasonably hinder the seller's rights and obligations under the agreement. For example, if the deal was for $200,000 cash, and the buyer assigned the contract to a third party who purchased the property, the seller is not inconvenienced in any way. Yet if the seller discovers that you made a huge profit, he or she may be upset. We have, on occasion, seen lawyers threaten (unsuccessfully) to sue buyers for misrepresentation after their contracts were assigned for a profit. This effort to bully the investor is silly, of course, since it would be no different if the buyer purchased the property for cash, then resold it a day later for a profit. As a practical matter, it may help to diffuse such an argument in advance with an explicit statement in the contract, "Buyer may assign this agreement to a third party for a profit."

Of course, such a clause may also alert a seller into thinking, "Maybe I should ask for more." Whether such a clause is necessary is a tough call, and it depends on the particulars of the deal. For example, if the seller is in foreclosure, divorce, or some other motivation that requires him or her to knowingly sell the property below market, it wouldn't hurt to include the clause. But if the reason you got a killer deal is because the seller is ignorant of market conditions (such as an out-of-state seller), you risk blowing a good deal. If you are a licensed real-estate broker, the seller may assume you are acting on his or her behalf to get the highest price, so you should disclose that you could get more if you listed the property.

The Earnest Money

Follow the guidelines discussed above, and never let the seller hold the earnest money.

New Loan Contingency

If you intend to obtain a bank loan to purchase the property, you should include a loan contingency clause in the contract. The loan contingency clause has been interpreted broadly by courts as putting the obligation on the buyer to make reasonable attempts to obtain a loan. Banks will lend to virtually anyone who has enough money to put down and is willing to pay a high rate of interest. The buyer should have a clause that reads similar to the following: "Buyer is not required to accept a loan with an interest rate higher than _____ percent over _____ years and payments exceeding $_____/month, and buyer is not required to accept any loan that requires more than $_____ in points, closing, or other fees."

Seller Financing

If the purchase includes some seller financing, the buyer should look for the following:

- The loan should contain no due-on-sale clause (so the property can be resold to another investor on seller-carry terms).
- The loan should be nonrecourse, which prevents a judgment against the buyer if the loan is in default. The operative language is: "Seller's sole recourse in case of default shall be against the property and there shall be no personal recourse against the borrower." Another way to limit your liability is to have a corporate entity, such as an LLC or corporation, sign for the obligation.

Appraisal Provision

If the contract calls for an appraisal contingency, the buyer would prefer one that does not require a licensed appraiser. This will give the buyer an out if he or she can find a local real-estate broker who will vouch that the property will not appraise.

Right to Choose the Closing Agent

We cannot tell you how much heartache and aggravation you will save by using a closing agent who understands the double-closing process (more about this later). As the buyer, insist on the right to choose the title or escrow company so that you remain in control. If the property is listed with a broker, he or she may have a company preference. Offer to pay the full closing fee (usually about $400–$600) for the right to choose—it is well worth it!

Right to Extend the Closing Date

Most contracts call for a specific closing date. If the buyer is not ready to close, the seller can hold the buyer in default. Here are some tips for buying time:

- Make the closing date "on or about" rather than "on or before." What does "on or about" mean? This is up to the judge, but we guarantee it will buy you some time (of course, when selling, make your closing date "on or before").
- Have the right to extend the closing date if it is not your fault: "Said date may be extended an additional fifteen (15) days if lender requires additional documentation, paperwork, or actions from the buyer and said delay is not due to the fault of the buyer."
- Have the right to extend for thirty days by paying the seller the equivalent of one month's mortgage payment.

Possession

As the buyer, you want possession of the property concurrent with the closing. Typical wording would be "possession by buyer to occur upon transfer of deed." If the sellers are living in the house, make sure you have the right to charge them a hefty daily rent if they are in possession after closing. Since you probably do not want to become a landlord and attempt to collect rent from your seller, it is best to inspect the property immediately preceding closing and confirm the seller has vacated. If the contract calls for allowing the sellers to remain in possession after closing, consider holding back some of the proceeds to ensure you will get possession when you need it. Many sellers underestimate the time they need to move, and the longer they are in possession, the more money it costs you.

Also, the contract should state that the property be left "broom clean and free from all debris." A cleaning crew and a hauling truck could cost you several hundred dollars if the seller leaves a lot of unwanted property behind.

Seller's Remedy Limited to Earnest Money

Unless stated otherwise, the seller can keep your earnest money and sue you for breach. Give small earnest-money deposits and use the phrase, "Upon default, seller's sole and only remedy shall be to retain buyer's earnest money." If the seller insists on a larger earnest-money deposit, insert a phrase that entitles you to interest at the highest rate permitted by law on your money. That way, the seller will be less likely to hold on to your earnest money for six months while you sue to get it back.

Weasel Clauses

As a buyer you'll want at least one contingency or "weasel" clause. If the buyer can get out of a contract without breaching, then the buyer is entitled to his or her earnest money. The less earnest money you put down, the less you need a contingency clause. If you do need a weasel clause, here are two favorites:

> "This agreement is subject to inspection and approval of the property by the buyer in writing prior to _____."
> "This agreement is subject to attorney approval within seventy-two (72) hours."

Access to Property Before Closing

If you intend to flip the property to another investor, you may need access to the property before closing. If you intend to rehab the property, you have to get access to obtain contractors' bids. Try using the clause: "Buyer shall be entitled to a key and be entitled access to show partners, lenders, inspectors, and contractors prior to closing. Buyer may place an appropriate sign on the property prior to closing for prospective tenants and/or assigns."

Create a Standard Addendum

If your deals often involve real-estate brokers, you might want to draft a standard addendum that contains your favorite clauses. You also will have to learn what specific clauses in the standard contract used by local real-estate brokers are favorable and unfavorable to you when buying and selling. Take time to meet with a local attorney who will review the standard contract and help you come up with a standard addendum. It is amazing what clauses people (including brokers) will accept when part of a so-called standard addendum. A few bucks spent with a savvy attorney can be a worthwhile investment.

BROKER CONTRACT VS HOMEMADE CONTRACT

Some people prefer using the standard real-estate contracts that local real-estate brokers use, while others use their own homemade version. If you are a licensed real-estate broker, we recommend you use the standard contract with an addendum. As a nonlicensee, you can use either. Our purchase contract is pretty short and to the point, so we generally give the seller a choice of which form to use (and guess which one they usually choose!).

Most of the discussion here has involved drafting a contract slanted in your favor when *buying*. When *selling* a property to another investor, you should use the standard real-estate contract that the real-estate brokers use in your area. This method will make financing easier for the buyer and for banks, and title companies are familiar with the form. Several words of advice when wholesaling (see chapter 9) to another investor: limit the inspection contingency to forty-eight hours, have a short time before the closing date, and get as much earnest money as possible. A serious investor should have no objection to inspecting the property immediately, putting up $2,000 or more as earnest money, and closing within a couple of weeks.

ELECTRONIC SIGNATURES

Many investors are now using electronic signatures, through online services such as RightSignature.com, DocuSign.com, or HelloSign.com. In 2000 the federal government passed the ESIGN Act, which gave electronic signatures the same legal weight as handwritten ones. State law, for the most part, has followed suit in recognizing the equivalent validity of e-signatures and traditional ink signatures. In most cases, you will be meeting with a seller face-to-face and doing it the old-fashioned way, but e-signatures can be efficient if the seller lives out of the area.

WRAPPING IT UP

- Take the time to learn about contracts.
- Work with a competent attorney.
- Choose the contracts that work best for your needs.
- Learn the local contracts brokers use.
- Create a standard addendum to the standard contract.

CHAPTER 8

Foreclosures

In this chapter we will explain what foreclosures are and take a look at the somewhat complicated auction process that occurs after a property has been foreclosed. "Chasing foreclosures" is jargon for following properties through the process while attempting to entice the owners to sell. Foreclosure properties can be the best (or the most frustrating) source of leads. The good part is that foreclosures often sell at steep discounts; the bad part is that once the foreclosure is filed, the information is public and other investors are competing with you. To work the foreclosure market successfully, you must understand how the foreclosure process works. Also, realize that property owners (especially owner-occupants) are protected to varying degrees from predators once their loan is in default, or even when they are behind on their payments.

Foreclosure is a legal process the mortgage holder can initiate once the collateral for a promissory note (i.e., the house) goes into default. The process is slightly different from state to state, but there are basically two types of foreclosure: judicial and nonjudicial. In mortgage states, judicial foreclosure is commonly used, while in deed-of-trust states, nonjudicial foreclosure is the most common. Some states permit both types of proceedings, but it is standard practice in most states to exclusively use one method or the other. (You can find a complete summary of specific states' foreclosure processes on page 262 in the appendix.)

JUDICIAL FORECLOSURE

Judicial foreclosure is a lawsuit that the lender (mortgagee) brings against the borrower (mortgagor) to get the property. Like all lawsuits, foreclosure starts with a summons and a complaint served upon the borrower and any other parties with inferior rights in the property. Most junior liens (i.e., mortgages and judgments behind the loan being foreclosed) are wiped out by foreclosure, though there are exceptions—liens that can be considered senior to a primary (first) mortgage. HOA dues (to a limited extent), county property taxes, and local assessments must be investigated. Also, existing property leases may survive the sale under the Protecting Tenants at Foreclosure Act of 2009, meaning the lessee may have the right to stay in the property after the sale. Of course, rent would be due to you as the new owner if you were to "inherit" a tenant. You could let the lease run its course or give the tenant a monetary incentive to leave early (colloquially called "cash for keys").

If the borrower does not file an answer to the lawsuit in a judicial foreclosure, the lender gets a judgment by default. A referee is then appointed by the court to compute the total amount (including interest and attorney fees) that is due. The lender must then advertise a notice of sale in the newspaper for several weeks. If the total amount due is not paid, the court appoints a person to conduct a public sale on the courthouse steps. Once started, the entire process can take as little as three months or as many as twelve, depending on the volume of court cases in the county at that time. Also, realize that lenders often wait for as much as a year before putting a property with late payments into foreclosure.

The sale is conducted as an auction, and the property goes to the highest bidder. Unless there is significant equity in the property, the only bidder at the sale will be a representative of the lender. The lender can bid up to the amount owed without actually having to come up with the cash to purchase the property. But the lender may choose to set the initial bid at an amount less than it is owed. The primary reason for this surprising tactic is simple: the lender does not want to take the property, since banks, credit unions, etc., are not in the business of owning and selling real estate. Another reason to start the bidding below what is owed is to create bidding interest so the sales price would end up over the minimum bid, and the lender would recoup all or more than the amount owed. Also, the lender may want to bid less than the full amount to reserve a right to go after the borrower for a "deficiency," which is prohibited in some states. A deficiency results when the amount yielded from the foreclosure sale is not enough to pay the amount owed to the lender.

NONJUDICIAL FORECLOSURE

Many states permit a lender to foreclose without a lawsuit, using what is commonly called a power of sale. Rather than a mortgage, the borrower (grantor) gives a deed of trust to a trustee to hold for the lender (beneficiary). Upon default, the lender simply files a notice of default and a notice of sale, which is published in the newspaper. The entire process generally takes 90–120 days and is less costly than a judicial foreclosure. However, the process at the end is still the same—an auction for the property.

REDEMPTION

In some states, the borrower may have a right of redemption after the sale (i.e., the borrower can repurchase the property). This right is important to investors because they stand to lose their interest in the property if their borrowers exercise that right of redemption. If that does happen, the buyer will be reimbursed the purchase amount, along with incidental expenses. In some states, the lien holders behind the mortgage being foreclosed also have a right of redemption.

The Internal Revenue Service, if it has a recorded lien against the property, has 120 days to redeem should it choose to do so. Fortunately, the IRS doesn't often redeem properties, and it does not sell its redemption rights to other parties. In this case, you will need to contact the local IRS office and negotiate the lien off of the property in exchange for a mutually agreed upon sum of money.

Redemption can be a technical and tricky process, so make sure you know the rules inside out before attempting it.

STRICT FORECLOSURE

Though less common, a few states permit strict foreclosure, which does not require a sale process. When the proceeding is started, the borrower has a certain amount of time to pay what is owed. Once that date has passed, title reverts to the lender—quickly, over and done.

REINSTATING THE LOAN

Many states permit a borrower to "cure" the loan before the date of sale. This process simply requires paying the amount in arrears, plus interest, late fees, and possibly attorney fees. Curing loans allows borrowers to keep their homes, or to at least regroup and have time to sell their homes on the open market without having a foreclosure on their credit reports. Reinstatement is good for market health because if there are too many foreclosures in a geographic area, you may have problems getting a house to appraise when it's time to sell.

An investor can also buy a house and then personally reinstate the loan. This scenario is known as buying "subject to" the existing mortgage as a means of alternative financing. The investor simply gets a deed from the seller *subject to* the seller's mortgage loan, then keeps paying the monthly mortgage payments to the seller's existing lender. While the mortgage document may contain a provision ("due on sale" or "acceleration" clause) that allows the lender to force an early payoff if the property is transferred without the mortgage being paid off, in our experience lenders rarely balk at this type of arrangement. If a property is already in default and it is suddenly cured, few lenders would then turn around and call the loan due in full. In any event, when the property is fixed and resold in a few months, the loan is paid off and there's little chance of the lender catching the transaction or taking action in time.

GOING AFTER FORECLOSURES BEFORE THE SALE

Buying from the owner before the foreclosure sale can be a much easier way to buy than a competitive auction. The best way to get in touch with owners is to knock on their door. Doing so can be dicey, since you may be dealing with a bitter, belligerent person. More likely, you will be dealing with

There is no law against buying subject to a loan. Many attorneys, brokers, title companies, and other so-called professionals will be appalled at the idea of buying a property subject to the existing mortgage loan without the permission of the lender. Many will even tell you that it is *illegal* to do so, until, of course, you ask, "What law am I breaking?" The answer is generally a blank stare because there is no law, federal or state, that prohibits this type of transaction. The lender's due-on-sale clause in a mortgage is not automatic; the lender must affirmatively choose to enforce the right to accelerate the balance of the loan. As stated earlier, very few lenders choose to do so. As a short-term strategy, the subject-to purchase is low risk and can be very effective.

people who are not being honest with themselves about their situation. Let the owners know that you are available, give them your business card, and check back from time to time. The more you follow up, the greater the chance you will make a deal. At some point, sellers in foreclosure do face reality, and they will usually sell to the first person who comes banging on their door. This approach can prevent the house from ever going to sale through curing the default, or through the process known as short selling.

GETTING PAID *NOT* TO BUY

Because many people in foreclosure are deluded into thinking they have options other than selling to you, offer them a buyout clause in your purchase contract. Your written contract will give the sellers the right to cancel if they obtain a written offer better than yours before your closing date. Make sure the buyout fee is enough to make it worth your while. Give the seller the choice between a buyout clause or a slightly higher sales price. Likely you will remain the seller's best option. Other investors may not bother to make offers once they learn the house is under contract. Besides, if the foreclosure has not been filed yet, and the house has not been offered for sale on the MLS, few people would even know the home was for sale.

FINDING HOMES IN FORECLOSURE

It is likely you will bump into foreclosures using the methods we teach for finding killer deals. In addition, there are specific places to find properties that are in foreclosure. Research online and visit your local courthouse or county office to find out how its sale process works and where it posts names of property owners in foreclosure. Usually the county website will explain the process, and they may even offer classes for people in foreclosure (which might be a good place to learn and meet sellers!).

You can also subscribe to one of the national or local foreclosure-listing services. These companies compile information each week and sell it for a reasonable fee. They often include data and details not available on county websites, saving you a great deal of time. They may also include tools for comparative market analysis (CMA) to help you quickly decide which properties to pursue.

FINDING PRE-FORECLOSURES

For every published foreclosure, there are many more owners who are in default or otherwise close to being in foreclosure. Since this information is not published, it is often more rewarding (and difficult) to find these properties. Why? As the only person making an offer to buy these homes, you will be able to close a high percentage of deals. Most of the techniques in this book will lead you to houses in pre-foreclosure status. Once you have systems in place to locate pre-foreclosures, you will be well on your way to success as a real-estate investor.

FORECLOSURE-PROTECTION LAWS

About half the states now have foreclosure-protection laws that require you to give a seller certain disclosures in writing and wait three or more business days before you can close or ask the seller to deed you the property. A state-by-state list can be found on page 264 in the appendix. Violations of these rules can result in a fine or even criminal prosecution, so look before you leap.

GOVERNMENT-OWNED PROPERTIES

Certain loan programs are guaranteed or insured by the federal government. The government becomes the owner of tens of thousands of properties each year. Many can be purchased at good discounts, if you know how to find them. The FHA, which operates under the HUD, insures certain loans targeted at first-time homebuyers in low-income neighborhoods. The VA guarantees similar loans for current and former military personnel and their families.

Most of these properties are listed and sold through real-estate agents. The property is first offered to potential owner-occupants in a bid process. When no suitable owner-occupant is found, the properties go on an extended listing, which is offered to everyone, including investors. These properties are attractive because you can place a bid on these properties with as little as $1,000 as earnest money, and if your bid is accepted, you have about sixty days to close.

The bidding process is somewhat difficult, and you need a savvy real-estate broker to help you along. The HUD/VA contract has no weasel clauses, however, so you will lose your earnest money if you fail to close. Furthermore, the HUD/VA contract is not assignable, so you have to do a double closing to flip the property to another investor. If you get the property at the right price, sixty days is more than enough time to make things happen. (We discuss double closings in detail in chapter 9.)

BUYING AT AUCTIONS

When the real-estate market is "down," there are many more properties available at a discount, but there are also more investors trying to get in on the opportunity to profit. Many investors buy and hold properties, either indefinitely or at least long enough for the homes to appreciate back to their previous values. As flippers, we compete with these long-term investors as well as with eager new investors. Together, these two categories of buyers are often willing to spend more to acquire houses.

A third group of investors (like us) focus on doing flips. These savvy flippers should have done well because there were plenty of homes to buy when prices dropped during the recent big crash, and as things improved, most regions (including ours, the Denver market) were healthy enough that you could sell a nicely renovated home quickly. As the market continued to improve, the number of auction properties for sale continued to decline. Homeowners were able to work out their issues, either directly with their lenders or by selling the home to pay off their debts.

Even though interest rates remain extremely low, some people continue to buy properties with adjustable-rate mortgages (ARMs) with little or no money down. Over time, we expect to see additional foreclosures as part of the normal real-estate pricing cycles, which usually run from six to ten years.

PREPARING FOR THE AUCTION

After locating where and when the auction will be held, you need to crunch the numbers. Investors are often shocked to find out that what started out as a reasonable payoff figure on the loan ends up being a huge number. If the loan amount was $100,000 when it went into default, the payoff could easily be $140,000 (including interest, lender fees, and attorney fees) when the property makes it to auction.

Let's say the bank sets the sale price at $100,000, and the house is worth $180,000 on the retail market. If you were able to purchase the house for $100,000 and then spend $10,000 on repairs, for a total of $110,000 invested, there would be a solid $50,000 profit potential (after $20,000 in carrying and sales costs)—certainly a good deal. Of course, other investors (including the lender) may agree, so the house could easily sell for more. With auctions, it is important to decide how much you are willing to spend ahead of time and not stray far from that number. If the bidding went up to $125,000 or more on that house, it would likely not make sense for you to continue to bid. Remember, just because someone else is willing to pay more, does not mean you should.

Check up on the property in a few months to see if the new owner flipped it and what it sold for. Usually there will be pictures on the MLS, so you can get a reasonable sense of the flipper's renovation costs and estimate the profit or loss. Use this information to help you make good decisions the next time you bid.

SHORT SALES

You will likely come across dozens of properties in foreclosure with no equity—that is, the seller owes more than the property is worth. In these situations, lenders are sometimes willing to accept less than the full amount due, commonly referred to as "short pay" or "short sale."

Negotiating a short sale with the lender is a difficult process. Finding a bank officer who has the authority to accept a discount is a daunting task. You will have to call around to locate the lender's loss-mitigation department. Each lender you deal with will more than likely have a special name for this department, so be patient when calling. Expect the process to involve a lot of waiting on hold and being bounced around an intricate maze of automated voice-mail systems. Once you get in touch with the right person, then the negotiating begins. Don't be surprised if you spend many months working on (and waiting for) a single short-sale transaction to close.

From the lender's perspective, a short sale saves many of the costs associated with the foreclosure process: attorney fees, the eviction process, delays from borrower bankruptcy, damage to the property, costs associated with resale, etc. Your job as the investor is to convince the lender that it will fare better by accepting less money now.

The lender will want some information about the property, the borrower, and the deal the borrower has made with you. Primarily, the lender wants to know what the property is worth. The lender will generally hire a local real-estate broker or appraiser to evaluate the property—called a broker's price opinion (BPO). You can also submit your own appraisal or comparable sales information. In addition, you will want to offer as much specific negative information about the property and neighborhood as possible. The highest contractor's repair bid should also be submitted.

In addition, the lender will ask for financial information about the borrower/seller. It's sort of a backward loan application in which the borrower must now prove that he or she is unable to afford the payments. This process may involve as much, if not more, paperwork than an original mortgage application! The borrower should submit a "hardship letter," which is basically a sob story about how much financial trouble the borrower is in. This may require a little literary creativity and some help on your part. Don't lie; just paint a picture that doesn't look good.

Finally, the lender generally wants to see a written contract between you and the seller. The lender wants to make sure the seller isn't walking away with any cash from the deal. Generally, the contract must be written so that the buyer pays all costs associated with the transaction, so that the net cash to the seller is the exact amount of the short pay to the lender (i.e., there is no extra going to the borrower). A preliminary closing settlement statement is often requested, which can be difficult, since many title and escrow companies simply won't prepare one in advance of closing.

Don't be surprised if your first short-sale bid is rejected. Lenders are hesitant to give you a steal. Many short sales fall through if the BPO comes in too high. You can't pull the wool over a lender's eyes; if the property isn't in need of serious repair, it is unlikely you can convince the lender the property is worth a great deal less than the appraised value.

Going through the short-sale process is not complicated, but it entails hard work. The success or failure of the deal depends upon how you present it to the lender. Many novice investors and brokers give up at short sales quickly because their first deal is rejected. Like any business, short sales take practice to master.

WRAPPING IT UP

- Learn how to work the foreclosure business.
- Look for pre-foreclosures.
- Short sales take time, but can be lucrative.
- Seek expert help to profit at auctions.

CHAPTER 9

Wholesaling

Wholesalers locate deals for other investors. They find a bargain property, sign a purchase contract with the owner, and sell the deal to that other investor without ever taking title. Wholesalers most often resell the deal in its "as is" condition.

Wholesalers can turn over as many deals as they can find, and some wholesalers have built impressive marketing operations that bring in lots of deals. The lifestyle of wholesalers is that of true entrepreneurs; they can work as much or as little as they like, with no boss, no employees, and the freedom to do as they please!

FIND THE BACK DOOR FIRST

Every wholesaler should have the means to sell properties quickly. A wholesaler should not enter into a real-estate transaction without an exit strategy, which is typically another investor who will rehab and flip it or rehab and keep it as a rental.

Let's look at an example. You find a property worth about $100,000 in its current state. It requires $10,000 to renovate the property. In its best condition, the property is worth $150,000. You negotiate a purchase price of $80,000 and sign a purchase contract with the owner. You find another investor who is willing to pay you $83,000 for the property and do the necessary repairs. Thus, you can sell your deal to another investor and walk away with a $3,000 profit using no money of your own. The other investor will make a nice profit as well.

Keep in mind that the investor you sell the property to will eventually make more money than you on the deal. Don't let that person's profit potential bother you. There is enough room for both of you to profit, and, unlike a retailer, you assume little risk.

WHOLESALING, STEP BY STEP

Step 1: Build Your Back-end List

Aren't we putting the cart before the horse? Absolutely not! The key to being a successful wholesaler is to have buyers lined up even before you have the deals. If you start looking for your investor after you have the contract, you are working against a ticking clock.

Wholesalers who hope to assign a contract or arrange a double closing may only have thirty or sixty days to find their buyer and tie up loose ends. In many cases, that may not be enough time to market the property properly and attract interested purchasers.

Every day that you don't have a buyer, you limit your options. As the closing date approaches, you may be forced to exercise a contingency clause or you may choose to line up financing and close on your own, hoping that you can find a retail buyer before too many payments trickle from your pockets. Neither option is desirable.

Know your exit strategy (or "who" your exit strategy is) before you even begin looking for your first deal. That means meeting investors who want to buy properties and learning their likes and dislikes. We've mentioned the benefits of joining an investment club, and here are a few more tips on how to find investors in your area.

You can find them on Internet discussion groups, or by reading the classified ads on Craigslist.org under the "Real Estate for Sale" and "Financial Services" sections. In addition, ask real-estate brokers, landlords, or apartment associations for names of investors in your community. If there are no such clubs in your area, consider forming one yourself. Run a classified ad in a local newspaper or on Craigslist. The ad can be fairly generic. Something like, "Investors wanted! Properties available way under market value! Call 555-5555."

Take the time to qualify the callers and investors you meet to ascertain their investing preferences. Here are some good sample questions to ask:

- How many houses do you buy each year?
- Do you have preferred locations and types of properties?
- What type of discount do you usually look for on properties?
- Do you have your own cash to close, or will you borrow it?
- How big a renovation can you handle?
- If I find a bargain, how quickly can you close?

Asking these questions will quickly generate a list of investors to call when a new project comes along.

Don't waste too much time with inexperienced investors; they probably don't have the means to buy properties from you. Build a master list of buyers from the people you meet and the calls you receive. Input names and contact information into a database. Ideally, you will use e-mail addresses almost exclusively. Time is of the essence when a deal comes your way, and nothing beats informing a hundred or so investors at the click of a mouse!

Step 2: Go Make Offers

In chapter 5, we discussed how to analyze a profitable fix-and-flip. The same formula works for a wholesale deal, and you should run the numbers as if you were going to fix and flip it yourself. The problem beginning wholesalers often make when attempting to buy properties is offering too little to make room for their wholesaling fee. This practice is *wrong, wrong, wrong*! Instead, get the property under contract, and just shave a little bit off the profit that your back-end buyer (investor) is going to make. Create an understanding that you'll bring in deals on a regular basis.

For example, if the potential profit on a fix-and-flip property is $25,000 for your back-end buyer, then if you took $3,000 of that profit as a wholesaling fee, everyone will be happy. But don't get greedy and ask for 50 percent of the potential profit as a wholesaling fee. Remember, the investors you are wholesaling to have to make a larger profit than you because they are taking a bigger risk and spending more time and money on the project.

Most investors think of wholesaling as finding a junker property and selling it to another investor, who will fix it up and sell it retail to an end user. The reality is, you can wholesale any property that someone else wants. For example, you could get a property under contract that would make a great rental after a minimal amount of upgrades and repairs and wholesale that to another landlord. In short, don't limit your wholesaling repertoire to just fix-and-flip deals; find out what your back-end buyers want, and fill the need.

Step 3: Get a Deal Under Contract

In a previous chapter we discussed real-estate contracts. Whichever contract you use, we explained that you must make sure there are important clauses in it, including the right to assign the contract to someone else. In wholesaling, there are two situations where the inclusion of this clause will be a problem. First, most lenders who accept a short sale will not allow the property to be resold or the contract to be assigned. Second, most bank-owned (or REO) properties will require an addendum that strictly forbids the contract from being assigned. We'll deal with that issue shortly.

Step 4: Wholesale Your Deal

There are three basic ways to wholesale a deal you have under contract:

1. Assign the contract
2. Double or "simultaneous" closing
3. Entity assignment

Assign the Contract

Assigning a contract is similar to double endorsing a check—you assign your rights under the contract to another investor for a fee. The investor closes directly with the owner in your place, like a pinch hitter. The main disadvantage of the contract assignment is that it is hard to sell. Unless the investor knows you personally, he or she may be wary of buying your contract.

The contract assignment requires the investor to conduct due diligence regarding the title to the property, the legality of the contract, and whether the seller will live up to it at closing time. Thus, you may not get as much money for a contract assignment as you would if you did a double closing (see below) and gave the investor a bona fide deed.

The second disadvantage of the contract assignment is that the investor knows what you are paying for the property. An unscrupulous investor may try to go around you and deal directly with the property owner. The solution to this challenge is to record a memorandum of agreement in county land records. You may recall that once recorded, this affidavit becomes a cloud on the seller's title. The cloud on title will effectively prevent the seller from selling the property to anyone but you. In this situation, the seller or the unscrupulous investor would have to pay you a ransom to step out of the deal (which is done by you signing a quitclaim deed).

Double Closing

The second way to wholesale a deal is with a double closing. As you know, a closing is a ceremonial process during which title is delivered by deed from the seller to the buyer. But in this wholesale method, you buy the property from an owner of a distressed home and sell the property to another investor in a back-to-back double closing (also called double escrow or simultaneous escrow in some states).

You do not need any of your own cash to purchase the property from the owner before reselling it to the retailer in a double closing. Here's how it works in eight steps:

1. You sign a written agreement to purchase a property from the owner.
2. You sign another written contract with the end investor, who thereby agrees to buy the property from you at a higher price.
3. The only party coming to the table with cash is this end investor, the retailer. Assuming the retailer is borrowing money from a lender to fund the transaction, the retailer's bank will wire the funds into the bank account of the attorney, escrow agent, or title company (called the closing agent) that performs the closing.
4. The owner signs a deed to you, which is not delivered but deposited in escrow with the closing agent.
5. You then sign a deed to the retailer that is deposited in escrow with the closing agent.
6. The retailer signs the bank loan documents, at which point the transaction is complete.
7. The closing agent delivers the funds to the owner for the purchase price and delivers the difference to you.
8. The closing agent records the two deeds, one after another, at the county land-records office.

As you can see, the wholesaler brought no cash to the table and received funds from the proceeds of the second sale. If the second sale does not happen, the first transaction, which is closed in escrow, is not complete. The deal is dead.

In the past few years, there has been a lot of negative press and misinformation about double closings. Many people have been indicted under what the press has labeled "property-flipping scams." Double closings are not the same as these illegal schemes, despite what some misinformed lenders, real-estate brokers, and title companies may tell you. The unlawful transactions work like this: unscrupulous investors buy cheap, run-down properties in mostly low-income neighborhoods. They do shoddy renovations to the properties and sell them to unsophisticated buyers at inflated prices. In most cases, the investor, appraiser, and mortgage broker conspire by submitting fraudulent loan documents and a bogus appraisal. The result? The buyer pays too much for a house and cannot afford the loan. Because FHA insures many of these loans, the government authorities have investigated this practice and arrested many of the parties involved.

FLIP TIP

Does a wholesaler need a license? Real-estate brokerage is an activity regulated by states on their own terms. Each state defines which activities require a license. The majority of states use "for another" language in their state broker-licensing laws (i.e., the statutes provide a laundry list of activities that require a license if you do it for another). Clearly, when you are putting a property under contract as principal, you are not wholesaling the property for another but for yourself. A contract to purchase property gives the buyer an equitable interest in the land (property). Thus, if you have an interest in the property, you are basically exempt from the licensing regulations, since you are selling your own interest, not someone else's. The bottom line is that if you don't act like a real-estate broker, the state agencies that license brokers will leave you alone. If you use the state or local board of Realtors' approved contract, it is important that you make it very clear to all parties in the transaction that you are not a broker and are acting on your own behalf as a principal and not for the seller or buyer.

Such activities amount to loan fraud, nothing more. The media have inappropriately reported the activity as illegal property flipping rather than loan fraud. Neither flipping nor double closings are illegal. Anyone who claims flipping is illegal is misinformed.

Unfortunately, this misunderstanding has not been without consequences. Many title and escrow companies will not do double closings anymore because of the risk of potential fraud. Other title companies simply require all parties to sign additional disclosures, so that all parties understand the transaction involves two closings, the second of which will fund the first.

Double closings are handled in two ways: wet and dry. A **wet closing** is when the wholesaler closes with cash, buys the property from the owner, and then resells it to the end buyer to get the original purchase money back. A **dry closing** is when the wholesaler uses the end buyer's funds to pay for the first closing. Title and escrow companies don't like dry closings, but they don't mind wet closings. Of course, wet closings require cash, which can be borrowed from transactional lenders who charge about 2 percent of the loan amount for funding the first closing for about an hour so the wholesaler can then resell the property and pay off the transactional lender.

Entity Assignment

The third wholesaling method is entity assignment. In states where filing of an LLC can be done online quickly and for a reasonable fee, you may consider setting up a single-purpose LLC for the purpose of a wholesale deal. In this case, the LLC signs the purchase contract as buyer, then you assign its ownership (called membership) to your end buyer. Since ownership of private LLCs is not public record, the seller would not know what you have done. This is particularly useful when dealing with a seller who refuses to allow you to assign the contract. To watch a video with more details on this process, visit Flippingbizbook.com.

WRAPPING IT UP

- Start by creating a list of potential buyers.
- Don't try to make too much money on each deal.
- Make sure to create your contract with the right exit plan.
- Learn the three ways to wholesale your deal to another investor.

CHAPTER 10

Contract through Closing

A closing is nothing more than a delivery of cash by the buyer and an execution and delivery of the deed from the seller. Yet many significant events occur in the period between contract and closing, often called escrow. Real-estate brokers, attorneys, and title-company representatives usually handle most of these tasks, but you should familiarize yourself with the process.

The three most significant events between contract and closing can be remembered by the hard-to-forget acronym ATM:

- **A**ll contract contingencies met
- **T**itle searches and title commitment prepared
- **M**ortgage paid off and, if needed, a new one approved for the buyer

All Contract Contingencies Met

If the contract calls for an **inspection** by the buyer, this should happen immediately, especially if there is an inspection deadline. As we discussed earlier, the buyer will most likely employ a professional house inspector to do a thorough inspection. The inspector will then write a complete report with photos and a narrative of all items that need work. The buyer will likely use this list to his or her advantage to negotiate a lower price or cash back at closing (called a concession). If the seller will not agree to make the necessary repairs or adjustments to the price, the buyer can cancel the contract and receive any earnest money back.

These are some of the most common major inspection items that will come up:

- Roof
- Furnace
- Water heater
- Electrical
- Plumbing
- Structural issues or leaks

If you are the seller, you must anticipate these issues, but don't be in a rush to fix everything that is wrong with the property. For example, if you know the furnace is twenty years old and has an average life span of twenty years, your buyer will likely insist on some credit for a new furnace. If the furnace is in working order and otherwise safe, the buyer may accept a $1,500 concession at closing. The point is, don't rush to fix *everything* before you put the house on the market, but rather consider the cost of doing so versus the cost of a concession. Fix the items that relate to safety, the ones that could scare off a potential buyer if left unaddressed.

FLIP TIP

Attention grabber. The buyer's inspector is paid to find things wrong, so expect that person to come up with a big list of items. From there, the seller will negotiate which items to fix and which items to offer a concession in price for. If you are the seller, as a negotiating strategy, consider leaving an obvious item (e.g., an old furnace) unrepaired so that the inspector focuses more on that item and less on the minor ones.

As part of the contract requirements, a buyer may require the seller to execute a state-approved **disclosure** form, listing everything about the property that the seller knows is working, not working, or has been repaired or caused problems in the past. For example, even if the buyer does an inspection, it may not reveal the fact that the property had water damage in the walls that was fixed and repaired with new drywall. If something happens to the property later and someone is injured as a result, the seller could be sued if he or she knew about some latent defect that was not disclosed. Thus, it is in the seller's best interest to disclose anything that is wrong or was wrong and was repaired.

In addition to the disclosure form, there are mandatory federal and state disclosures that the seller must give the buyer. Under federal law, the seller must provide a lead based–paint disclosure and a copy of the pamphlet *Protect Your Family from Lead in Your Home.*[1]

In addition, your state may have other required disclosures, such as the following:

- Presence of termites or asbestos
- Seismic hazards (whether the property is in an earthquake zone)
- Megan's Law (whether there are child predators in the neighborhood)
- Presence of radon gas
- Whether the property is in a special taxing district
- Whether the property is in a flood zone

Check with your division of housing or real-estate commission for the required disclosures. If you are selling a property with a real-estate broker, he or she should be aware of all required disclosures.

If you are the buyer and intend to wholesale the property, it won't make sense for you to spend the money for a formal, thorough inspection as outlined above. Instead, conduct your own basic inspection, bringing interested investors with you when you do so. In fact, your contract with the seller should include a provision allowing you to show the property to prospective buyers during the escrow period between contract and closing.

---

1. A sample lead disclosure and pamphlet can be downloaded from the EPA's website at https://www.epa.gov/lead/real-estate-disclosure.

Title Search and Commitment

A real-estate contract usually requires that title to the property be marketable—that is, it must have no serious defects that would prevent it from being mortgaged or sold at a later time. Buyers want a marketable title so they can feel secure that no one will sue them or claim an interest in their properties.

A title search is an inspection of the public records that relate to a particular property. While a deed is evidence of ownership, it does not represent the complete picture; some liens are not recorded in the county records, such as unpaid property taxes, HOA liens, and municipal water/sewer liens. You have to check directly with those authorities to find out what is owed.

Every county in the US has a place where records of title are publicly recorded. In most cases, it's the office of the county clerk and recorder or the county courthouse. Most areas of the country now use computers to index documents.

Understand the Terminology

The giver of any interest in real estate is called the grantor; the receiver of the interest is the grantee. On some documents, the grantor and grantee are called by other terms. For example, on a deed, the grantor is the seller, and the grantee is the buyer. On a deed of trust, the grantor is sometimes called the trustor, and the lender is the beneficiary.

The most common indexing system is by grantor and grantee. All documents conveying property interests are recorded by the grantor's last name in the grantor index. The same transaction is cross-indexed by the grantee's last name in the grantee index.

Conduct a Title Search

A title search is important because it will determine if a property's title is good and marketable. To determine that, you must follow the chain of title as it changed hands over the years. A break in the chain of title creates a gap, which can result in confusion over ownership. Theoretically, the chain of title could be followed back to the Native Americans, or at least as far as the ascertainable records will show. In practice, the chain of title is only searched back about fifty years.

A title search can be conducted with a title company for a fee. Or, as an educational exercise, you can do it yourself. If you are willing to spend time at the county recorder's office, you can usually find a title-company employee who would be willing to assist you. In addition to the chain of title, make certain you also check for unpaid property taxes, assessments, HOA dues, water and sewer charges, restrictive covenants, court judgments, bankruptcy petitions, and other possible liens that are not recorded in county land records. If this process sounds confusing, don't worry—it is! Be smart and pay for a title search when you buy properties. Do not, however, waste time checking title until you have a signed contract with the seller.

Save Money on Title Insurance

Title insurance, like any insurance, defends and pays claims against the insured. In the case of real estate, the buyer is the insured. Thus, if anyone makes a claim against the buyer's interest in the property, the title-insurance company must defend that claim and pay any damages suffered by the buyer because of the claim. Consequently, the title company may seek damages against the seller. Many sellers have a false sense of security when buying title insurance because they think they are being protected. Holding title in a land trust would be similar to holding title as a company and can help limit your liability in this respect because the title company will not have recourse against you personally (see chapter 17).

Typical claims involve liens not discovered until after the closing, forgeries, errors from previous deeds in the chain of title, and easements or rights-of-way that were not known. If you have little money invested in a transaction, you have very little to lose. For example, if you as buyer give a seller $1,000 to deed you the property, what is the limit of your loss? The answer is obviously $1,000, so why would you pay $700 for a title-insurance policy if no risk of a title problem was apparent? As you become more experienced, you will see that purchasing a title-insurance policy is not always necessary, particularly when you intend to flip the property to another investor. That investor will undoubtedly buy title

Ask for a reissue rate. If you do purchase a title policy when doing a double closing, ask for a discounted rate. If the property was sold or refinanced within the past few years, most title-insurance companies will offer a discounted rate, since their risk is lower. Make sure you ask—they won't always offer it up front! Also, ask for a hold-open policy. This type of policy costs an extra 10–20 percent up front and will cover title on resale within twelve months (some companies will cover you up to twenty-four months). The policy may be called by another name in some states, so ask your title-insurance representative. Because the seller usually pays for title insurance, your cost will be 10–20 percent of a full policy.

insurance if he or she intends to resell the property after putting up several thousand dollars for repairs.

Let's be clear, however: we do not recommend you buy and sell property as a beginner without checking title or buying title insurance. This technique must be learned through experience and knowledge. Always do things the conservative and safe way when starting out.

Mortgages Paid Off

If you are paying off existing mortgages or other liens, contact the holders of these mortgages or liens for payoff information. Make certain you verify that the holder of the lien or mortgage has an original document that can be delivered to you when the underlying obligation has been satisfied. Be sure to get original promissory notes back marked "paid in full." If you are dealing with private mortgage or lien holders, remember to ask for a discount on the principal owed as a way of maximizing your profit. The answer may be "no," but you never know what you'll get unless you ask!

Before closing, the seller has to pay off his or her existing mortgage, unless the sale is a seller-financed or a lease-option transaction. The seller can use the buyer's funds from the sale of the property to pay off the existing mortgage and release the mortgage lien (or deed of trust) from the property before it is deeded to the buyer. Contact your lender (or lenders if you have a second mortgage or home-equity line) and ask them to provide a payoff statement for the loan. You'll want to make sure the payoff statement is good through at least the closing date, with daily (per diem) interest listed on the statement in case your closing date gets postponed.

While getting a loan is primarily the responsibility of the buyer, it is also your problem as seller. What if they can't qualify for the loan and don't have another lender lined up as a backup plan? In other words, you have to take charge of the situation to make sure the loan gets closed. Have a provision in your contract that gives you the right to communicate with the buyer's lender during the process so you can keep tabs on what is going on and what documents or lender requirements have to be taken care of.

COMMON COSTS INCURRED WHEN BUYING

Closing costs, as well as who customarily pays for them, vary from state to state. In most cases, there's no law that prevents you from negotiating who pays the costs, so it never hurts to ask the other party to pick up a fee. As an alternative, a lowball price with an agreement that *you* will pick up all fees may close a deal. Some typical fees you should expect to incur when *buying* a house are listed below.

Inspection Fees

For about $300 in most areas, a home-inspection service will carefully evaluate the property and prepare a detailed report with its findings. A professional inspection of a property, while not required by law, is a must when you are buying a fixer-upper. Most inspectors offer a cheaper "mini-inspection" that only looks at the major items: roof, foundation, electrical, plumbing, etc. You don't need an inspection of cosmetic items or appliances as you're likely to replace those anyway.

Appraisal

If you are borrowing money, whether from a bank or hard-money lender, they will undoubtedly require an appraisal. If you are paying all cash, an appraisal is not a necessity if you've followed our advice about analyzing deals.

Loan-Origination and Lender Fees

If you are borrowing money from a hard-money lender, expect to pay 3–5 percent of the loan as a loan-origination fee. In addition, you'll have to pay for half the typical closing costs of the closing agent (attorney, escrow company, or title company), which range from $300 to $1,000, depending on what state you are closing in. If you are dealing with an institutional lender, expect to also pay for typical "junk" (administrative) fees, which could add up to as much as 2 percent of the loan amount.

Survey

A lender may require a survey of the property to assess the lot lines and whether there are any structures (e.g., garage, fence, or shed) that are over the property lines. If the property was built in the last forty years and is in a well-defined subdivision, it's not a necessity that you have a survey. In an older urban neighborhood where houses are close together and structures are close to the lot line, a survey may not be a bad idea.

FLIP TIP

HOAs and CCRs. Make sure you know what you are getting into when you buy a condominium, townhome, or house in a covenant-protected community. You have to abide by homeowners' associations (HOAs), which have recorded covenants, conditions, and restrictions (CCRs) with the county recorder's office. CCRs may limit what color you can paint the outside of a house or require HOA approval before commencing work, which could substantially delay your rehab project. In addition, a financially insolvent HOA will make reselling the property very difficult, especially when dealing in condos and townhomes. Make sure to request HOA financials and any information related to recent or expected special assessments.

THE CLOSING PROCESS

In the old days, before land records were formally recorded, a seller would simply take a bundle or stick or a clump of dirt and hand it ceremonially to the buyer. Now, closing has become very complex and is a document-signing nightmare!

Closing refers to the closing of escrow on a property. When you go under contract and the buyer gives earnest money to the title company or escrow agent, it is said that escrow has "opened." When the seller signs and delivers a deed to the buyer, escrow has "closed."

In addition to a deed, the parties will also sign a number of related documents, such as the following:

- **Closing instructions**, which authorize the closing agent to collect and disburse funds and record documents
- A **closing statement**, which is a summary of the numbers of the transactions for both parties (formerly the HUD-1, now called the Closing Disclosure)
- Various **affidavits**, under which the seller promises he or she hasn't hidden anything from the closing agent or title company prior to closing (For example, perhaps the seller made an oral agreement with a neighbor for an easement across the back of the property to allow that person access to a fishing pond. That agreement must be revealed.)
- A plethora of **loan documents**, including promises to come back and correct any errors made in the closing documents

Closing is officially complete when the deed is given to (or recorded for) the buyer, and funds are given or released to the seller. If a buyer or seller is out of state or cannot attend the closing, the process is done "in escrow" (in pieces and parts, the sum of which make a full closing).

WRAPPING IT UP

- Both the buyer and the seller can use professional inspection results as leverage.

- Become familiar with key closing documents, processes, and expenses.
- Both buyer and seller should pay special attention to loan progress before closing.

PART III

Getting to Work

CHAPTER 11

The Rehab: Planning It

In this chapter we'll discuss how to assess a property's initial repairs, decide what to fix, and determine how much it will cost. We'll also look at potential hazards and deal breakers. Before you make an offer and seal a deal, you should be thinking ahead and applying these concepts. Walk away from a potential buy if there are too many hurdles in the way of your making a profit, and move on to the next house. If the seller has equity in the house, however, you can always make a lowball offer. You might end up with a deal after all.

HOW MUCH REHAB KNOWLEDGE IS NECESSARY?

Many real-estate investors have become wealthy without having any knowledge of construction. An even greater number, however, have lost considerable money because they didn't have enough construction experience. If you intend to fix up properties yourself, then start with a basic rehab job that requires cleanup, simple updates, carpet, paint, and landscaping. These cosmetic items do not require any special knowledge, just labor and the cost of materials. Smaller jobs take less time and knowledge and generally can be done without a permit. Even if there is some permitted work done, such as replacing a furnace or roof, you can get by without using a licensed general contractor. Your electrical, plumbing, HVAC, or roofing contractors can each pull the permit for their specific projects. Typically, these permits are over the counter, so there is no review process to delay the project.

Keep in mind that older houses tend to hold more "secrets." This means your inspector may not discover existing structural problems such as subpar repairs, faulty wiring, or other issues that will be expensive to address. Keep extra room in the budget for surprises that will show up during the rehab process.

Of course, "old" is a general term. Homes built in the last ten to fifteen years are seldom viable flip candidates. The main exceptions are auction and other foreclosure properties. In these cases, you may find a newer house (or one in excellent condition, for that matter) that has no real repair issues. The issues are with the seller's ability to make the mortgage payments. Or the problem may be a lack of equity that has led the seller to walk away from the property. These homes can still be purchased at a discount and sometimes placed on the market right away with little or no renovation needed.

The next class includes homes built from the mid-'70s to late '90s. Here you'll occasionally find deals, and these homes have fewer potential hazards to worry about compared to older homes. If they've been poorly maintained, you still will need to go through an extensive renovation, but most likely you won't have to tear into walls to fix structural issues or replace plumbing, electrical, or heating systems. The newer the home, the less likely you are to find major environmental hazards. You could run into asbestos or radon, but they are seldom deal killers.

Houses built from the '50s to early '70s account for most of the potential flips. These houses can be expensive to renovate, with potential for additional "surprise" problems. In general, they need more substantial updates than newer homes. The structural walls may be concrete or cinder block, which lacks insulation and is harder to work with than newer generation framed walls. The electric systems are often lower capacity than what buyers find acceptable, and there may be ungrounded circuits. Plumbing supply lines may be galvanized pipe, and waste lines may have some sections of lead pipe. Often these plumbing systems must be replaced. Asbestos was used in drywall and joint compound, floors, insulation, and some exterior siding in those days, so expect to find some in the house. You don't usually have to remove it, but it can limit your ability to make major changes without running into additional complications and cost. Don't consider this a complete list, but just a few examples of how things get more troublesome and expensive with older homes. The good news is that the foundations and bones of these houses are usually good.

The final category of homes is anything built from the late 1800s to the 1950s. Anything older than that is beyond our experience, since Colorado, where we live and work, doesn't have homes as old as those on the East Coast. Sometimes the systems on these sixty-plus-year-old houses have already been updated, but usually there is a mix of old and new, and lots of detective work needed to see what's really going on. You'll have to decide how far to go with repairs, but be warned that improvements can get expensive very quickly.

If you did replace "everything," you would likely overimprove the house and would not be compensated for your additional time and money. It's practically impossible to find all the flaws in an old house without completely gutting it (i.e., without removing most of the wall-covering materials).

Old houses have old foundations, of course, which are difficult to bring up to today's standards. Many buyers will overlook sagging floors and other issues that tend to give these houses character, so don't be overly worried about every possible defect. Besides, you can usually correct sagging or bowed floors with little effort. If you intend to do an addition, however—which is beyond what we do in most of our flips—realize the cost will be higher than doing similar work on a new home. It's difficult to add on to really old houses. Also, be aware that if you do, you will be required to bring many areas, including insulation, plumbing, electric, and egress, up to current code. If the home's location is really spectacular you may be better off doing a "scrape" (building a new house). If so, bring in an experienced contractor-partner for a share of the profit.

So, the rule is: don't treat a flip as you would your own dream house, but also don't take shortcuts or leave known flaws without disclosing. Once you purchase the house, you'd be wise to continue the inspection process, which would potentially require tearing into walls and paying for expert help. If your house was built before the mid-'70s and you plan on disturbing more than a very small painted area, you should test for lead-based paint and asbestos. Test for these items before purchase if finding either of them would affect your purchase decision.

ESTIMATING REPAIRS

Every successful real-estate investor must learn how to budget repair costs. You will need to break down all labor and materials costs, then factor in how long the repairs will take. Your initial (prepurchase) estimate will serve as a rough draft. Then, if the numbers look good, you can spend money on a professional home inspection, followed by specialized inspections and estimates as needed.

Both beginning and experienced investors habitually underestimate the time and expense needed to complete a renovation. Always estimate repairs conservatively, taking into account the worst-case scenario. There's a saying in business that certainly applies here: "Takes longer, costs more." Start with the inside and work through the project room by room, step by step. Refer to the checklist on page 271 in the appendix, create a repair estimate, then add at least a 10–15 percent margin for error (the older the house, the larger the margin).

Before making offers, we quickly run through the cost of repairs. You'll eventually be able to throw a ballpark estimate almost by feel. Usually a typical 1970s three-bedroom, two-bath ranch will be about $25,000–$35,000 to prep for sale (slightly higher in areas where city permits and regulations are very strict). We run through the repair numbers based on demolition and trash removal, general interior, kitchen, bathrooms, framing, electric, HVAC, floors, plumbing, drywall, paint, general exterior, roof, and landscaping.

Time management is also a key factor, especially if you are working with borrowed funds. Set the closing date out longer if you are not going to have the crew available right away. No sense owning a property that's just sitting there. Be ready to go once it's officially yours. If you are a wholesaler and underestimate the repairs, an experienced retailer will notice and won't be enthusiastic about doing business with you in the future. Refer to the repairs checklist on page 271 in the appendix. It's something we use on every project, big or small.

DETERMINING THE COST

Estimates will vary by geographic region because of the availability and cost of labor and materials. You'll also want to get a feel for what grade of materials makes sense for your area and the home's after-repaired value. Around our hometown of Denver, it is difficult to find a nice, livable home for under $250,000. In areas with less expensive homes you may be able to get by with less expensive materials and some used items. The problem with used items, however, is that they take extra time to source and bring to the job site. Also, if the items don't work out for the intended use, you won't be able to return them. If you insist on sourcing used items, try Habitat for Humanity's ReStore or other community-based nonprofit organizations. We no longer purchase used appliances or materials for flips unless it's a special appliance or fixture that would be expensive to purchase new. If you have the time, you can also shop for bargain appliances in overstock stores and in the clearance area of major appliance retailers. We especially like the Sears outlet stores.

Shop around for kitchen cabinets and bath vanities. We often find nice vanities in the clearance section of Home Depot or Lowe's. We tend to stay with stock cabinets for kitchens because they are inexpensive and readily available. Sometimes we'll have to special order one or two cabinets that are not in the store, but we can start assembling the kitchen even while waiting for the missing cabinets. Speaking of assembling, some investors like IKEA cabinets. We have no problem with IKEA products in general and suggest you visit a store for ideas. Their mock-up rooms can also help you visualize how to work with small spaces. Their cabinets take a lot of time to assemble, which we don't think is worth the effort—unless you have ample time to do it yourself.

You may wonder if you should replace an electric range with a gas range. In most cases, we would say no. If it's a more expensive house, however, then it may be worth the upgrade. In general, if the electric panel is workable but is being overtaxed, it should be converted. But changing to a gas range may allow you to avoid that expensive upgrade of the electric service. By the way, replacing an electric panel has become more expensive in our area because the utility company requires a meter-disconnect switch to be added as part of the update.

LABOR COST

The labor-time estimates in our checklist are for an experienced handyman or tradesman. Actual installation times will vary. There is no good excuse for poor workmanship. Even with inexpensive homes, hold yourself and your contractors to high standards. In almost every case, it takes little or no extra time to do the work right. Your contractor should correctly miter trim, install doors and cabinets with nice reveals, properly mortise door hardware, level floors prior to installing tile, and align electrical cover plates. A contractor who fails to do these basic things either doesn't care or lacks the necessary skills to work on your houses. You can be sure that such a contractor will take other shortcuts that won't be readily apparent.

Remember also that labor rates vary greatly according to many factors, such as skill level, licensing requirements, experience, contractor

---

FLIP TIP

Venting, inside or out? Depending on the degree of prep needed for each project, the estimates on page 271 in our appendix checklist may be too low. For example, replacing a range vent hood in a kitchen is a relatively simple task. The estimate assumes there is already a hood in place, however. If the house has an antiquated fan vent in the ceiling (similar to a bathroom fan), there will be additional work to wire the new hood and install ductwork to the outside of the house. Some homes will have self-venting hoods that recirculate the inside air. If it's not too difficult, we suggest you upgrade to an outside vent. This project may not give an immediate return on your investment, but it will help to make the house safer. Part of the satisfaction of doing flips is in making the house a better home for families in the years ahead. If the house has a gas range, then building codes require that it vents to the outside, so taking the steps to install the proper duct work is even more important. The simple lesson here is to think ahead when estimating.

demand, and company overhead. Ideally, you'll hire contractors who are working at the top of their ability level for each project. For example, you don't want to pay seventy-five dollars per hour to an electrician to install switch cover plates when you can pay a handyman fifteen to thirty dollars an hour to do that task. That handyman can likely replace devices (switches and receptacles) as well.

You can also err by being overly frugal—for example, paying a high-school student who's never done home repairs ten dollars an hour to install cover plates. If the student does not understand how to shim the receptacles out when necessary, is not comfortable removing a device to adjust or replace it, or, worst of all, doesn't recognize if there's a problem in the junction box, then you will have issues to address later. In summary, hire competent people to fill each role. Your workers must know enough to know when they should ask for help. Hiring the right people is part of the team approach to rehabs, and always remember that each member of the team needs supervision and direction from others.

ACQUIRE FIRSTHAND EXPERIENCE!

If you have never picked up a hammer, a repair checklist may not mean much to you. You don't have to acquire the physical skills necessary to do each job, but you should understand the overall process. Once you're familiar with the mechanics of each part of the job, you will become confident estimating repairs and negotiating with contractors. There are lots of home-improvement shows on television, and even shows specifically about flipping. *This Old House* is an interesting place to start. Books and videos on basic home improvement are also available from Reader's Digest, Taunton Press, and Time Life. *Fine Homebuilding* is an excellent magazine, offering online as well as print subscriptions. Major home-improvement stores such as Home Depot give free classes on everything from tiling kitchens to replacing windows.

In fact, you should spend a few hours in home-improvement stores such as Home Depot, noting the cost of various items you are likely to purchase for your projects. The finishes you choose should be in keeping with the home's price point. As you go up in price, you may choose to make upgrades such as granite countertops, stainless steel appliances, and nicer trim. The problem is that you'll be tempted to make the home too nice and take on projects that won't yield a good return on investment. On the other hand, if you skimp too much you may not be able to sell the house.

Once you know the cost range of replacement items, the next step is to determine how much labor will be involved in replacing or installing the items. Always assume you will hire out the labor when calculating total repair costs.

We try to avoid too many generalizations because even the most basic "paint and carpet" project will likely cost a minimum of $20,000. A more extensive renovation involving a new kitchen, and possibly opening up a wall or two, would jump up to the $30,000–$40,000 range. Once you get into gutting a house, which entails removing a lot of drywall and replacing electrical, plumbing, and HVAC systems, you'll be in the $50,000-plus range. Building a full-on addition or doing extensive renovations in a higher-priced home will get you well beyond that.

Like any art, mastering the budgeting takes practice and experience. Our goal is to get you thinking and looking for things that may need repair or replacement, so you can come up with a rough estimate.

GET BIDS FROM CONTRACTORS

When starting out, whether you intend to do a job yourself or hire help, have two or three contractors bid on the work. Never just one. Spend time with each contractor and ask questions. If one contractor claims a particular project is difficult and expensive, then have the contractor talk through the specific issues with you. If another contractor says the job is simple, repeat what the first contractor said and listen to the response. This contractor's answer will help you to determine if one contractor is more experienced than another, or if someone is fibbing. Aim for simple, fast, and cost-effective repairs.

Sometimes, it's better to hire an expert who does not personally offer repair services to assess a problem. Then you can acquire repair bids based on a clear understanding of what needs to be done. We employ sewer video camera services, roofing-certification companies, structural engineers, and general property inspectors. As circumstances arise, we'll bring in other experts. For example, we had a tough time getting contractors to agree on how to deal with a basement that had water issues. There had been previous mitigation work done on the property, which was unsuccessful, and we had bids up into the tens of thousands of dollars to do elaborate repairs. We brought in a consultant who offered sound advice about a relatively simple fix that worked great. We've had similar results with foundation problems, where the contractors wanted large sums, but we later found less expensive solutions. Similarly, different structural engineers will come up with various ways to address issues. So don't hesitate to bring in another engineer if your first one comes up with an outrageously expensive fix.

TO FIX OR NOT TO FIX

Many seminars teach investment students a cookie-cutter approach to rehabs. While you should be systematic in your own approach, never forget that every property is different.

Government regulations have increased the cost of rehabbing properties. You'll need to navigate the turbulent waters of health and code regulation and compliance, while balancing costs and schedules. Pay strict attention to health and safety issues in and around the property. After all, people's number-one concern is the physical and mental well-being of themselves and their loved ones. In most cases, you will need to disclose those issues, even if they have already been mitigated. Do the research to understand the legislation in your state that affects rehabbing properties. Let's look in more detail at some of the most common health problems in rehab homes.

Mold issues due to water damage or lack of cleaning can become a major problem. However, "black mold" is considered to be a threat to health and can be an expensive issue to handle. If the mold is localized in a small area such as under a bathroom sink, you may not need to bring in a professional for remediation. Household bleach and other cleaners will kill mold. On nonporous surfaces like tile, mold can be removed with mild cleaners. If the mold is on walls, it's best to remove all the affected drywall and inspect any covered areas in close proximity. If the mold is in a larger area and has been disturbed or is present in porous surfaces, it is a more serious issue. Call in a pro to help you assess the problem. These companies test air quality and will verify if it is indeed black mold you are dealing with.

Only one time did we *not* purchase a home specifically due to a mold issue. The basement of that house had a moisture problem, and the mold had been left to thrive for a long time. It was growing on the basement ceiling, and even the framing was covered with residue. I didn't see how we could remove the mold with complete certainty, so we passed on the deal.

Lead-based paint was commonly used before the 1970s and has since been phased out. You cannot tell if a house has lead-based paint unless you test for it. In 2010 the EPA issued a federal mandate requiring contractors renovating, repairing, or painting structures built before 1978 to test for lead. There are several options for testing. First, you can purchase a do-it-yourself home test kit, but such tests do not meet EPA requirements. Second, you can have the contractor with the proper certification test for lead. We don't recommend either of these options because of the chance for error and future liability. We believe the best option is to pay a company specializing in this type of testing. Their equipment penetrates multiple layers of paint and is quite effective at detecting lead. Typically, you will test a home if you are planning on removing drywall or replacing windows. In our experience, however, lead does not affect renovations as often as statistics seem to indicate.

If you buy a property that has lead-based paint, coordinate your renovation plans with a professional remediation company. Some methods of removing paint actually increase the risk of lead exposure. If lead paint on ceilings and walls is in good repair, then painting them or covering them

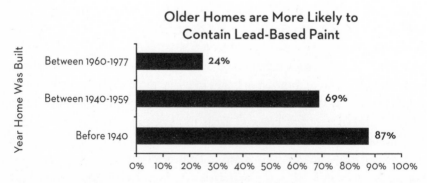

*Source: EPA.gov.

with wallpaper may be all that is needed to keep the lead in place. But if the lead paint is chipping or peeling, or if it's on a surface such as a windowsill or stair rail where children can be exposed to it, or on surfaces that rub each other, then it should be removed or covered.

Asbestos, now widely recognized as a health hazard, was used frequently through the 1970s because of its effective insulation properties. You may find it in various areas of a building, but most commonly wrapped around ductwork, in old glue-down floor tiles, and in drywall and joint compound. If you have a popcorn ceiling texture, there is a high chance it, too, contains asbestos.

Don't panic if you find asbestos in your house. When possible, leave it alone, but if you need to remove it, you'll need to do some assessment first. There are removal guidelines based on the percentage that is present and on whether it's been disturbed. Have the areas you're planning to demo tested by an industrial-hygiene firm. After the firm collects and analyzes samples, you should receive a written report explaining where and how much asbestos was found. The report should also include recommendations about how to contain or remove asbestos. OSHA has guidelines for unlicensed individuals removing materials that contain a low percentage of asbestos. The contractor should help you with reasonable solutions and should be licensed for the type of work performed. Some abatement companies will prey on people's fears and run up larger bills than necessary. Your local health department should have a list of certified companies. Hopefully, you can simply contain what is there, but if you must bring in an abatement company, budget extra time and expense for the removal.

Radon gas is another common rehab health issue and is not limited to older homes. Many buyers test for dangerous levels. Mitigation is not a lender or code requirement, but it may be necessary to reduce radon levels if it's important to your buyers. The EPA states that levels of 4 picocuries per liter (pCi/L) or more should be addressed. Some areas of the country, and even particular neighborhoods, are known for high radon levels. Even if nearby homes have high levels, your house could be within the acceptable range. Homes with finished basements are the most likely to have radon issues.

We don't test for radon prior to purchase or even before listing our properties for sale. Remember, radon removal systems can be installed for about the same cost after renovations are complete, typically for around

$1,000. If having a system installed becomes a matter of postinspection negotiation with a potential buyer later, it can be addressed then.

Lead in water is another potential health pitfall, one that certainly has the nation's attention after the severe problems in Flint, Michigan. So you must make sure your house's water supply line is not made of lead pipe. It's possible to have high lead levels in water regardless of the supply-line piping, but this issue is not one that has affected our sales over the years. If a buyer did test for and find unacceptable lead levels, there would be filtration options to alleviate the problem. If you happen to renovate a property with its own well or other source of water, then water quality can also be an issue. Before purchase you should have the well's viability tested by a reputable company.

ADDITIONAL OLD HOUSE ISSUES

In addition to health hazards, there are other often-overlooked concerns when evaluating potential purchases. Faulty **sewer lines** are quite common. Sewer issues are easily discovered by having a company inspect the line using a snake with a video camera attached. If you do have the line scoped, have the contractor note the line's path to help with later repairs. This inspection service costs $100–$150. The higher end of the spectrum occurs if the sewer line is blocked. If that's the case, try to have the blockage removed, but if the line cannot be cleared, assume it is broken. If the house is more than thirty years old or has a sewer line that is close to large trees, definitely spend the money to have the line checked by a professional.

Replacing a sewer line usually can run from a few thousand to as high as $10,000. This price includes adding outside cleanouts. You may be able to do a repair for less, however, if there is only one bad section or if the house was built without a basement and the line is not buried very deep. Unfortunately, some sewer lines are longer or deeper than others. If the line goes under concrete or nice landscaping, or, worst of all, is damaged at the city tap (where it joins the sewer main line), the price goes up. In some circumstances, such as when you would have to control traffic on a busy street in order to make the repair, it may be best to install a liner into the damaged pipe. We've spent as much as $12,000 in these difficult cases. Most clay lines have some low spots (bellies) that hold water and root invasion through small cracks or pipe joints. In these cases, it's best to not repair the line. If the issue comes up when you sell the home, you can negotiate a settlement or do the repairs prior to closing. It doesn't usually add too much cost to repair a sewer line after completing the home renovation.

In some areas, you may need a **termite** inspection. Given the right conditions, termites can flourish in many climates. Some termites are extremely aggressive and can do tremendous damage to even newer homes. Look carefully for signs of infestation, rotted wood, and elevated moisture levels. You can purchase a basic yet effective pin-type moisture meter for less than fifty dollars. In addition to pin-type meters, the professionals use radio-frequency (RF) meters that can pick up moisture hidden behind dry exterior surfaces. Knowing a home's moisture levels will let you know if conditions exist that could lead to a termite infestation (or moisture problems). An inspector should be able to tell you what, if any, treatment is required and give you an idea of the cost. An easy way to determine if you have a big termite problem is simply to take a screwdriver and randomly jab it into wooden joists in the basement. If the screwdriver goes up to the handle, you've got a problem!

Foundation issues sometimes exist in new and old homes alike, especially if the soil contains clay, which tends to swell when it becomes moist (expansive soil). Many areas require soil tests when building new homes, but this has not always been the case. Typically, settling results from poor drainage or from not adequately compacting soil during the backfill process. Most homes' foundations are not tied to the concrete slabs, so a little cracking in the slab shouldn't be a major issue when it comes time to sell.

Poor drainage can lead to settling on homes built even on good soil. Address the drainage to keep water away from the foundation and you'll reduce the likelihood of future occurrences. If the home has substantial evidence of movement such as notably bowed or cracked foundation walls—or on brick houses, cracked or uneven grout lines—you'll need to bring in a structural engineer to determine the best course of action. Repairing and stabilizing foundations can be very expensive, and some buyers won't purchase homes with prior issues. Be wary of purchasing homes with major foundation problems.

Electrical issues are quite important since they are also safety concerns. Even outdated electric systems can be updated without spending a fortune. In most cases, there will have been some updates done over the

FLIP TIP

A good foundation. Make sure your home inspector has experience with foundation issues. Most inspectors can recognize an issue, but few can diagnose the solution. Don't let a panicked inspector scare you away from buying the house. In dealing with all this, do *not* get a free opinion from a foundation company, since they will offer the most expensive solution. Instead, pay an engineer who does not sell foundation repairs to give you an objective opinion.

years, so you shouldn't have to replace all the wiring. If you discover slipshod electric work, then carefully evaluate the entire system. Examples of poor electric practices include connecting two conductors to one breaker (double lugging) or connecting wires outside junction boxes (open splices). Other common mistakes include using 14-2 wire in circuits protected by 20-amp breakers and wrapping splices with electrical tape instead of using wire nuts.

In today's age of electronics and convenience, homeowners place large demands on their homes' electric systems. Your home will need more circuits than older homes tend to have in order to support items such as microwave ovens, hair dryers, and air conditioning. Many years ago, homes were wired using a design known as "knob and tube." This wiring has exposed conductors and is something you will need to replace if found. We don't see this style of wiring often, since it was phased out in the '30s. If we do find it, it's usually just in one area of the house. If the house was built before the '20s, it likely didn't even have electricity!

You may also find rigid conduit, which can be OK. It's possible to pull new conductors through the conduit if necessary. Homes built in the '30s and '40s used flexible metal conduit called BX (also known as armor clad). This conduit may contain a ground wire or use the armor as its ground. Overall, it causes few issues, other than being a bit difficult to work with. Romex-style wiring has been prevalent since the '70s and can usually be left intact. Cloth-covered wire, however, should be evaluated by a licensed electrician, and it may be worthwhile to add ground wires if there are only two conductors. Some Romex is grounded with a smaller gauge wire, which is not ideal but is usable.

Aluminum wiring was often used for branch circuits from 1965 through 1972. It is still used for feeders and service drops, which is not a problem. Old aluminum conductors can become brittle and oxidized, leading to arcing at connections and potential fire hazards. To address aluminum branch wiring issues, replace wires and devices where possible, then "pigtail" any remaining aluminum connections with copper wire. These repairs, when handled by a specially trained electrician, are generally considered safe.

In addition to the types of wiring, evaluate the breaker panel to confirm it is not damaged and is adequately sized. One hundred amps is the minimum acceptable size for electric service in today's homes. The panel should have enough room inside to be accessible and should contain at least six breakers. Many home inspectors think that panels made by Federal Pacific (FP) should always be replaced, but the problem units tend to be the really small panels that are overfilled with wires. In fact, you can still purchase FP panels and breakers today. Ideally, the panel should have a main breaker that shuts off every circuit, although it's not mandatory to have a main disconnect. Most panels are either outside or in a garage, but panels located inside a home are fine as long as they are readily accessible.

We often replace all the switches and receptacles (collectively known as devices) in a house with new white ones. We use receptacles that are marked tamper resistant, since these devices offer shock protection and are required by building departments adopting the 2011 National Electric Code (NEC). We also use ground-fault circuit interrupters (GFCIs) in areas where they are required by code.

Many home inspectors do not realize that GFCIs work on ungrounded circuits. The confusion results from the simple electric testers that most home inspectors use. These testers trip GFCIs by shorting to the ground wire. If there is no ground wire, the testers falsely indicate a problem. If this issue arises when you are selling a home, point out that every GFCI has a test button which will verify if the device is wired correctly. If the inspector doesn't agree, provide a link to the manufacturer's website or a copy of the installation instructions.

If you do extensive renovations, you may be required to use arc-fault breakers. These breakers actually detect the arcing that can start fires. They are a great safety feature but, at thirty dollars each, are roughly ten times the cost of typical breakers. The building department may also ask you to install hardwired, interconnected smoke detectors, as required by the NEC. If you are required to use interconnected smoke detectors, see if the building department will allow you to use RF units. These smoke detectors use ac power, but communicate with each other wirelessly, greatly simplifying installation.

Most homes you renovate will have at least some **plumbing** issues to resolve. We already addressed the sewer line, so now we'll discuss the additional plumbing systems. Cast-iron waste pipes (drains) typically last fifty years or more, so the inside waste lines are usually not problematic. They should be evaluated, however, since older lines can rust through. In addition, lead pipes and old-fashioned drum traps should be removed. When you update plumbing fixtures and change their locations, you will need to tie the new drain lines to the existing pipes. You can use either PVC or ABS plastic pipe. It's often less expensive removing the cast-iron pipe rather than mixing old and new. Be wary of mixing PVC and ABS pipe; building inspectors do not like to see the two glued together. You may find copper waste lines in homes built in the '60s. This material doesn't pose any problems. Any newer homes will primarily have PVC or ABS, with the common exception of a cast-iron sewer line exiting through the foundation wall.

Water supply lines were typically made of galvanized iron pipe through the early '60s. These galvanized lines may have already been replaced, or at least partially so. If not, you'll likely need to completely replace the supply lines, since galvanized pipe corrodes and can become restrictive. Replumbing a ranch home with a crawl space or unfinished basement is relatively simple. But if the plumbing is hidden in finished walls, such as in a two-story home, the cost will go up substantially.

By the way, the water heater should have a label showing its warranty or expected life, in addition to a manufacture-date sticker. Often water heaters will last well beyond the posted tank life, but if the unit is more than fifteen years old or is showing signs of corrosion around the bottom, it should be replaced.

After the '60s, copper supply lines were used, and copper is still popular today. Copper pipe is quite reliable. The major concern is that if the pipes had been allowed to freeze, then there could be lots of leaks. If you are able to inspect the home with the water on, you'll know. But if the home is winterized, then you won't find out for sure until after you purchase it. Polybutylene pipe (poly) was installed in up to ten million homes, mostly from the '80s through 1995, when it was pulled from the market. This pipe had failure issues and was the target of a class-action lawsuit. To be safe, replace it if you find it in your house. Look for gray or white flexible pipe and couplings.

The last type of supply line we'll discuss is cross-linked polyethylene (PEX). It's been around for decades and has been quite popular in the US since around 2000. PEX is a flexible plastic pipe that is typically red or blue, though sometimes it's white. PEX is an excellent product. It is less expensive than copper, both in material and installation costs, and is usually not affected by freezing temps. It has passed copper in popularity.

Exterior plumbing is primarily for sprinkler systems. In most cases, we don't repair sprinkler systems. In Colorado they are winterized for about half the year and normally need attention each spring. If the house is going to be on the market in the summer, however, it makes sense to repair the system. If the system is older and has not been maintained, it may be best to remove it.

Roofs on older homes offer special challenges. If the roof is severely damaged, then at least some of the plywood decking would need to be replaced. The decking in homes built since the '60s and '70s is plywood, but older homes may still have the original planks for decking. If the house has skip sheathing (decking), the building department may require you to replace the old decking with plywood as part of a roof replacement.

Construction methods also impact renovations. Many years ago foundations were not much more than piles of rocks, or at best bricks that would eventually crumble. Some foundations are beyond repair, so evaluate carefully. Framing techniques have evolved over the years but don't greatly affect most renovations. Older framing did not include fire blocking between floors. Older lumber was slightly thicker and wider than modern dimensional lumber. Some homes have cinderblock exterior walls, which can add challenges when making changes. Also, lath-and-plaster walls are more difficult to work with than drywall. Simple projects become more difficult when the walls crumble as you cut into them, and when you replace a section of a plaster wall with drywall, it will have to be shimmed. As we've stated, every aspect of renovation gets more complicated—and more expensive—with older homes.

WRAPPING IT UP

- Learn about repairs and labor, and know what they cost.
- Don't overlook potential hazards.
- Be aware of challenges with older houses.

CHAPTER 12

The Rehab: Doing It

This chapter provides specific information on how far to go with updates and repairs. Every property renovation requires sometimes difficult decisions about what to fix, how nice to make the house, and what artistic and stylistic choices to make. We try to stick with what has worked in the past. Every project is unique, however, and it is always a challenge to turn a dilapidated house into an inviting home.

HOW NICE SHOULD YOU MAKE IT?

Quality workmanship shows. Even first-time buyers recognize shoddy workmanship. Your buyers may initially miss problems, but the defects will probably be caught by their professional home inspectors. These issues may jeopardize the sale. Other well-hidden shortcuts could eventually lead to lawsuits, fires, or other tragedies. Fortunately, you will be compensated with personal and financial satisfaction when you repair it properly the first time. Remember, it is your responsibility to deliver a safe and sound home.

Beginning investors often spend too much time and money on unnecessary projects. These beginners then make the mistake of asking premium prices for their properties. They end up wasting time and money waiting for their houses to sell and eventually face the reality that they must lower the price. It's fine to pick out a couple of highly visible areas to splurge on, just do not go overboard. Only do things that add value and marketability to the house. A rule of thumb is to tackle only those projects that will add twice the renovation cost to the home's value. Of course, some projects simply must be done for the house to sell.

You never want to have the most expensive house in a neighborhood—just the cleanest. Standard items should be consistent with those in neighbors' homes. For example, window air conditioners may be the norm in one neighborhood, but central air may be standard in another. Don't bother installing central air conditioning in a window-unit neighborhood. Items such as new windows, sprinkler systems, security alarms, and storm doors are seldom worth the cost and effort to install. On the other hand, be generous on inexpensive items and projects that add curb appeal. Spend a little extra on exterior door hardware, house numbers, a nice front door, and the front landscape. Replace lock sets, switch plates, toilets, faucets, light fixtures, and other cosmetic items.

INTERIOR UPDATES

Let's walk through the basic rehab process on a typical three-bedroom, one-bath ranch starter home (approximately 1,200 square feet). We will assume the house has working mechanical systems and is structurally sound. We will also assume that you are no Bob Vila but that you can handle basic tasks such as replacing a bathroom vanity and installing a medicine cabinet. If you cannot or choose not to do these things yourself, then factor in the cost of a handyman's services. If you want to be your own general contractor, a detailed list of items and prices can be found on page 271 in the appendix.

Some investors recommend you start with the outside of the house to attract potential buyers as early as possible. We disagree. Never draw undue attention to the fact that you are doing extensive repairs. Working on the inside first will allow you to maintain a relatively low profile. If nosy neighbors or potential buyers stop by, tell them to come back for a tour in

Be trendy. Today's most popular hardware trend is to use satin-nickel finish. Typically, we replace the lock sets throughout the house. Go ahead and replace hinges as well. Oil-rubbed bronze is also a popular choice, but some items such as faucets will cost more in this finish. Chrome remains popular as well and can look great if you go with a modern look throughout the house. You can also mix finishes. For example, the door hardware can be satin nickel and light fixtures oil-rubbed bronze. It's fine to present more expensive finishes and fixtures in the powder room, master suite, or kitchen.

a couple of weeks. By the time they return, you will have cleaned up the debris, animal odors, and unsafe conditions left by previous inhabitants. Buyers lack the imagination to see the potential of a property in the early stages of renovation. Once you show them the house in a rough state, they won't ever come back.

Most homebuyers are couples, and the first place they want to see is the kitchen. The kitchen should be relatively modern and bright. Updating the kitchen, while keeping existing cabinets, should cost about $2,500. But if you replace the cabinets and install granite countertops, you'll likely spend closer to $7,000.

Granite slab **countertops** are popular but expensive. Still, they are a great place to splurge, and buyers love rimless undermount sinks. Do your homework and find a company that will discount prices for common granite colors. You can get a similar look using granite tiles for countertops and backsplash areas. Formica countertops have come a long way and are a good substitute for granite in lower-price-point homes.

Cabinets are important, and hopefully the existing "boxes" will be in salvageable condition. Cleaning natural finish cabinets with lemon oil–based products will often bring back their natural luster. If cabinets are dull or dark brown, spray them with high-gloss white paint. Start with an oil-based primer, sand as necessary, then paint. Also, replace knobs and hinges. Damaged cabinets can usually be repaired if they are going to be painted. If the house has a dropped soffit over the cabinets, remove it for a more contemporary feel.

Replacing cabinets is another option, but taking this step means you are going beyond a really basic renovation. We often replace cabinets, which has the added benefit of allowing us to update the kitchen layout. Remember that relocating appliances increases project cost; it's expensive to make plumbing and electrical changes, in addition to drywall repairs. For higher-price-point homes a nice upgrade is tall upper cabinets instead of the typical thirty-inch units. Changing to thirty-six-inch or forty-two-inch uppers will add storage space and impress buyers.

Commercial-style kitchen **appliances** remain popular. We usually add lower-end stainless steel appliances for a designer look, except on low-end homes. Replace any appliance or fixture that doesn't look clean and fresh. Black, white, or stainless are acceptable finishes, assuming all the appliances have the same finish (it's fine if the appliances are not all from the same manufacturer). You can buy a new stove or dishwasher for a few hundred dollars at a retail chain store. For the same price, you can buy a slightly better model at an appliance store specializing in overstock or scratch-and-dent units.

Don't forget to budget for a range hood as well. Installing a microwave hood can be a nice upgrade. These hoods are designed to go under a short upper cabinet, however, and may look awkward if they are too close to the range. The manufacturer will have guidelines regarding installation height. Also, microwaves draw high amperage and should be on a designated 20-amp circuit. Unless the refrigerator is nice and clean, throw it out. An ugly fridge looks worse than no fridge. We usually sell our flips without a refrigerator, especially if the kitchen is small.

Install a contemporary **faucet**. Faucets can cost several hundred dollars, so don't get carried away. You can usually find a nice one with built in sprayer for around one hundred dollars. Chrome finish is fine in a kitchen. If the existing sink is stainless steel, you can usually clean it up. Expect to replace the disposal, since it's not worth trying to reinstall an old, corroded unit. You should also replace the water shutoff valves and flexible supply lines throughout the house.

Replace any dated **light fixtures**, including fluorescent lights. Surface-mount lights are not expensive. Opt for either two-bulb fixtures or LED models to ensure adequate light. Energy-efficient LED fixtures have come down in price, so you may want to install them throughout the house. We try to match light fixtures throughout, with a few exceptions. For example, we use low-profile fixtures in areas with low ceilings.

Chances are you will need professional assistance on **electrical** projects at first. Take time to learn about electric systems and always respect potential dangers. We always replace old ivory or brown switches and receptacles. Even if you choose not to replace switches and receptacles, install new plates throughout the house. Some rehabbers leave the old, ugly switch plates or install white plates over ivory switches. Buyers will notice this obvious shortcut.

Nice **bathrooms** are an absolute must. You may not be able to expand a bathroom, but make sure it is inviting, modern, and bright. Start with a thorough cleaning. Use vinegar and lime/rust removal products to clean up porcelain fixtures. Remove old caulk; then bleach out any white or light-colored grout. We replace tubs that do not clean up well. The new tub itself is not too costly, but installing one requires replacing the tub surround and redoing the floor. In many cases, you'd be replacing these items anyway, but if not, replacing a tub becomes a relatively expensive project. If the tub is in poor condition or is not white, but is a good design and has a nice surround, have it refinished. Old claw-foot tubs add character and are worth restoring. Although it will cost several hundred dollars, refinishing a tub is simpler than replacing it. A tile surround can usually be refinished in white or repaired and regrouted. Any plastic or fiberglass surround in poor condition should be replaced. Adding a contemporary tile surround really improves the look and feel of any bathroom. Take advantage of the opportunity to insert a nice border or accents.

Replace the toilet and seat if they can't be cleaned to like-new condition. We seldom leave old toilets in our properties. In addition, replace the faucet, sink, and vanity if they are at all dated or damaged. There are many inexpensive off-the-shelf options to suit your home's style.

Throw out old window coverings. In most cases, we just leave window coverings off. We selectively install new ones based on the home's price point, each room's views, and security issues. Home Depot or Lowe's cut nice-looking, relatively inexpensive blinds to size while you wait.

Paint colors matter. Modern water-based paints cover well and are easy to apply. Traditionally, painters used semigloss paint in the kitchen and bathrooms. But paints have improved so much that we now use eggshell sheen on walls throughout the house. Like semigloss, it can be wiped clean, but it covers flaws better than semigloss. We prefer warm, neutral colors. We usually paint walls an off-white or light-beige color. Light-gray shades are also popular if you are going for a modern look. Typically, we paint ceilings with flat white paint, trim and doors with white semigloss paint. To reduce costs, we often paint basement walls and ceilings the same color. When using just one color in a basement, choose white to brighten up the rooms a bit. White ceiling paint on closet walls and ceilings is also fine.

You can paint over wallpaper that's properly hung and not textured using primer for the first coat. We never seem to see wallpaper that we like enough to keep "as is." If the paper is textured or is peeling, remove it. You

---

FLIP TIP

Paint by the numbers. Check your local home-improvement store or paint supplier for bargains on returned paint that was mistinted for a customer. So long as it is in the right shade of beige or white, it'll work fine for you and save you a few bucks.

---

can purchase a steamer for about one hundred dollars. The steamer should pay for itself quickly. In less expensive neighborhoods, paint over paneling if it is in decent condition. Caulk the seams and nail holes, prime, then reapply caulk to the areas you missed before painting. Or you can easily remove the paneling if there is drywall behind it.

Ceiling fans are nice upgrades for bedrooms and other rooms, unless the house has low ceilings. Confirm that ceiling junction boxes are designed to work with fans, and replace if necessary.

Replace **trim** if it's in poor condition or is dated looking, such as streamline or clamshell style, which have a taper or radius from edge to edge and are very plain. Replacing trim is an optional project but can really dress up a house. We usually choose a 1" × 4" profile craftsman-style preprimed MDF (medium density fiberboard) trim over traditional colonial-style trim.

Look for opportunities to **add functional square feet** to a house without actually having to do an addition to the house. Often you can open up a wall or doorway between rooms, which gives the house a brighter, more contemporary feel. You may even want to create a luxury feel by combining two bedrooms into a large master bedroom. This project may be as simple as removing a non-load-bearing wall, which is not too difficult. To be safe, consult with a structural engineer or competent framer before removing any walls. You can also enlarge a bathroom as part of the master-suite project, but adding a bathroom tends to be expensive.

We are by no means saying you should reconfigure every house, but we are encouraging you to think creatively. Even a nice master suite won't make a two-bedroom house more desirable than a three-bedroom house. Sometimes we add finished square feet by raising the finish level of existing basements or sunrooms or by converting an attic into a living space. For example, a sunroom may have a sloped concrete floor and no heat source. By leveling and carpeting the floor, then adding a heat duct to that room, you improve the entire home's livability. Converting an attic into a living space is a little more complicated but can add substantial value to a Victorian-style home.

Make sure that all interior **doors** work properly, and replace the lock sets. We usually replace the hinges as well. When possible, we restore vintage hardware that has lots of character. Most towns have resources to buy old hardware and doors if you are missing a few bits and pieces. Replace damaged or flush slabs (those without raised panels) with new six-panel, hollow-core doors. Or, you might consider Santa Fe or other door styles, especially if you have to replace every door to have them all match.

Bypass (sliding) or bifold closet doors are both fine. Use whichever type offers the most convenient closet access. If the house has odd-sized closet doors, then bypass doors will be easier to fit to the existing openings. In many cases, you will have to either resize the existing openings or cut down the doors to fit.

Flooring is a major expense in most renovations. Hardwood floors are often hidden under outdated carpets. Hardwood is highly desirable and can almost always be restored. Refinishing floors, however, is not a do-it-yourself project. The cost of equipment rentals and the disappointing results that often follow are good reasons not to tackle the project yourself. Professionals will repair, sand, and refinish the floor for as low as $1.50 per square foot. In some cases, you can spend even less for a "screen and coat." This process cleans up scratches and looks great if the floor was in pretty good shape to start with. You'll be surprised at how good a pro can make even a severely damaged floor look. For a little extra money, professionals can replace damaged boards and apply a coat of tinted stain to hide pet and water stains. Dark floors are popular right now, so don't worry if you need to go with a cherry or light-walnut look.

There are quite a few product choices available for polyurethane flooring, so discuss affordable options with your installer. In some cases, we'll install new hardwood floors—usually in relatively expensive homes.

There's another consideration if you plan to install new hardwood or tile floors and are also replacing cabinets. We prefer to install the cabinets first. Use plywood to raise the cabinets by about three quarters of an inch to match the new floor height. We've found this method reduces flooring costs and minimizes damage to new floors. After the hardwood floors are finished, touch up base trim, install fixtures and kitchen appliances, and take care of punch-list items that didn't quite get done in time. In most cases, we have the finisher put down one or two coats and then come back in a week or so to put down the final coat.

We're not huge fans of laminate flooring, "engineered" hardwood flooring, or prefinished solid-hardwood flooring. These products can be installed by a do-it-yourselfer, but the results are not always perfect, particularly in large areas. We do recommend hardwood laminates over man-made surfaces. Most buyers prefer traditional hardwood.

Tile remains a great choice for kitchens and bathrooms. Ceramic-tile floors and surrounds are desirable upgrades. You can learn to install tile or find an affordable tile installer (setter). Porcelain tile is a type of ceramic tile that is made from a different type of clay and is fired at a higher temp than ordinary ceramic. Porcelain tile may be superior, but don't pay a premium for it. For our purposes, consider porcelain and ceramic the same. Opt for a nice mid-priced tile and avoid cheap tile that looks like it's been screen printed. Natural stone is a great option but may be a more expensive choice. With any tile, capitalize on the opportunity to be creative with patterns and design. Try to keep grout lines at the current trend of a quarter inch or less. Spend the extra money for a quality installation with cement underlayment ("backer board") on all tile floors and surrounds. Installing tile on concrete should cost less than installing tile over other substrates. Tile is also great to use for the laundry room and entryways.

Resilient flooring is a growing category. There are newer products that lock together as tiles or planks, and there are many styles of sheet-vinyl available. Luxury vinyl tile can be made to look like wood or stone and has become popular even in expensive homes. You should be able to install this flooring yourself, though some people think the "click-and-stick" tile is more difficult to install than engineered or prefinished wood flooring. We remain partial to ceramic tile, but sometimes choose vinyl flooring for the kitchen, bath, entryway, or laundry room.

We advocate installing new **carpet** throughout the remainder of the house. Only on rare occasions have we been able to keep the existing carpet in a flip. Don't carpet bathrooms or laundry rooms.

Light beige is a safe bet for a carpet color and can actually make a room look larger. Some feel beige is boring, so consider other neutral grays or taupe to add a designer touch. Twisted pile is by far the most popular type of carpet. If you find a great deal on a patterned Berber or even shag pile (which has become popular in luxury homes), then go for it. You can find quality carpeting at bargain warehouses. Ask for overruns or other discount offerings. If your house has multiple flooring materials, then you can save even more using remnants from a partial roll. Be wary of combining rolls, as they may not be a perfect color match, and the difference will show in the seams. Many carpet stores will discount the price of the carpet if you hire their carpet installers. Home Depot and Lowe's also run specials that include whole-house installation for about one hundred dollars. It's a great price if you are carpeting a large area. Be wary of up-charges—extra fees for stairs, basements, or tricky areas.

Select carpet that is at least one grade above the FHA minimum standard. Visit an established carpet supplier to learn about price points, grades, and materials options. Relatively inexpensive carpet should look great when first installed, though it will start to look tired sooner than more expensive carpet. Spend a little extra on the pad, and the carpet will feel like a higher grade than it actually is. Don't make the mistake of buying the cheapest carpet you find; the money you save will be lost many times over if the property does not show well.

Make sure every property you sell has sound **mechanical systems**. Some type of central heating system is mandatory. A furnace is a commonly replaced item. Pay an HVAC contractor to make sure the furnace (or other heat source) and water heater are safe and will pass a home inspection.

Boiler systems tend to be quite reliable, and old systems can usually be brought up to good working condition by a competent plumber or HVAC technician. Even if the furnace or boiler works well, it's a good idea to add an outside-combustion air source. This source would typically be two metal ducts that go from the home's exterior to the ceiling and floor of the mechanical room. If you do replace the furnace, an 80 percent efficiency unit should be your first choice, but some areas now require high-efficiency direct-vent models. These units cost at least 50 percent more than less efficient models. Typically, the existing ductwork will work with your new furnace, but you may need to replace the exhaust-vent piping. It is usually easier to upgrade these items before listing the property for sale. But replacing a furnace after renovating a house is not a huge problem if you are not replacing the ductwork. If the furnace is working satisfactorily and you are on the fence about replacing it, hold off. As we mentioned earlier, you can always negotiate the replacement or allowance with your potential buyer.

Adding air conditioning may be a worthwhile improvement in some areas, depending on the neighborhood. If most homes in the neighborhood have central air, then so should yours. Decide if AC makes sense for your project, and budget accordingly. Usually, you will need to replace the furnace when you add central air. If air conditioning is involved, the cost compared to just replacing a furnace is about doubled. Window-type air conditioners may be worth keeping if they are already installed and working. They are eyesores, however, and block some light from coming in the windows. Follow your intuition, but remove existing window units if they are visible from the street.

Your house may have a swamp cooler (also called an evaporative cooler). Some people love swamp coolers, but in our experience they tend to be old and in disrepair. We usually throw them out, especially if they are window units. If you're not familiar with them, swamp coolers cool the air through evaporation of water. If the home has a rooftop unit complete with ductwork and permanent wiring, you may be better off repairing it or replacing it. Otherwise, you'll incur substantial cost to remove it.

As you may expect, we usually remove old water softeners, humidifiers, hot tubs, water features, and even swimming pools. All of these items require maintenance and are simply not worth repairing if neglected. If your rehab house has a nice hot tub or pool you want to keep, then remember to budget for repairs needed to put it in tip-top shape.

Good enough. When replacing major items such as furnaces, carpet, and roofs, it is not necessary to go with the best quality or grade. Do what is consistent with the neighborhood. If you overspend on quality items, you are appealing to the intellects of your buyers instead of their hearts. People buy on emotion, so instead of overspending on major items, overspend on minor items such as light fixtures, door handles, and sink faucets.

Safety items can never be ignored. Always install battery-powered smoke detectors in each bedroom and hallway. Replace old, yellowed detectors with new ones. You will also need to install carbon-monoxide (CO) detectors. These devices detect potentially lethal carbon monoxide and are now required in the majority of states. You will most likely need to place units in the hallway immediately outside each bedroom. Battery-powered units are acceptable.

Each bedroom must have a closet and an egress window or egress door. There are specific guidelines regarding egress-window size, height from the floor, outside-well dimensions, and ladder requirements. Grates over basement windows must be operable from the inside. Obviously, egress doors must go to the exterior, not interior passageways. Nonconforming bedrooms without proper egresses will lower the property's appraised value, so provide at least two conforming bedrooms if possible.

Make sure the property has securely locking exterior doors. Dead bolt locks should allow the occupant to open the latch from inside the premises without a key, due to fire-liability issues. Buyers expect you to provide window screens and unseen things such as adequate insulation. There are a few specific requirements for garages as well. Automatic garage door openers should have an electric eye safety device and a properly adjusted clutch. Garage service doors (hinged) leading into a house must be fire rated and should have self-closing hinges. The shared wall separating the house from the garage should also be fire-rated drywall or, at a minimum, extend to the rafters.

In addition, stairwells and decks should be protected by adequate guardrails. Stairs should have proper handrails, and stair treads should have consistent and proper rise and run. Most homes you sell will be subject to FHA guidelines. FHA appraisers have some flexibility in what they deem unsafe, so when in doubt, err on the side of caution. These safety guidelines are a good starting point, but take the time to learn the basics of modern building codes.

Strong **curb appeal** helps sell any property. Focus on exterior items such as paint, entryway, landscaping, roof, windows, gutters and downspouts, and mailbox. Sometimes we will add shake shingles on the face of gables, or spruce up the front porch to give the home a bit of style. If the house has been poorly maintained, you may need to replace siding or repair brick that has cracked due to settling. We usually replace some amount of exterior trim on every flip. Go ahead and replace all the siding or trim if you find that more than 20 percent of it is damaged. Masonite siding and trim is relatively inexpensive and a good choice for flips. Cement-based siding holds up really well but is more difficult to install and is not worth the extra expense. T1-11 siding comes in sheets, and its vertical grain tends to make a house look like a manufactured home. Other than on garages or outbuildings, we avoid using this material for siding.

Exterior painting goes a long, long way. We generally paint the exterior of the home an attractive neutral color. Light colors tend to make a house look larger. Match colors to the roof and any stone or brickwork. Accent the house with basic earth tones such as beiges and greens. White is fine for trim and is a good choice with white gutters and downspouts. Avoid light-blue paint. Even though it's a common color choice, some people hate it. Flat sheen is the norm for exterior paint. Don't buy the cheapest paint or spend too much on ultra-expensive paint brands.

The key to a good paint job is taking the time to prep. Before you paint, clean the exterior siding with mild soap and water. If it cleans up well, you may not need to paint the entire exterior. Take a small piece of painted material to the paint store for an electronic color match. Then purchase a gallon or two of paint to touch up problem areas. Even with a good color match you'll want to paint a complete section of the home, so there are no obvious transitions. Remove any loose, peeling paint, then feather edge with sandpaper. Replace damaged boards, and use caulk where necessary. Then prime over repairs or other raw wood. We don't like to paint brick because it's as close as you can get to a no-maintenance surface. But if it's an ugly color, you can paint over it. Limewash is often an attractive and inexpensive vintage solution for painting exterior brick. And if the exterior of the house is a nice cedar shingle or has vinyl siding, use a pressure washer and elbow grease to clean it up rather than paint it.

You only get one chance to make a first impression. A cheap **front door** makes a house look cheap, and an old front door makes a house look old. If the front door is worn or very basic, spend $250 for an attractive new one. Paint it a bold burgundy or hunter green, using a semigloss sheen.

Be sure that the entryway is well lit with an attractive porch light. Many homes have functional but unattractive aluminum storm doors. Discard these doors or leave them in the garage for future owners. Remove antennas, satellite dishes, or other unnecessary items that are visible from the street.

If the front stoop has cracks or settling that makes it unsightly or dangerous, replace it. Make sure the rise of each step is less than eight inches. You could have a small concrete stoop repaired with a mixable concrete such as Quikrete. As a last resort, you can paint concrete. Assess all the concrete, including driveway and basement. If there are substantial repairs, bring in a contractor to bid on doing all the concrete repairs at once.

A wooden **porch** is fairly easy to repair. Use redwood or pressure-treated lumber and apply stain-and-weather treatment. A plain or tired looking front porch should be given a facelift. For instance, replacing spindly columns with more robust ones can improve the look of the house. If there is a front railing, make sure it is sturdy and attractive.

In many neighborhoods, everyone on the block tends to have the same black mailbox. Stand out. Be bold! Spend about thirty dollars for a unique mailbox. For another fifty dollars, you can buy a nice wooden post for it. People notice and appreciate these special touches.

Landscaping should highlight the house without overpowering it. In most areas of the country, the front yard should be green and lush. You may have to resod the lawn, but try to salvage it first. You may be able to overseed the grass, but the growth process takes at least six weeks, so planting seed is not an option on all projects. Even a weed-infested lawn can look presentable if it is well watered and cut low. One of your first steps when rehabbing a property should be to spray and pull weeds, then set up sprinklers on timers to bring back the neglected lawn.

Organic mulch can cover many faults in a yard. Mulch is a natural-looking substitute for grass and flowerbeds. Use it to create beds and borders around the house's foundation and cover previously weed-infested areas. We avoid the red-dyed mulch since it doesn't look natural. Use bricks or inexpensive landscape timbers to make interesting beds and borders. You can even transition to mulch without edging if you prefer. Don't use gravel instead of mulch; it costs more and is difficult to work with. Gravel is also harder to remove if a buyer wants to do something different in an area. Keep in mind that new home buyers have to do their own landscaping. So if you offer a nice clean palette for your buyers, you should be fine. A backyard that is nothing but mulch is much nicer than a muddy or weed-infested area.

If the front yard lacks greenery, plant a few inexpensive shrubs across the front of the house. Cut trees that are too close to the house. Remove overgrown shrubs, or trim them back to a manageable size. Be creative in working with what's there and you should not have to spend much for landscaping. Geraniums or other annuals add color during the warm months. Just use your imagination and you'll be surprised how much a little effort will improve the outside of a property.

The condition of a house's **roofing** is often overlooked by beginning investors. Note that many areas require removal of all existing layers when installing a new roof. This job should be left to the professionals, but shop around for a good price. Choose a roofing company that can provide referrals, and require the contractor to pull a permit. As with other trades, there are many fly-by-night roofers who will perform sub-par work. Clarify what materials will be used and how your roofer will address problem areas. We usually replace the drip edge and other flashing with white or brown painted metal when installing a new roof. Have the roof inspected by a licensed roofer to see if it can be repaired and certified. Certifying a roof costs several hundred dollars. The cert will state the roof complies with FHA standards and has a life expectancy of one or more years.

It costs about $3,500 minimum to replace the roof on a basic 1,200-square-foot ranch house, and in many cases $5,000 or more. We typically use dimensional asphalt shingles, which improve the home's curb appeal, for a slightly higher cost over basic three-tab shingles. Sometimes the roof will sag due to lack of support or moisture damage to the decking (sheathing). Remember that a wood shake shingle or tile roof is much more expensive to repair or replace than an asphalt shingle roof.

Replacement **windows** are a nice albeit expensive upgrade to a house. In the past, we often replaced windows on flips. But auction buyers we worked with who had purchased literally thousands of investment properties told us they seldom if ever replaced windows. So we decided to save those dollars and have had little negative feedback. If you do need to replace windows, keep in mind that replacement, especially on older houses, is not a job for the beginning rehabber. New windows must be special ordered to fit existing openings in most cases, and the work may require a permit.

Wood windows are usually not difficult to repair. Sandpaper and soap can be used on old windows to get them working again. Remember to test for lead-based paint if you may be sanding or removing old windows. Hire a professional to replace broken windowpanes, counterweights, and screens. Insulated glass windows sometimes lose their seal and develop a hazy appearance. Hire a glazier to replace fogged glass, since home inspectors tend to notice it.

Consider adding exterior wooden shutters. Shutters come preprimed and are easy to install. If the house has storm windows in need of repair, it may be better to remove them altogether.

A missing section of **gutter or downspout** can be installed quickly. If most of the gutters are bad, hire a professional to install new ones. Seamless gutters cost about $3.50 and up per linear foot installed, and they look much better than sectioned gutters. If the house doesn't have gutters, but has no drainage problem, don't bother installing them. Make sure that downspouts have proper slope and extend several feet from the house.

When you improve a property, you also improve the **neighborhood**. If you are renovating a house that has been in disrepair for some time, you will soon make friends with the neighbors. If the house next door looks like a junkyard, then offer to clean it up. We've been helping out neighbors for many years, and they tend to be quite appreciative. You can also repair fences, do landscaping, or paint exteriors for adjacent property owners at a reduced cost.

WRAPPING IT UP

- Upgrade the right things to be consistent with the neighborhood.
- Don't cut corners, especially on safety issues.
- Be generous about installing basic cosmetic items.
- Consider fixing the neighbor's house or yard if it looks bad.

CHAPTER 13

The Rehab: Managing It

So you've created a plan, outlining what you are going to fix up and estimating the cost. Some people like to be hands-on; others are all thumbs and have no business doing fix-up work. Determine whether getting involved in the rehab area of your business is the most effective use of your time. Remember, if you can hire a contractor to handle your projects, you will have extra free time to find and negotiate more deals.

You may decide to take on a partner who will handle the rehab business while you take care of financing, paperwork, selling, and finding the next deal. Whichever way you choose, always be involved in managing the process at some level, or it will get away from you. You can't afford to fall behind your schedule, do poor-quality work, or go over budget. If you are not a regular presence at your work site, or ideally a fixture, then workers will become distracted and potentially lethargic. Try to have a positive impact on your entire team.

TIMING IS EVERYTHING

Establishing a time line is a key element of your success. Instead of creating an arbitrary period such as one month, start with a time goal. Let's say five weeks for our sample flip. Then as you go through each phase of the renovation, adjust your time line as necessary.

You should also create scale drawings to share with your team. These plans will help everyone stay on the same page and will also help you when creating lists of needed building materials (material take offs). Create a site plan to clarify issues with fences, walkways, landscape borders, and items to be removed or protected.

Plan ahead so the correct materials will be at the job each day, and do your best to stay ahead of the workers' needs. Stockpile materials in batches, ideally by having them delivered. But don't introduce extra clutter and increase the risk of loss by delivering everything to your house on the first day. Hold off on items such as flooring, cabinets, hardware, appliances, and other items until you are almost ready to install them.

HELP WANTED

You will likely be paying others to do most, if not all, of the repairs. Over time, you will develop a network of helpers. You can find handyman types to fill most of your needs through HomeAdvisor.com or AngiesList.com. You may find less expensive help on Craigslist.org, but you will have to determine—perhaps through trial and error—which workers are good and which are not so good.

We are able to keep contractors busy for long periods, so we run our own ads offering full-time work. You can also visit local construction sites to find skilled tradespeople such as roofers, framers, and ceramic-tile installers. Often these people are willing to moonlight and will save you money compared with using large companies. Don't be afraid to work with sole proprietors, since they tend to have low overhead and high loyalty. Sometimes you will have to refer to YellowPages.com or a Google search for specialized help. We try to hire folks who are not only skilled, professional, and reliable, but also inexpensive. Yet we're realists and know that in most cases you can't have it all.

Eventually, you'll need a good, dependable general contractor with the experience and skills necessary to manage larger, more complex renovations. General contractors will also be helpful with permit issues, materials acquisition, and locating the right subcontractors for each task. Choose your general contractors carefully, and make sure they have the licenses and insurance necessary for your project.

PAYING FOR LABOR

Treat every aspect of a renovation as a simple challenge to get the maximum value per dollar spent. Generally, you can save money on labor by paying cash. But there are tax ramifications regarding cash payments, contractor labor, and employee issues, so consult a tax adviser before you get in over your head. Try to find general labor for about fifteen dollars an hour, depending on your local market and the supply of labor. Unskilled laborers can do a great job if they are willing to work hard and learn along the way, and if you monitor them closely. You may also find someone who is semiretired and wants to work part-time. We've found some great workers like that, but try to avoid the person who wants to manage everyone else instead of being hands-on. You don't need an additional manager in your operation.

Expect to pay skilled laborers twenty dollars or more per hour. Many times, you will undertake jobs that require the services of licensed tradesmen. Expect to pay extra for those individuals, and trust us—it's worth it; the last thing you want to do is skimp on jobs that can endanger the lives of the workers or the ultimate occupants of the house.

Licensing requirements vary according to trade and locale. For example, electricians, plumbers, and HVAC techs are usually licensed by the state. Some contractors such as asbestos mitigation companies and septic system companies are licensed by local health departments. General contractors are usually licensed by their local building departments. Most building departments require contractors to pass a standardized test, and many departments have additional requirements regarding experience and insurance. Smaller building departments usually offer reciprocity to contractors licensed in other geographic areas, but there are still annual fees involved. Depending on the work needed, you may be able to get a license yourself by simply paying a fee. For example, you may have to get a demolition license to start such work in areas that require demo permits. Be wary of contractors who claim they are licensed for work that doesn't even require a license, such as drywall, gutter installation, painting, flooring, or carpentry.

ALWAYS GET IT IN WRITING

For larger projects, you can reduce risk and often save money by getting a written bid and paying contractors for the complete job versus paying on an hourly basis. But never pay in full until the work is completed, and when permits are involved, wait until the work passes inspection and the job site is completely clean. Later, when you know your contractors better and can calculate the time involved in each task, you can pay based on time and materials. Create a written agreement with each contractor you hire (see sample contractor agreement on page 274 in the appendix). Spell out exactly what the contractor is to do, how long it will take, and how he or she will be paid. Clarify when progress payments are to be made, who will be doing the actual work, who will pay for materials, and how you will handle changes along the way.

General contractors use change orders, which basically amend the original agreement as changes arise. Investors often get sticker shock at the end of the project from change orders that were not negotiated up front. Remember, if you don't ask the cost of the change order, you will get charged whatever price the contractor decides to charge you. Written change orders can be effective, but try to implement them in such a way that work is not interrupted every time a small issue comes up, particularly one that can delay the work if not dealt with promptly. Our sample contract in the appendix clearly addresses how change orders are dealt with, along with emergency exceptions.

Have each contractor complete a lien waiver when you pay them. This document states that payment has been received for the services rendered and releases you, the owner, from any obligation or debt that could potentially create a lien on your property. See ZLien.com for state-specific lien forms. If the contractor is hiring subcontractors, the subcontractors should also sign waivers. In addition, make a custom lien-waiver stamp. If you neglect to get a regular lien waiver, your backup method is to stamp

---

FLIP TIP

The final payment. Don't ever pay contractors in full without walking through the entire house with them and identifying all the minor unfinished or poorly finished items. Create a final "punch list" of these items, with a deadline by which they must be done. Hold back a significant amount of money (at least $1,000) so that the contractor doesn't skip off to the next project without finishing up. The punch list should include closing out permits, cleaning the paint from the sinks, removing rubbish, and making sure no packaging or extra materials are left behind.

---

the back of each check with lien-waiver language that the contractor assents to when endorsing the check (for sample language, see page 281 in the appendix). While helpful, lien waivers are not a substitute for hiring the right people in the first place, or for paying your bills on time.

Do *not* pay contractors too much in advance; *do* create monetary incentives for them to stay on schedule. Make sure every contractor you hire understands your work standards. We do not allow contractors to smoke inside our houses or to drink alcoholic beverages during the workday or on site at any time, for obvious reasons. If you work with a general contractor, or contractors who have to buy materials for your job, then you'll have to bend the "do not pay in advance rule." When working with an unproven contractor, you can offer to pay the vendor directly for materials, or deliver materials to the job yourself. In general, progress payments are the norm in construction, but be careful not to pay too much up front.

WHO'S RESPONSIBLE FOR WHAT?

It's critical to clarify the responsibilities of each person involved in your home's renovation. If your business partner or general contractor is going to manage the project, then you essentially have just one person to oversee. Don't assume that that person has everything under control and will always make good decisions. Even someone who is from a construction background, but is new to flips, will need to understand how critical the time line and budget are. Be clear about how much time each partner is expected to devote to the project and how much time each will spend on site. You may have assumed that your partner would be there forty hours a week helping with the construction, while your partner was assuming a ten-hour-a-week commitment. Or some partners may assume that they'll manage and write checks, while you assume they'll be hands-on. Either way is fine, of course, but communicate and sort out the plan ahead of time.

Schedule regular meetings at the property. Even if you are not experienced in construction, you can pick out and deliver materials to the job site. This effort will save the general contractor lots of time, raise your awareness of expenses, and reduce the chances for miscommunication. You will also learn a great deal and reduce costs by helping out around the project, even if it just means cleaning up and organizing the job site.

Remember, general contractors do more than just manage subcontractors. They should also manage workflow, schedule inspections, and help you make better decisions. Their relationships should get you desirable labor rates from reliable contractors. Their influence should also be helpful when asking for favors from contractors when emergencies come up or when you are running behind schedule. Problems or disagreements on how to handle some aspect of a repair will always come up, so we instruct contractors to go directly to the general contractor first but to let us know if they can't resolve the issue among themselves.

You'll also need to clarify the responsibilities of each sub you bring on a job. For example, if you have a plumber doing *all* of the plumbing on your house, make sure you're in agreement about how to handle the rough-in (initial piping) and trim (final assembly and fixture installation). Don't assume that the plumber will be doing any framing prior to installing a tub, or will install the vanities, instead of simply installing the water shutoffs, supply lines, faucet, and drain assembly. Remember that the plumber will have to come back to do the trim once the other trades, such as electric, HVAC, and drywall, are finished. We suggest that the plumber who did the rough-ins also install the trim on your first projects, so you can verify everything was done properly. You don't want your handyman arguing with the plumber about who made the mistake when something doesn't work. Once you have a team you trust, you will find it easier to split up tasks and keep things moving forward quickly.

How you approach your investment business is entirely up to you, which is part of the fun of being an entrepreneur. It really comes down to your own skill sets, how much time you have, the cost, and your personal preference. Be honest with yourself, and if your project is not going well, make changes. On multiple occasions we've helped other investors who were several months into projects but making little progress. They were either too busy with other areas of their lives to get things done in a timely manner, or they didn't have the experience or resources to manage the work on their own.

PLANNING THE RENOVATION PROCESS

A vacant house will not make you any money, at least not right away, so make it your priority to complete the renovation as soon as possible. Don't wait until after closing to start planning. If there is a chance you'll need building permits, then visit the building department and see what you can do to get the ball rolling. Plan to begin work immediately after purchase, but be prepared to cancel or postpone deliveries and subcontractors if the property does not close on time. Verify the electric, gas, and water will be working when you take title to the property. If the gas is off, then you may have to arrange for a licensed plumber to test the gas lines before the utility company will turn it on. There is no reason to wait until closing to have the utilities turned on.

LOCATE SHUTOFFS

Locate the main electric panel as well as the gas and inside water shutoffs before starting work. Also locate the city water shutoff near the street. You may need to stop the water flow from a broken pipe, and you don't want to rely solely on the main shutoff inside the house. You certainly don't want to flood the house, so test the inside shutoff to make sure it works.

RUBBISH REMOVAL AND DEMO

Plan to remove trash and other personal property on the first workday. If there are items you can donate, arrange for a charity such as Goodwill or Disabled American Veterans to pick up items at the house. We've filled up multiple forty-yard roll-off Dumpsters with nothing but personal property from a single home. You should also plan to remove carpets, other flooring, appliances, cabinets, and plumbing fixtures right away. Arrange for someone to take away the appliances and other scrap metal. It's surprising how much metal you can get out of a house, and you don't want to fill up a Dumpster with metal that someone will take away for free.

As discussed earlier, maintain a low profile during the renovation. We often hire a service to help with demo and haul the trash away in a trailer. This service may cost more than a roll-off, but it is convenient and works great if there is not a good spot to place a Dumpster. Put all additional trash in an inconspicuous place such as the backyard or an extra bedroom. Neighbors are likely to complain if you create a mess or have obvious potential safety hazards.

Be ready to start any remaining demolition right away. Your area may require a building permit for demolition if you are gutting a house. Be wary of hidden wiring and gas pipes, and don't tear out walls or other potential structural items unless you are experienced in demolition techniques. In many circumstances, overzealous people have removed load-bearing walls and compromised a house's structural integrity as a result. As we've discussed, don't disturb items that may contain asbestos, mold, or lead-based paint without testing first. We get rid of old doors, but you can wait to take them off if you want to use the hinge mortises as a template for new doors. It's helpful to have a working toilet and sink as well as lights, so if possible keep these "luxuries" available throughout the project. Some projects will require a porta-potty. Keep the furnace operational if it's wintertime.

As you clean up the house, keep your eyes open for any repair issues you may have missed. Cover windows from the inside so that no one can see your building materials and nice tools. Replace broken windows at once, and secure the house. You do not want vandals or curious children inside the property. We often brace exterior doors with two-by-fours so they can only be opened from the inside. Obviously you will need to leave one door operable. If you are lucky enough to have an attached garage, the overhead door is ideal. Once the house is emptied, you can alleviate most odors by airing it out for a few days and by spreading baking soda over plywood floors. If you think there were bugs or critters living in the house, now is the time to fumigate. Stay out of the house for at least twenty-four hours after using any type of spray bomb. If you have removed any plumbing fixtures, then you may need to cap the supply lines so you can test the plumbing and be able to use water as needed.

WILL YOU NEED BUILDING PERMITS?

Years ago, it seemed that most projects we took on did not require building permits. But now most do involve some degree of permitted work. In the past we didn't need permits for changing windows or for a basic kitchen remodel. That is not the case anymore. Depending on your locale, you may be required to hire a general contractor for what seems like a simple remodel. Don't count on being able to pull homeowner permits unless you intend for the property to become your personal residence. Sometimes we'll intentionally forgo certain updates just so that we don't cross the "permit line."

Fortunately, most building departments are reasonable. When the building department requires improvements in addition to the work you planned, costs can be substantial. For example, you may be required to bring a basement up to today's code if it was originally finished without a permit. Or the building department may ask you to bring a basement up to current code because you are doing some other projects in the home.

We sometimes have the inspector visit our projects early in the renovation process to see how we should handle gray-area issues. Unfortunately, there are no guarantees that the initial inspector's advice will hold up once the permitting process and work inspections take place.

If you start a project without permits and receive a stop-work order from the building department or a public utility, you'll be in a tough spot. If the department believes you didn't realize you were doing work that required a permit, then they will likely be helpful. But if you blatantly tried to get around their guidelines, they could make you redo a great deal of work, or at least charge you extra fees. Do your homework, and get it right the first time. In hundreds of projects we've done, we've received stop-work orders only twice. Once, a neighbor reported our project because "he had to get a permit when he remodeled his house," and the other time an inspector for our permitted work noticed the house had a finished basement that was never permitted. Both times we were able to work with the building department and move forward with minimal inconvenience. We have taken on many projects that were already subject to stop-work orders, where we had to go in and regain the building department's trust.

One of our more interesting projects was no simple flip. Someone had built foundations for two homes on his land in a nice neighborhood and then moved two houses onto the foundations. The problem is the owner never received permission from the local planning department. The project was condemned, and the houses sat vacant for twenty years. We secured the property with a purchase contract, then met with the city planners during our contract's inspection period. The planning department was anxious to get rid of that major eyesore, and we laid out a plan for how to proceed. They did decide later that we should update the storm drains and sidewalks on the rather large lot, which cost us more than $10,000. Fortunately, there was ample profit in the deal, so it worked out fine.

One time, we built two spec homes on an existing lot, and well into the permitting process the county planning department decided we should install a new sewer main line in case someone else wanted to build new homes in the area. The sewer work was going to cost around $40,000 since we were required to use a county-approved contractor. Fortunately, we were able to work out a compromise that cost us less than $20,000. On another occasion, an investor had paid an unlicensed contractor to rebuild a small addition on an older home. After the addition was framed in, the building department placed a stop-work order on the property. The foundation was not built to code, they said, and we had to completely tear down the addition and start over.

These examples underscore an obvious but important point: there is additional risk when dealing with larger projects, planning departments, and building departments.

DO EVERYTHING IN THE RIGHT ORDER

There is an order to the way things should be done in a rehab. Let's say you were finishing a basement. The first step would be to obtain a permit. This process could take anywhere from a few days to several weeks. Once the work starts, the framing would be done first, then the plumbing, HVAC, and electrical rough-ins. Next you would call in for plumbing, electrical, and HVAC inspections. Assuming everything passes inspection, you would call in for a framing inspection. The reason a framing inspection comes after the other inspections is to make sure various contractors did not weaken the framing by cutting the joists or studs. Next would be an insulation inspection, followed by a drywall inspection. This inspection process can really slow down the workflow since some projects cannot be started until other work is complete.

And if, for example, there was going to be an egress window added, then a structural engineer would have to sign off on the header or lintel designed to go over the window. The project could not even start without that engineer's letter in the permit application. If one contractor is delayed, or something doesn't pass inspection, it holds up everything. In some cases, there are separate final inspections for plumbing, electrical, and HVAC. Finally, once the basement is painted, carpeted, and 100 percent complete, there comes the final inspection.

JOB-SITE ORGANIZATION

Let's get back to managing a project by looking at our basic rehab example. Now that the house has been cleaned out and secured, organize your working environment. Find the best areas to store building materials and tools, and, if possible, set up a simple workshop. It's always helpful to have a workbench, which can be made by putting plywood on top of sawhorses. We like to organize supplies in small totes so that materials are easy to find. For example, you could label separate totes for cleaning supplies, painting supplies, drywall supplies, fasteners, plumbing, and electric. The same approach works for tools. Keeping basic tools and supplies on hand will reduce work interruptions and the number of trips to the store. At a minimum, make sure you have trash cans, brooms and a dustpan, a shop vacuum, ladders, and portable fans at every job site.

THE ROUGH-IN PHASE

You've completed the demo phase and created a good work space. Now it's time to start putting things back together. It's also a good time to have a new roof installed if needed. But if the roof doesn't leak, it can be done a little later. Don't schedule other work for the day or two the roof is being replaced. Not only is it unsafe to work around a roofing crew, but the installers' pneumatic nailers and hammers are noisy.

It's best to take care of as many repairs and updates as possible prior to drywall and painting. There is no foundation or framing work in this example, but if there were, now would be the time to do it. Complete carpentry, electric, plumbing, and HVAC repairs. Repair or replace anything that's tired or broken, install switches and receptacles, bathtubs, tile surrounds. Wall tile can be installed directly on water resistant drywall (sheetrock), but cement backer board is a much better choice, and may be required by code. As with any tile work, make sure the edges are backed by solid framing and all other areas are completely sound before installing the backing. Expect to replace at least some subflooring that is either water damaged or was destroyed when the old flooring material was removed. All the aforementioned projects can lead to drywall repair, so we tackle them first.

THE DRYWALL PHASE

Next up is drywall repairs, including texturing walls and ceilings as necessary. Many homes have a sprayed popcorn-style ceiling texture. This texture may contain asbestos, so remember to have it tested if you plan to remove it.

Most contractors can do drywall work, but professionals do it faster and better. Pros also use a tool called a banjo to install joint tape, instead of the self-adhesive mesh tape aimed at do-it-yourselfers. If you pay attention, you will notice that a good drywall finisher does not have to do much sanding. On larger jobs it's best to have a pro do the work. Ask for a bid on the complete job, including texturing. You'll save money and achieve better results than if you'd paid someone with less experience to do the job on an hourly basis.

TRIM STAGE

Repair damaged trim, doors, and other woodwork. We usually paint all trim, although in older houses it may be worth restoring it to a natural finish. This type of restoration work is tedious, but natural finishes really highlight a home's character. Install new door hardware, then remove the lock sets prior to painting.

New ceiling lights typically have a larger footprint than the old ones, so we usually keep the old lights hooked up until after the house is painted. Install basic porcelain bulb sockets temporarily when you remove the only light source in a room. If you're replacing all the trim, it generally makes sense to purchase doors complete with jambs (i.e., prehung). These doors can be installed more quickly than actual doors (slabs), and it's nice to have new jambs along with new trim. When keeping old trim, just replace the slabs. If you are installing new flooring, other than just carpet, hold off on installing trim. Go ahead and paint and then install the floors, followed by prepainted trim. That way you won't need to install quarter-round molding to cover the edge of the flooring material. Of course, you will have to go back and touch up the trim, taking care not to damage the new flooring.

PAINTING

Once you have completed the bulk of the inside construction and any drywall repairs, fill in remaining gaps, cracks, and other imperfections with painter's caulk. Make sure all windows are operable. Clean grease or smoke residue off relevant surfaces, and use an oil-based, stain-blocking primer to cover crayon marks, ugly wood finishes, or other damaged areas. Paint walls that have been newly textured or repaired with inexpensive PVA primer.

When installing new trim, it will save time to prepaint it and then touch it up after installation. We used to purchase paint from specialty suppliers but have found over the years that it's easier to buy it from the big-box stores. Home Depot offers up to a 20 percent discount if you join their Pro Xtra loyalty program.

FINISHING TOUCHES

Ideally, you would install bath vanities and kitchen cabinets after painting. But you can install cabinets, countertops, backsplashes, and plumbing fixtures prior to painting if it's more convenient. Once the paint is dry, you can install lights, electrical cover plates, plumbing trim, bath accessories, and other hardware. If you have hardwood flooring, minimize the foot traffic by doing as many projects as possible before the finish coats are applied. After all the messy inside work is completed, bring in the carpet installers. Throughout these later phases, put down rosin paper to protect wood floors and self-adhesive film to protect carpets.

Spray it on. Painters almost always spray the inside of houses to save time and money. Spraying the doors also looks nicer than painting them by hand. If you are painting an entire house yourself that has essentially been gutted, then consider renting an airless paint sprayer. If the house has no carpets and most of the cabinets and fixtures have not been installed, the job will go quickly. Use drop cloths to protect floors, and mask other areas with paper and tape as needed. You should be able to paint a 1,200-square-foot house in a day once the prep work is done. You may even be able to paint the inside and outside of the house on the same day. There is a learning curve with using any new equipment, but even a beginner can achieve excellent results spraying a house. Try to paint on a warm day, ensure adequate ventilation, and wear a canister-style respirator. There is no one right sequence for painting, but we typically start with the ceiling and work our way down.

EXTERIOR PROJECTS

Replace damaged trim and siding, and repair any other unsightly areas of the home's exterior. It costs less to replace severely damaged wood than to try to restore it. Go over any repairs with exterior primer. Replacing exterior doors can require interior work, so in most cases we replace exterior doors early on in the rehab process.

Brick and stucco cracks and other problems can be repaired with the help of a professional. If sections of brick, stucco, or exposed foundation have moved and created large cracks or gaps, then you will likely need to repair the foundation. We once purchased a two-story Victorian home that had the complete front exposed because the brick exterior wall had collapsed. It was true brick construction, as opposed to brick veneer over wood framing that is common today. It looked like a dollhouse with a cutaway view of the sagging second-story floor. During our prepurchase inspection period, however, we were able to get a bid to have the foundation and brick wall repaired by a reputable company. We renegotiated the

FLIP TIP

Schedules and lists. Many tasks can be worked on simultaneously, as long as workers won't be getting in each other's way. Don't have lots of people inside if someone is doing noisy work such as operating a jackhammer, or is making lots of dust or smoke. Always keep a list of projects that can be done anytime, so that workers can stay busy if they get held up on a particular task. You'll also want to take advantage of any nice days during the wintertime to work outside. It may seem obvious, but maintaining a flexible schedule will reduce your downtime throughout the project. Post a clipboard or dry-erase board in a convenient area so that everyone can see the daily tasks. Workers should write down notes, including any items they need you to purchase. We also communicate with key team members via shared Google Docs. There is a variety of project-management software, some specifically developed for home remodeling. For our needs, however, simple checklists work well.

purchase price and were able to save a charming home from being demolished, while making a nice profit for ourselves.

If you plan to replace the roof and gutters, then it's best to replace the gutters first. Let the gutter installer know you plan to replace the roof so the gutters can be set to the correct height.

We usually wait until later in the project to replace concrete. If sections of a driveway or even a concrete porch have settled, it may be possible to raise them back into position through a process called mud jacking. Have a professional company assess the concrete at the beginning of your project so you have time to schedule the work. Depending on the neighborhood, we may choose to leave a driveway or sidewalk intact even if it has a few cracks. Fill any cracks with an elastomeric caulk to prevent further damage.

As with the interior, small things on the exterior can really make a difference. Sometimes installing a front door with windows (lites) helps to brighten up the inside of the home as well.

If you need to replace a deck, remember that redwood is expensive. Trex or other composite deck materials are even more expensive and require more joists than wood, so we shy away from these products.

LANDSCAPING

In the last chapter, we discussed your home's back and front yards in some detail, so we won't repeat it all here. Our primary point about landscaping is simple: with a little imagination and very little money, you can create a welcoming, clean exterior for your property, one that makes potential buyers eager to step inside to see more.

TOOLS

You will need to invest in quality tools if you plan on doing work yourself. You may want to acquire tools if you intend to take on the role of general contractor. We prefer to buy rather than rent equipment, which saves time and money in the long run. But realizing you cannot buy everything at once, start with the basics and always invest in well-made, established name-brand tools. Of course you should first attend free workshops or otherwise learn how to use any new equipment safely. Power and hand tools are dangerous in their own right, more so if they are of questionable quality. Budget an extra few hundred dollars into each job to buy the tools you will need along the way. In a few years, you will have the equipment to tackle most projects yourself or to supply your crew with what they need to do the jobs safely and effectively.

If you take pride in your tools and if you will be the only one using them, then it makes sense to buy them new. But if you plan to have the equipment on site for your subcontractors to use, then buying used tools through Craigslist or from a supplier's rental department makes good financial sense. We've purchased many factory-refurbished tools directly from the manufacturer and through specialty tool suppliers. We would always choose a commercial-quality used tool over a subpar new tool. Avoid pawnshops, since they tend to charge too much for tools that have been used hard. Be wary of Harbor Freight and other bargain-priced power tools, since they often fail at the least opportune moment.

Start your collection with traditional carpenter's tools. We'll describe a few favorites, and hopefully our opinions won't offend anyone. A Skilsaw worm-drive circular saw will last a long time and is the choice of most framers. A traditional or sidewinder circular saw is great for long, precise cuts, guided by a straight edge. We keep a finish blade on ours. A Milwaukee Sawzall reciprocating saw is another favorite, and will be quite helpful in the demo phase of construction. Milwaukee is also known for making quality drills, and you will find a heavy-duty half-inch-drive drill to be quite useful. Like many US companies, Milwaukee has moved its manufacturing overseas, but it still makes fine products. Bosch also makes excellent tools, and we especially like their jigsaws and rotary hammers. A rotary hammer is essentially a heavy-duty hammer drill used for drilling in concrete. Porter Cable is another company with a great reputation, and we prefer their belt sanders and routers over other manufacturers' versions. Be aware that routers are one of the more dangerous tools in the hands of an unskilled operator. The Fein MultiMaster is the original oscillating multi-tool. It comes in handy for all kinds of intricate detail work. We've tried the competitors' models, but they don't seem to hold up well. Even though the blades are expensive, these little guys can be a lifesaver.

Battery-powered tools are convenient and super helpful as well. Unfortunately, batteries are only good for about three years and keep evolving, so these tools become obsolete. We don't recommend you purchase used rechargeable tools. We like Milwaukee and also Makita; however, you could buy a less expensive brand since you'll only expect to use it for a few years. Ryobi and Ridgid both make tools that are decent quality yet on the affordable side. You'll want to purchase a compound miter saw as well. A sliding compound miter saw set up on a work stand will get lots of use on any rehab project. Though these key tools will handle most projects, you'll soon find yourself needing additional ones. A table saw is a must-have once you start replacing siding or trim. You will also save time by using pneumatic nailers. You can start with a small, portable compressor that comes with nailers. We've had great success with Hitachi and Senco nailers, and Bostitch also has a good reputation. Eventually, you should invest in a high quality pancake-style compressor. We prefer those made by Rolair because they are quiet and seem to last forever.

We won't go into what hand tools to purchase, but there are a few other items worth mentioning. You will need an assortment of ladders. Ladders are rated according to their capacity, and it's worth spending extra for type 1 or 1A. We feel that fiberglass ladders are safest, because, unlike aluminum, fiberglass does not conduct electricity. The only aluminum ladders we use are the versatile ones that were once made only by Little Giant, although other companies now sell similar designs. You'll need an assortment of landscape, cleaning, and specialty tools. We spend extra for durable tools made with fiberglass handles or all-steel construction rather than those that have plastic parts. The list of specialty tools is endless, but you'll find a self-leveling laser level especially useful. We use one to help evaluate home foundations and floor settling prior to purchase.

Lastly, you'll need a way to store and protect all the equipment. We paint all our tools so they are easily recognized. Also, we engrave a contact name and number on most tools. A lot of work-site theft is by workers, so don't make it easy for people to "accidentally" take the wrong tools home. You can't stop a professional thief from snatching your equipment, but you can deter less-skilled prowlers. Purchase a large job-site box and keep your tools locked up at all times. Place it in an area away from exit doors, fill it with tools, and, if necessary, other heavy items. Attach ladders, a compressor, and other tools to it with heavy, locked chains. We've experienced several break-ins over the years, but have never had anyone get into a job-site box or steal anything of real value. Another good practice is to leave expensive specialty tools at home except for on the days you actually need them. At times, we've used a portable alarm system as an additional theft deterrent. For about a hundred dollars, you can purchase a simple system. Pick one that uses a remote siren so that it will be somewhat difficult to disable. We have also installed surveillance cameras or fake units on our properties. Keep entryways well lit, and consider installing a motion-sensing light in the backyard. One last thing, take pictures and keep a written inventory of your tools so that you have records for taxes and potential insurance claims.

Even if you are a wholesaler and never plan on rehabbing a property, keep a clipboard, tape measure, flashlight, screwdriver, and crowbar in your car for inspecting houses that are boarded and abandoned or have no electricity. If you're really tight on space, look into telescoping ladders. These units will fit in almost any vehicle's trunk. Your smartphone will work fine for taking basic pictures.

SAFETY ITEMS

Purchase a few safety-related items if you do rehab work. Safety glasses, hearing protection, gloves, and a charcoal-canister respirator are important for you and your crew. Consider having workers wear hard hats when applicable. Be sure to keep a five- or ten-pound dry-chemical fire extinguisher and a first aid kit at each job site. Fire safety is an important issue, and we know a carpenter who lost everything when his shop burned down due to excess sawdust catching fire. If you need to run space heaters, make sure they are placed in safe locations. Propane or kerosene heaters are effective but also need adequate ventilation when used indoors. We are fond of the newer LED work lights because they don't draw much current and are not a fire hazard like halogen lights.

An organized job site is also a safe one. Let your crew know that you expect the work site to be cleaned daily and that you won't tolerate nails left in scrap lumber, or other careless habits. We once worked with a building inspector who had been severely injured at someone else's job site years ago. He stepped on drywall that was covering a hole in the floor and fell through. Set up temporary railings and proactively avoid dangerous situations. Remember, you are not the only one working on the property, and every worker should rightly assume that the job site is safe.

AUTOMOBILE

It's not practical to load up your sports car or luxury SUV with building materials on a daily basis. Serious investors either drive pickup trucks or employ workers who do. You don't need to buy a new vehicle right away. But transporting your materials and equipment will eventually become an issue, so be prepared to have the right vehicle. Even if you don't see yourself in the contractor role, you may want to purchase a trailer to move building materials and possibly staging items.

WRAPPING IT UP

- Start with a plan.
- Keep in touch with everyone involved.
- Understand your role in the renovation process.
- Always take safety precautions on the job site.

CHAPTER 14

The Rehab: Staging It

Once you finish the renovation process, you should have a sparkling-clean, "new" property to sell. You only have one chance to make a first impression! If you've watched any of the shows about flipping houses, then you've seen the mad rush to make houses ready for an open house. Avoid this drama, along with potentially costly mistakes, by allotting adequate time to prepare the house. We advise you take an extra week for the final prep before putting your house on the market. Make a strong, positive impression to ensure your property stands out from other listings. The goal is to present your property to potential buyers in a way that screams, "This is your dream home—buy it!"

Staging is the process of decorating a home specifically for resale. There are many books and even television shows on this subject. We've been staging our homes for more than twenty years. We believe that the process of applying finishing touches and going that extra mile to make your home stand out is worthwhile. An empty, vacant house, especially a modest one, tends to lack character inside and will come across as stark. White paint and neutral colors certainly don't help add personality; each room will blend together in your buyer's mind. The following steps have proven to be effective for us. Use them as a starting point in developing your own process and style. Now is not the time to question your remodeling choices. But do make small adjustments to accentuate the positive attributes of your home. Draw the buyer's attention to interesting details, and show buyers how to optimize the living space. For example, if there is only a small niche available for dining, then stage the area with an appropriate small table.

Take advantage of the clean-slate potential of a vacant house to appeal to the buyer's senses. Your property will show well, and buyers will realize they need to offer a fair price if they want to own it. A vacant home will not be cluttered or clash with most buyers' tastes, and it will be easy to show.

WALK THROUGH THE HOUSE LIKE A BUILDER

Prior to bringing in decorations, you'll need to do a thorough inspection and cleaning. Fortunately, many items in the house will be brand new, and the house should already be in broom-clean condition. Do a walkthrough of the entire house, noting any issues that still need attention. Create a written list based on your room-by-room evaluation. Your list should include details such as drywall and texture touch-ups, paint overspray, poor coverage, or mismatched sheen. Sometimes you won't notice issues such as visible drywall seams or base colors bleeding through new paint unless you visit the property in various lighting conditions throughout the day. Caulk sometimes shrinks, so look for cracks and voids.

Walk throughout the house at a quiet time to listen for squeaks in doors, creaky floors, or any other sounds that can be eliminated. As you walk through each room, test that every door and every window works properly. Doors sometimes bind up, or require paint touch-ups if they were closed before the paint was completely dry. Doors may also need to be trimmed if they drag across the new carpet. Each door should have an even reveal around the edges and should latch without requiring excessive force. Pay close attention to the front door, since you want to make a good first impression with potential buyers. We remove window screens and store them together to be installed after the home is under contract (windows look clearer without screens). Make sure all cabinet doors and drawers are properly aligned and operate as they should. Note any scratches on cabinets, trim, and wood floors. A little furniture oil, stain, or a stain stick can address small blemishes. Look inside drawers, cabinets, closets, and other cubbyholes for any debris.

Turn on the water heater, and set it to a reasonable temperature. Test hot and cold water flow on every faucet. Now would be the time to open up any drain traps you might have blocked. Traps need water in them to effectively block sewer gases, and of course they can get clogged with construction debris, so we often cover or block them. Flush each toilet a few times to remove sediment from the tank and to ensure the waste lines are not blocked. It's common for faucets to get blocked with construction debris and spit out brown water or sediment when they haven't been used for a while. It's also common for shower scald valves to prevent the water from coming out hot enough, so adjust as necessary. We've had multiple occasions where hot and cold water were reversed—usually on a tub-and-shower valve. Once we even had hot water going to the toilet, a "luxury" most home buyers would not appreciate!

Run the furnace and confirm it is working and not excessively noisy. Sometimes a furnace will become noisy if it has ingested paint spray or excessive dirt during renovation. Check to see that lights and receptacles (including GFCIs) are in good working order. Make sure every lightbulb in the house is good. Test each smoke and CO detector. Don't forget to test the kitchen appliances. Run the garbage disposal; it can be damaged if there is metal debris in it. Don't forget to go through unfinished areas such as the attic, basement, crawlspace, outbuildings, and garage.

CLEAN YOUR HOUSE BETTER THAN "GOOD ENOUGH"

Once the house is empty and you have completed all planned projects, expect to take up to ten hours to thoroughly clean it. We prefer to bring in a professional cleaning crew.

Even if you bring in a pro to do your cleaning, it won't hurt to keep a few basic items on hand. You'll need a shop vacuum. Purchase a HEPA filter to use for your final cleaning. You will also need a canister or upright vacuum for carpets. Of course you'll need cleaning products; nontoxic Simple Green all-purpose cleaner has been our favorite for years. Buy a large bottle of concentrate, along with a couple of commercial-quality spray bottles. One bottle should be highly diluted, and with care it can be used on walls and just about everywhere else. Another bottle that's more concentrated will work on greasy spots or other grimy areas.

You may want to purchase window cleaner and possibly an extendable wand with hose attachment for hard-to-reach windows. For the bathroom, you'll need a brush for floors and tile and also a toilet-bowl brush. For special needs, try CLR to remove difficult stains such as calcium and rust. Use Goof Off (contains xylene) or mineral spirits, which is a milder solvent, or, safest of all, citrus-based solvent to remove dried paint, stickers, and stains. Wear gloves, have adequate ventilation, and wear a respirator when working with most solvent-based cleaners. Be careful with these strong cleaners, since they can remove cured finishes and may bleach carpet. Scotch-Brite or other abrasive pads, a small brush, terry-cloth rags, and paper towels will handle most projects.

Also, pick up a pack of razor blades to scrape paint and other residue off hard surfaces. Replace blades often when scraping glass, and spray the surface lightly with liquid to prevent scratching. Oil-based cleaners are great for restoring gloss to wood flooring, trim, and cabinets. A dry mop will be helpful for floors. As with other tools, organize your supplies in a single tote, and put together a smaller tote or bucket to take from room to room. Keep a broom, upright vacuum, and basic cleaning supplies at the house for touch-ups prior to sale.

Sanding hardwood floors and drywall creates dust that will continue to appear for weeks after the rehab work is complete. To address the dust issue, make sure the furnace filter is clean, and vacuum out the furnace and accessible ducts. Next, vacuum the entire house, and avoid using a broom for any remaining cleaning. The house should be completely empty of tools or supplies. From this point on, you should avoid wearing shoes inside, and you should protect carpets with self-adhesive plastic if you haven't done so already.

Next, start at the top and work your way down as you make your way through each part of the house. Remove all dust from vents, ceiling fans, cabinets, and horizontal surfaces. If walls are dusty, wipe them down lightly with diluted cleaning solution. Remove stickers from appliances and fixtures. Remove paperwork and packaging from the oven and dishwasher. In the event someone turns on an appliance, you don't want to ruin the manual or start a fire! Clean the inside and outside of kitchen cabinets, and don't forget the tops. Wipe down countertops, using granite polish if applicable. Clean windows inside and out, including the tracks. Go over tile, vinyl, and wood floors with a slightly damp mop. If the carpet is new, vacuum up all loose strands.

PREP THE EXTERIOR

The outside of the house is the first thing potential buyers see. Walk all the way around the property and make sure there are no visible trash cans, garden hoses, or other eyesores. Follow the same process you used inside the house; start at the top and work your way down. Sweep the roof and clean the gutters. Paint, tuck-point, caulk, or replace any weathered penetrations such as flues, chimneys, or roof vents. Remove any paint overspray, and touch up paint and caulking where needed. Vacuum out any debris in window wells, and add some gravel. Sweep all walkways, and remove any paint or other stains from the concrete if possible.

ACCENTUATE THE POSITIVES

Builders spend thousands of dollars on interior decorators and expensive furnishings for their model homes because they know emotion sells properties. You do not necessarily need to furnish the entire house, but you should add nice touches. The key to staging is to accentuate the home's positive attributes, while making it feel comfortable to potential buyers. The idea is to have buyers fall in love with your house. They will want to purchase the house based on an initial feel. Remember, buyers think they know what they want, but studies have shown that most people lack vision. You want to help these people feel like they are living in the home.

Now you can bring in the staging items. Most of these things can just be set in place, but you'll need basic tools to hang pictures, mirrors, and other wall art. In order to minimize wall damage, we use hangers that work with small nails. Our staging supplies tend to get banged up and dirty, so we also clean each item as we place it in the house. Keep your eyes open as you stage the house because you will continue to notice little projects to address. We will highlight a few specific areas in the home, then leave it to you to be creative with other living spaces.

Entryway

Make sure the house is an inviting place to enter. Start with exterior lighting. The walkway to the front door should be well lit. If there is a dark or potentially unsafe approach to the front door, add low-voltage lighting. It does not have to be elaborate or expensive. Just place four to six solar-powered lights along the walkway so visitors can see where they are going. To ensure that real-estate agents leave the front porch light on, tape the switch in the "on" position. For a few dollars, you can purchase a photocell light socket that you screw into the bulb base. This device will turn the light off during daylight hours. You may want to tape another interior light switch in the "on" position as well. Agents will invariably forget complicated showing instructions such as what lights to leave on or setting an alarm. Make sure the doorbell has a lighted ringer and makes a pleasant tone. Many buyers like to ring the doorbell before entering, so do not let them start their tour by finding a broken doorbell. Place new doormats at each entrance. Mats welcome visitors and also help protect carpets and other flooring.

Foyer and Family Room

Buyers should walk into a home that is a comfortable temperature. Nothing says "cheap investor" like a house that is freezing cold. If it's summer and your home does not have air conditioning, open the windows early in the morning to bring in a little cool fresh air. Add stunning accent rugs to the foyer. Provide a small table so brokers have a place to leave their cards. Place a Plexiglas holder containing copies of informative property flyers on the table. This table is also an ideal spot to leave additional items the buyer would appreciate, such as homeowners' association information, loan options and payments, and information on neighborhood schools and amenities. You can also include a notebook containing home information such as product warranties, location of shutoffs, and a sprinkler-system map with winterizing instructions.

If there is not an obvious focal point, such as a large picture window with a nice view, then you'll need to create your own focal point. Accent great features such as a fireplace by placing figurines, candles, or other art on the mantel. If there is a wood-burning fireplace, place a few logs inside for effect. You may want to place fire tending tools on the hearth, or perhaps a pair of vases to draw attention to the feature. Even if there is no inherent focal point, use a love seat with side tables, or even a large plant to add interest to a plain room. Include a small bookshelf or an additional table complete with coffee-table books. You'll want to make it enjoyable for potential buyers to spend time in the home. The more time they spend there, the more likely they are to bond with their surroundings.

Kitchen

The kitchen is the heart of the home, so make it look lived in. Place dish towels, a paper towel holder, and glass jars with colorful contents on the counters. We usually set up a small cutting board with realistic-looking faux bread, fruit, and cheese on the counter. Highlight and add warmth to windows with tinted glass vases or sun catchers. Sometimes we'll place floor rugs in the kitchen.

Bathrooms

Place matching towels, soap, and tissue dispensers and a candle in each bathroom. A decorative, cloth shower curtain and satin nickel–finish curtain rings look much nicer than a plastic liner. Pull curtains aside to show off attractive tile work. Confirm every toilet-paper holder is filled. In bathrooms that don't have a good spot for a wall mounted toilet-paper dispenser, include a free-standing pedestal version. We usually include a small, decorative trash can as well but forgo the fuzzy toilet-seat covers! Lastly, check the toilet seats each time you visit the property, and close the lids.

Unfinished Areas

Make sure these spaces are completely clean. It's surprising how many listings have construction debris and other unsightly items lying around. We've encountered sewer-line debris, mousetraps, animal remains, furnace filters, ducts full of construction debris, building materials, cigarette butts, and drawers full of sawdust. Remove or repair unsecured wires, open junction boxes, or extension cords going to dilapidated light fixtures.

Your goal is to show every space in the best possible way. The only evidence of renovations should be well-marked cans of extra paint, spare shingles, tiles, and similar items stored in an appropriate place.

Landscape

We all know that curb appeal sells homes, so make sure the front yard looks great. If you have a front porch, consider adding a swing or a small table and chairs to serve as a gathering place. Every home needs an area to gather outdoors, so it's especially important to emphasize front-yard living space if the backyard is small.

As long as it's clean and not full of weeds, the backyard should be fine. You can improve an uninteresting yard with natural barriers and accents such as bird baths or whimsical lawn decorations. Adding a picnic table and chairs will give the back patio a sense of purpose, but is not mandatory. Chain-link fences are functional but not very appealing. If you have one, consider spray painting it green or brown, or if you need to block an unattractive view, insert slats through the links to create a low privacy fence.

Decorations

Try to decorate in a way that complements the home's style, architecture, and age, yet allows the home to stand out from others. In older homes we often add nostalgic decorations such as faux-antique Coke signs, weathered barn wood, or real antiques. A warm yet understated look with some degree of continuity between rooms contributes to a comfortable feeling and flow.

Place a few pictures, wall hangings, and a mirror or two throughout the house—one item in each bedroom and at least two in the kitchen and family rooms. Hang the pictures on the walls at or below eye level, lean them against the walls at floor level, or perch them on shelves where possible. Paired pictures, wall art, or small shelves at varied heights add dimension to plain rooms.

Displaying vases, bowls filled with potpourri, and candlesticks are just a few ideas. Bottles filled with gourmet cooking oil, colorful popcorn, or peppercorns are also an interesting touch. Dried flowers, pinecones, and other items found in nature can be placed almost anywhere. You can get such decorations at Michaels or Hobby Lobby. Stop by thrift stores, garage sales, and discount chains (e.g., Marshalls and Ross Dress for Less) that carry discontinued or slightly damaged items. Artist easels make nice stands for heavy pictures or for placing pictures in areas with concrete walls.

We include lots of realistic fake plants but shy away from cheap artificial plants or ones that are so colorful they appear too good to be true. An unfurnished room will be more appealing with a large plant or arrangement in the corner. Small plant stands will add charm and keep plants off the floor.

Bring nature inside to evoke passionate feelings about the home. Real plants are wonderful, if you are willing and able to care for them. A small water feature adds soothing background sound while being a nice touch. We like framed art involving leaves or scenes of nature. Even the frames can be a focal point if they are made of interesting wood. Dried flowers or tall grasses in large vases of various heights also add dimension.

Overall, we try to continue the same theme throughout each house. But you can experiment with adding a little extra color in finished basements, rec rooms, or kids' rooms. Basements can be a little drab to start with, so bold accents can bring an element of fun to the space. There may be an open hallway that you could showcase as a potential reading nook or home office. Resist the temptation to use tacky cardboard props such as computer monitors or televisions. For bedrooms, a few pillows and a nice comforter folded in the corner will give buyers the general idea.

Furnishings

There is no absolute need to furnish a house with bedroom furniture or other large pieces. We always opt for a clean look over cluttered. If you do choose to go all out and completely stage a home, however, make sure you don't use furniture that is too large for your home. The last thing you want to do is make the rooms appear small. For high-end homes, you can rent complete bedroom sets, but sometimes an air mattress on four milk cartons with attractive sheets will do the trick.

Small or odd-shaped spaces can create decorating challenges and often leave buyers with a negative impression. If your property has such an area, make an extra effort to furnish it in a way that shows there is a solution. Displaying a dining-room table, complete with chairs, place mats, and a nice setting, creates a homey atmosphere. We have sold several homes with the staging items included. It wasn't our plan to sell them that way, but the buyers insisted.

Floors

With hardwood floors, use rugs as accents. Larger rugs can hide unattractive floors, but don't try to hide obvious defects that should be disclosed to potential buyers. For example, if there is a section of exposed plywood in the middle of the family room's hardwood floor, you should repair it instead of covering it with a rug.

Lighting

Equip each room with a light-sensing nightlight so potential buyers can find their way around. Remember that many showings take place after dark, so the house should seem safe and be easy to view at any time of day. These lights help buyers find switches when entering dark rooms and help to make hazards such as stairways apparent. If there are no overhead lights in the bedrooms or other rooms, add floor lamps, plugged into switched outlets if possible. If a hallway or other space has no light switch, installing a wall-mounted, remote-control switch is a simple fix.

Use the optimum lightbulbs in every location. We recommend that you replace compact fluorescent bulbs (CFLs) since they don't immediately light up when you flip the switch, and they also cast a dreary light. Use the brightest bulbs that each light fixture can safely handle. New fixtures clearly state the maximum wattage bulbs they are designed for. Going over the maximum could overheat the fixture and lead to a fire. GE Reveal halogen bulbs offer a little extra brightness compared with standard bulbs and have a nice color balance. LED bulbs are a good option to increase the brightness of low-wattage fixtures.

The Power of Smell

Appealing scents can leave a lasting impression on people. You want potential buyers to associate a pleasant fragrance with your property, even if that association is on a subconscious level.

FLIP TIP

Leave a note. We suggest you place a few small handwritten notes or printed signs throughout to point out various features. These notes will make it seem like a guided tour and highlight selling points that may otherwise go unnoticed. For example, you can point out a special thermostat, air conditioning, appliance features, wiring upgrades, cable or computer outlets, architectural highlights, or other hidden attributes. Clarify the purpose of dimmer switches, special lighting, and gas-fireplace or swamp-cooler controls—items that could be confusing without a little explanation. Don't go overboard and point out obvious features. Most starter homes are purchased by families with children, so it pays to note safety features such as tamper-resistant receptacles or range controls mounted where they can't be reached from below.

Even though the house is immaculate, there will be lingering fumes from new paint, carpet, adhesive, and floor finishes. If possible, open all windows during the final few days of preparation, keeping air moving throughout the house. If necessary, bring in portable fans to help circulate fresh air. Or try a neutralizing product like Zorbx. Use natural cleaning products for any cleaning touch-ups to avoid a hospital-like smell.

ENGAGE OTHERS TO HELP WITH APPEARANCE

Because the idea is to upgrade the appearance of the property, don't use tired or cheap-looking items or those that might appear too personal in taste. Even if you feel qualified to make all the decisions regarding your decor and presentation, and don't want to bring in a staging expert, it would be wise to get second opinions from interior decorators, friends, or real-estate professionals. Have them walk through the house after you have done the "final cleaning" and before you've finished decorating. They will be amazed at your progress, but remember that you need critique more than flattery at this time, so ask for their honest opinions.

If you are seeking inspiration, try *Pottery Barn* or any number of home magazines. Look at publications that are specific to your region or

style of home. If you are looking for modern, try ScandinavianDesigns
.com or AllModern.com.

Although we've been outlining how to stage a house yourself, you
could consider hiring a professional staging company to decorate and furnish the entire house. Depending on the home's size and price range, this
may make sense. It is not uncommon for sellers to pay more than $3,000 to
professionally decorate a $250,000 home. There are various levels of stag-
ing, such as a consultation, basic package for key areas, or all-inclusive
plan covering the entire house. A couple of websites with excellent information are SimpleAppeal.com and StagedHomes.com. Houzz.com also
provides lots of ideas and is possibly our favorite of all the design websites.

OTHER CONSIDERATIONS

Remember that properties being shown require ongoing cleaning to look
presentable. Properties that have been renovated will continue to show
residual dust. Some listings have signs asking people to remove their shoes
or wear booties. While this practice points out clean or new carpets, it
does not invite potential buyers to "make themselves at home." Builders
showcasing immaculate, new homes do not ask buyers to remove their
shoes. A house can survive a little foot traffic.

It is amazing how much of a mess inconsiderate people can make
when looking at properties. They sometimes track in dirt, leave their trash
behind, leave water running, and do not flush toilets after using them. One
of our listings had major water damage because someone left a window
open during a tour. When it got cold later that night, a pipe burst and damaged the bathroom and hardwood floors. In addition to the cost of repairs,
several potential buyers were left with a bad impression, so we had to take
the property off the market while repairs were completed. Visit your property often to clean floors, dust, tend to lawns, and check for any problems.

WRAPPING IT UP

- Clean the house really well; then clean it some more.
- Find ways to add curb appeal inexpensively.
- Stage every house to present in its best light.

CHAPTER 15

The Rehab: Selling It

Congratulations, you've gone through all the steps to find, purchase, and prepare a property for sale! The hard part is behind you. All your work will pay off, but you'll still need to sell the property. If you've taken any marketing courses, you are probably familiar with the four Ps: price, product, promotion, and place. Selling real estate concerns the first three, as *place* is related to product distribution. We believe a well-prepared home will practically sell itself. That is because the *product* element was done well. You purchased in a good location, then made the right repairs and improvements. Yet there are quite a few details that, if not handled correctly, can easily make the difference between a tidy profit or a marginal loss on the sale.

Many people have predicted that brokers and the MLS will become less important in selling properties due to the widespread availability of information. But the vast majority of home sales continue to be by brokers using the MLS. You will need to decide whether you intend to work with a broker to sell your property. Then you'll need to determine your home's listing price. Price is important, and that's why it's one of the four Ps. No one knows for sure the maximum price a house will sell for. Still, an experienced broker is your best bet for selecting the optimum listing price.

Your broker will also be immensely helpful in handling the third P, promotion. You want to reach as many qualified buyers as possible, and though there are many channels for marketing properties for sale, your local MLS is still the best of all. In the years ahead, the MLS may become less important and may become accessible to non-agents. For now, however, you most likely will need to work with a broker to get your property included on the MLS. Other consumer-friendly sites have risen to the number-two position. There have been some interesting battles for supremacy among websites such as Zillow.com, Trulia.com, Redfin.com, and Realtor.com. Zillow Group now encompasses Trulia, though the two companies operate somewhat independently. And, of course, there are other ways to let the public know about your hot, new listing. For example, you can advertise locally, post a yard sign, and even use word of mouth. Include all these channels in your marketing mix.

There are many other marketing considerations. In addition to being well-represented online, your property should be easy to show. A potential buyer should be able to arrange a showing at his or her convenience. If you require consumers to do too much work, they will simply go away. Someone will also have to handle potential offers and get the property sold after it goes under contract. Many properties go under contract only to have issues come up that prevent the deal from closing.

WHAT DOES THE BROKER ACTUALLY DO?

Your broker should be instrumental in the process of selling your property. You can bet that successful investors are either brokers themselves or have cemented long-term relationships with their favored brokers. We've covered the basics of broker legalities and representation in earlier chapters pertaining to buying properties. This chapter is focused on the sale (listing) side of your transactions. It takes quite a bit of time and experience for anyone to market a property well, then negotiate and close the sale.

FLIP TIP

Red tape. Here in Colorado, the standard approved contract has grown to eighteen pages long. The basic Purchase Contract does not include the various required addendums, such as the Seller's Property Disclosure, Lead-Based Paint Disclosure, Source of Water Addendum, Square Footage Disclosure, or Closing Instructions. Once you get your property under contract, you will be expected to negotiate through inspection issues, provide title insurance, and eventually show up for a closing to sign additional, lengthy documents. Your broker should help to keep things moving forward. Sometimes a small error on a contract does not create a major problem. Other times a seemingly small oversight can kill a deal, allow buyers to walk away without penalty, or land you in court.

MARKETING

Pricing a property is as much art as science. As a seller, you have to compare your property to others, take a "snapshot" of current market conditions, then consider timing and other factors to determine the asking price. Of course you want to make a profit, but real estate is a commodity, and the market determines the value of every home. Don't base your listing price on your cost. A comparative market analysis or appraisal may be a good starting point to justify your listing price, but these assessments by no means guarantee the actual sale price. For example, if you were selling a rental property with positive cash flow and had no immediate need to sell, then it would be in your best interest to list the property after New Year's Day. Perhaps it would make sense to wait until spring if you lived in an area such as Colorado. Then again, your personal need for a quick closing might override your desire to receive the maximum sales price. Most flips fall into this category. Work together with your broker to determine the price, and trust his or her expertise when making the final decision.

Property values fluctuate, of course, and are not entirely predictable. Most of our flips go under contract in the first or second week, but that's not always the case. Sometimes we can't determine why there were no offers, so we may hold to our price, but usually we make aggressive price changes to move the house. Demand for a given property is quite elastic, meaning demand goes up as price goes down and demand decreases as price goes up. Homes in the upper price points of a given market have fewer potential buyers and will also tend to take longer to sell. Once your property is on the market, you will get feedback from buyers (via their brokers), and you can use that information to decide if you'll need to adjust the price.

What we generally call marketing is actually promotion, the third P. Your goal should be to maximize the exposure of your property to qualified buyers. We've explained that it's worthwhile to list your property on the MLS. It's also worth noting that brokers primarily work with qualified buyers who are ready to purchase a home. When you have a showing with a buyer represented by a broker, you can count on that buyer being genuine and serious. It's true that many buyers are quite involved in searching for properties on the Internet, but even their brokers will be highly involved in the eventual purchase process.

Photos are another important part of promoting your property. Your broker should represent your house using quality photos posted on the MLS and other Internet sites like Craigslist. These pictures can also be used for a brochure and property website.

Signage is also important. Having a sign in front of your house is the best way to reach people in the immediate neighborhood. In addition to the sign, it would be worthwhile to visit neighbors or mail out a new-listing announcement. Of course, you can place a sign out front without a broker, but don't expect many brokers to call you.

Open houses are another way to promote homes. While we tend to focus on other marketing, open houses can create excitement and might bring in that perfect buyer. Open houses are especially important if your house is not listed on the MLS. If you choose to have an open house, your broker is the ideal person to interact with potential buyers.

Each interaction with prospects is an opportunity to move toward a sale. Your broker should be available to answer questions and make it easy for buyers to see the house. A broker should offer other brokers the option of setting up showings online or over the phone.

NEGOTIATING ON YOUR BEHALF

Your broker is your advocate in negotiating offers. The highest offer is not always the best. Your broker is responsible for evaluating offers and helping to determine which one makes the most sense for you. A broker should be able to determine which offers have the best chance of closing based on a buyer's credit and motivation. Buyers with excellent credit may have other contingencies you don't understand. If you go under contract and the deal falls apart, it's unlikely that later offers will match your first offer. Even if there is just one offer, it may not be in your best interest to accept it. Most offers are countered, and price is only one detail that may be changed in the counterproposal. There are seemingly small adjustments your broker can negotiate that could affect your income or determine if and when the deal will actually close.

Once you are under contract, the real fun begins. Some people say their home is sold once it's under contract, but that statement is far from true. While the majority of properties that go under contract do end up closing, there are quite a few that fall out of contract and have to go back on the market. A great broker will navigate the stormy seas between getting the property under contract and getting you paid at closing. Buyers often question their own judgment after they commit to purchasing a home. Home inspectors create additional stress by pointing out flaws in the property. Appraisers and loan-related issues also come into play. Then there are the stubborn sellers. Any number of issues can derail the most solid deal. You may never realize or appreciate the difficulty of your broker's job.

PICKING THE RIGHT BROKER

As you've seen, your broker can make or break a deal, so choose wisely. Find a broker who is a good fit not only for your immediate needs but also for building a long-term relationship. You are looking for an experienced professional who understands the business of real estate. You should realize that your buyer's broker may not be your ideal listing agent. Loyalty does matter, of course, so you may want to offer the listing to the broker who found the deal for you. If that broker fits your listing needs, then by all means stick with him or her. The broker you rely on to handle most of your listings may not have the time to help you find properties. That broker may find you deals occasionally, possibly through word of mouth, but is most likely not willing to make scores of offers on your behalf.

Find out more about the company the broker works for and why he or she chose that company. The biggest and best brokerages with strong brand image may be a plus for you. An office with lots of top producers may be able to connect you to buyers before you formally list your property, or find you deals that never hit the MLS. Smaller independent brokerages are thriving, however, and are another good option; independent brokers tend to have a wealth of experience. Ask your broker about his or her specific credentials and designations. Don't be afraid to ask how the broker splits commission with his or her company. Less-experienced brokers tend to pay a large portion of their commission to their company. On the other hand, top producers usually pay higher fixed fees but are able to keep most or all of their commissions. Don't make the mistake of basing your choice of broker primarily on the commission charged. It is often worth it to pay an established broker a higher commission rather than saving a few bucks with a newbie. Don't be afraid to ask for a discount on the commission, but don't be shocked if the broker says no. The broker should understand that you intend to be a repeat customer and that you are a motivated seller. Brokers should not have to worry about clients pulling their listing from the market and should be confident that clients will be respectful of their time. You can propose a creative way to allocate the buyers' broker's commission if there is no buyers' broker. For example, if the buyers' broker's commission was going to be $6,000, the listing broker could accept $3,000 of that, and credit you the remainder.

Ask the broker exactly what services you would receive. It's common to have different plans available based on the level of service provided. We believe in full-service listings, where the broker is responsible for marketing and managing all aspects of the listing. We don't expect a broker to hold open houses every weekend or provide expensive marketing. But if you find yourself with a high-end or luxury property, additional services may be justified. Discuss the options of how your broker would represent you and manage your listing. Broker relationships vary among states, but we prefer agency brokerage (i.e., the listing broker represents the seller and the buyers' broker represents the buyer) over transaction brokerage (the broker represents neither party), since you want the broker to be your advocate. You may prefer to sit back and listen to the broker's listing presentation, then ask pertinent questions to fill in the gaps. The important thing is to get all the information you need and make sure both you and your broker are on the same page.

Discount brokerages or limited-services listings are worth considering. A limited-services listing would save you money on commission by having you handle some of the listing workload. The primary value of a limited-services listing is getting your property on the MLS. You can decide what services to include, but you would also benefit from having a licensed broker prepare the contracts and help with negotiations. If you work or live near the property, you could meet potential buyers there and could arrange broker showings.

NEW-LISTING TIME LINE

It's wise to speak with brokers several weeks before you are ready to list. That way, the listing broker can walk through your property before the work is completed and give you a professional opinion of the house and offer ideas for adjustments.

Wait until the property is 100 percent ready for sale, then finalize the listing price, and sign the listing agreement. Creating the documents is the easy part. Review the sold comps and expired listings nearby. Ideally, do a preview of any new listings you did not see before. Now is the time to adjust your asking price based on today's market, which may have changed since you purchased the home.

Once the paperwork is done, your broker can get to work and should immediately install the yard sign. We believe in spending extra for a sign that stands out. By the way, be wary of walk-up buyers who want to come in and look around. If you are alone, invite them back for a scheduled appointment with you or your real-estate broker. It is not worth risking your safety. And if the house is not yet on the market, get their contact information and invite them to the open house.

It's also time to enter the property on the MLS. We like to enter new listings on a Thursday or Friday because most agents look on the MLS for weekend showings. Also, remember to avoid holidays. Consider pushing back the listing a couple of weeks if it's near the end of the year. Thanksgiving to New Year's Day is a tough time to sell. Vacation markets are unique and may have different ideal times to list. Review the listing information for accuracy and content. Your broker should engage potential buyers by providing compelling remarks about the most interesting and important features of your house. Ideally, the comments will help the buyer to picture living in the "appealing, immaculate, renovated, updated, spotless" home without sensing the comments were just fluff. We are not big fans of using all capitals or too many exclamation points. In marketing, you can emphasize only so many points, or you end up emphasizing nothing. Sometimes we'll mention what may be a problem with the house so buyers know what to expect. For example, we heard about a home that had virtually no backyard and languished on the market for months with no buyer. Finally, the seller and broker decided to include the comment "no backyard to worry about" and were able to find a buyer in a few weeks.

The broker or a service the broker has hired can now take photos of the property. If snow or dreary weather is in the forecast, we usually take exterior photos ahead of time. Sometimes if timing is tight, we enter a property on the MLS with one or two pictures. We then add a comment that more pics are on the way. Don't settle for photos with your broker's reflection in the bathroom mirror, or of open toilet seats, or flare from using a flash. Exterior shots should include a nice sky background, and in most cases should be taken from a slight angle, not shot from directly in front of the house. The angled perspective will result in a more interesting composition. It's a challenge to take flattering pictures of small rooms or to show the views from inside windows. But a professional should be able to do a bit of postprocessing with photo-editing software and deliver pleasing results.

Tempting as it may be to manipulate images and remove unwanted features such as a giant radio tower behind your house, we think that doing this would anger buyers once they see the actual house. There's a balance between highlighting the positive attributes and misleading buyers. We upload ten to twenty photos of most houses we flip. That way we can highlight the homes' best features and still leave a little bit to the imagination. Some people believe the more photos the better, since so many buyers preview properties online. You do want potential buyers to spend lots of time looking at your property, but only when there is something interesting to see. Providing lots of photos of stark bedrooms that all look alike may bore your prospect and cause them to go on to the next listing. Another option is to provide "virtual staging." There are companies that can alter pictures to make it look like a house is completely staged.

There are many options for additional marketing bits. Companies such as CirclePix.com provide pictures and also offer brochures, property-specific websites, and virtual home tours. Brochures allow prospective buyers to leave with information they can refer back to. They are especially helpful for open houses, since potential buyers may not have an MLS printout provided by their broker. Providing brochures is an example of balancing buyer convenience with your desire to engage the buyer in a conversation that could lead to a sale.

We occasionally place flyers outside the house in case a neighbor or someone driving by has interest. Displaying flyers in front makes it easy for a person to learn about the home. You may want to omit the price, however, and thereby require curious persons to reach out directly to your broker. If you do provide flyers outside, then make sure you regularly restock the supply. Otherwise, people will be frustrated to find an empty flyer dispenser. You can also laminate one flyer and securely attach it to the dispenser.

Virtual home tours are becoming quite popular and definitely have their place in home marketing. We have not provided video of simple flips in the past. But we do use video of homes when there is a lot to see and take in. Based on their present popularity, providing video tours may become a mandatory practice in the near future.

If you decide to have an open house, holding it on the first weekend the home is for sale will create additional buzz about your property. Advertise the open house through the MLS, Craigslist, and other channels. We place signs with directional arrows around the neighborhood and attach a few helium balloons to get people's attention. Once inside, visitors should be greeted by a friendly face and the smell of freshly baked cookies. Make sure someone keeps a record of people attending so the broker can follow up with prospects at a later date. Many brokers have their assistants or other brokers handle open houses. It would be best to have your broker at the open house in case the perfect buyer comes along.

Track showings and feedback. Make sure your broker follows a solid process to get feedback from buyers' brokers. We use a brief survey that is automatically sent to each broker up to three times. If we've only had a few showings, then we'll call the brokers to ask personally for their opinion of the property. Your broker should share these unbiased opinions of the house with you. Actually, the opinions are not completely neutral, and most brokers will tell you the house is at least a little overpriced. Give it a couple of weeks and consider lowering the price if you have lots of showings and no offers. Even slightly overpriced properties should receive offers. Generally speaking, expect to receive an offer for every ten to twenty showings. If you are not getting more than a couple of showings a week, there may be a serious issue with the property or price.

Hopefully, sooner or later you'll receive an offer on your property. Any offer is worth negotiating, but if you can't come to an agreement with the buyer, you'll have to move on. All other things being equal, cash offers are best, followed by conventional loan-financed offers, then FHA- or VA-financed offers. Speak with the buyers' lenders, and don't be afraid to counter offers with adjustments, such as giving less time for the inspection, appraisal, and closing. If you are fortunate, you'll receive multiple offers. Most closings occur about five weeks after the property goes under contract. Get it under contract and congratulate yourself, but *don't* consider the house sold. You still have a ways to go.

In our market, about 30 percent of the contracts that are accepted fall apart before closing. Buyer's remorse is common, since people are not accustomed to making such important decisions quickly. Loan problems are also common due to stringent lender guidelines and appraisals coming in at or above purchase price in a market with rising property values. As we discussed earlier in these pages, after the house is under contract, there will be a property inspection, followed by the buyer asking for additional concessions. Your concessions can be to make repairs or offer allowances, effectively lowering the sales price. Even if there are inspection issues or the appraisal comes in low, you should try to keep the deal alive. Usually the first offer will be your best. If the contract falls apart and you have to put the house back on the market, it will be difficult to regenerate the excitement of a new listing.

If you don't receive the earnest-money check personally, confirm that the buyer has deposited funds with your title company or broker's office. Once your broker changes the status of the property on the MLS to under contract, showings will come to a halt. If you have the opportunity to secure a backup offer, then do so. It will put you in a strong position with the first buyer and increase your chances of a quick sale if something goes wrong with offer number one. You'll need to provide the buyer with disclosures about the home and possibly with records showing what work has been done. The buyer (and lender) will require title insurance and will have to secure homeowners' insurance. The lender will require an appraisal and possibly a survey or short-form version called an Improvement Location Certificate.

There is an issue known as "seasoning" that can apply when you flip a property in just a few months. Seasoning is basically the minimum time the lender wants the seller to have owned a home before reselling. To ensure there was not an inflated appraisal or other loan fraud in play, the lender may require you to submit renovation receipts along with a letter justifying the increase in your home's value. Your broker should stay in touch with the lender along the way to make sure the loan is proceeding as desired. It's common to have some drama with the loan, such as last-minute requests from the underwriting department.

If all these steps go well, there will be a final buyer walkthrough, followed by a closing. The closing is where you show up, meet the buyers, and sign a lot of papers—though not as many as the buyer. At the end of the closing, you'll hand over the keys, and you should receive a check in return. If everything went as planned, your proceeds, and, more importantly, your profit will be substantially greater than your broker's check.

SELL IT ON YOUR OWN?

We had intended to write a full chapter about selling your houses yourself. As we outlined the sale process, however, we realized there are so many good reasons to use a broker that we should focus primarily on that path. If you are in a really desirable area and are determined to sell it yourself, at least hire an attorney to handle the paperwork. Many people hire a real-estate agent to do the contracts at a 3 percent fee—that's $6,000 on the sale of a $200,000 house! A good real-estate attorney can represent you from contract through closing for about $1,500–$2,000.

There is a simple lesson here: if you want to do it yourself, then become a licensed broker.

WRAPPING IT UP

- Don't worry; the house is going to sell.
- Don't underestimate the value of listing with a broker.
- Marketing matters, and the MLS is still the best marketing channel.
- Selling a house is a lot of work—employ at least some professional help.

PART IV

Minding Your Business

CHAPTER 16

Success in a Changing Market

We get a lot of questions from people asking, "Will your approach work in my market?" Just as often, we hear uninformed statements such as, "This approach won't work in my market!" The truth is, flipping—buy low, sell high—works in every market, but you need to understand your own particular market and take advantage of the techniques in this book.

There are many ways to describe real-estate markets (e.g., hot or flat, rising or falling, buyers' or sellers'). Remember, to survive and profit as a flipper, you must buy at an appropriate discount, allowing you to sell the property for a profit. Flipping can be the least risky way for a beginning investor to make a profit in an uncertain market simply because of the relatively short amount of time he or she will own the property. Unlike the stock and commodities markets, real-estate markets don't rise and fall rapidly. For long-term investing, discussed later in this chapter, additional market factors are important to your buying decision. Flippers who plan for short-term real-estate market fluctuations are speculating, which is outside the basic model of flipping. We don't speculate; we invest, improve, sell, and profit.

WHAT IS THE IDEAL MARKET FOR FLIPPING?

Let's be clear: there is no such thing as an ideal real-estate market for flipping. It tends to be more difficult to find bargains in rising markets. Many would-be flippers complain about these high-priced, limited-supply markets that typically favor sellers. These conditions have been common in many parts of the country in recent years, providing certain challenges to acquiring properties at below-market prices. Once a property is secured at an attractive price, however, even if it takes relatively long to renovate and sell a property, you can ask a premium price, sell quickly, and reap a substantial profit.

In contrast, when property values are falling, more so-called bargains become available. Yet you need to assess the true value of these properties based on when you expect to sell the property. Thus, your purchase must be made at a steep discount to allow for a profitable sale later.

BASIC STRATEGIES

Some basic strategies can be used successfully in virtually all market conditions. Most of the following discussion is based on selling properties to owner-occupants, although similar rules apply to wholesaling properties to other investors.

Become educated in your local market first by understanding the large-scale trends—from global down to national, regional, and specific neighborhoods. Learn about target neighborhoods, enlisting the aid of successful real-estate professionals along the way. These professionals will help interpret market indicators, such as the average length of time houses are sitting on the market this month versus last month or last year. Armed with this type of information, you will be able to make good decisions.

Inventory Trends

Inventory, simply defined as the number of properties offered for sale, is a good indicator of current market trends. If inventory is low because of building restrictions or geographic limitations, then high demand will lead to rising prices. In rising markets, sellers often capitalize on the excitement of new listings to get properties under contract quickly, at premium asking prices.

There are also seasonal fluctuations in inventory, such as fewer listed properties in the winter than in the summer and a surge of listings in the spring. Properties sell year-round, though investors should plan to reduce the price for winter listings, or at least know that properties take longer to sell during those months.

Speculation on Market Appreciation Can Be Risky

In the period between 2003 and 2007, some speculators made a bundle buying up preconstruction condominiums in hot markets, then selling them for 25–50 percent profit after the project was completed, often a year later. Properly timed, a preconstruction condo purchase can be lucrative if there is limited supply (such as beachfront) and a strong local market.

But the basic premise of such activity violates our number-one rule, which is to make your profit when you buy, not when you sell. If you are paying full price at what could be the top of a saturated market, you may find yourself stuck buying an overpriced property or bailing on a large earnest-money deposit.

If you do sign a contract to purchase a preconstruction property, make sure the builder does not prohibit you from flipping the property. Also, have a plan B—if you can't sell it, can you complete the purchase and rent the property to ride out a market cycle? Check the fine print to see what you are committing to and how much money you have to put up before the project is completed. And be mindful that construction projects often get delayed for a variety of reasons, so make sure you are dealing with a reputable builder.

Condo Pros and Cons

Condos have made a strong comeback in recent years, partially because of the popularity of buying second homes, particularly in resort areas. Whether this trend will continue is uncertain, but keep in mind that condos are generally tougher to sell in most areas than single-family homes. And because condominiums involve a homeowners' association, you'll have to deal with management issues, rules, and costs that may be out of your control.

When buying condos, consider who your prospective buyer will be when you resell. Is the property priced so high that your pool of buyers is limited? It may be in the median price or below, but how many people live in one-bedroom condos? Is the development so old that the HOA dues are high and will continue to rise as the development ages and needs repairs?

For the most part, condos tend to fit into two categories—rentable and livable. Cheap condos that rent well often don't appreciate much in value. You can get away with buying a $50,000 condo and renting it for $500 a month forever. But in twenty years, it may barely have appreciated above inflation. A different condo near downtown or the beach may rent for negative cash flow and appreciate 10–15 percent per year. In short, the normal formulas that apply to single-family homes aren't as consistent with condos, which is why investors need to approach condos with extreme caution.

Falling Markets

Often, property values are flat or falling in a particular area. This type of market offers great opportunity to the savvy investor. When property values are falling, inventory often rises, and many sellers become highly motivated when their properties fail to sell quickly. Motivated sellers will do whatever it takes to sell their property. Whether sellers need to move from the area, are struggling financially, or have other pressing reasons to sell, there is a good chance they will accept a below-market offer. Investors know a weak market can offer extraordinary deals, though flippers need

---

FLIP TIP

No vacancy. Be aware that some HOA rules restrict the rental of units, so make sure you check the limitations before you purchase a condo that you plan to rent. Also, many lenders have limitations on financing condos, such as a requirement that a certain percentage of the units be occupied by owners.

to proceed with caution. In a falling market, even a few months' delay can turn a sound deal into a headache. It always pays to know the market and purchase the property at a low enough price that it will net an eventual profit, even if the market continues to fall. There is a common myth that you cannot make money by flipping properties in a bad real-estate market. In a bad real-estate market, you can often buy junker properties for fifty cents on the dollar and sell them for sixty cents. It's all in how you do the math.

It is also worth noting that markets can and will change. If the market rebounds after a purchase, then all is well for the investor. But if the market takes a downturn after a purchase, there can be trouble ahead. It is common for a market to show signs of slowing over several months. Sometimes the early signs come from national economic trends, such as rapidly rising interest rates or sweeping changes in tax policies that affect homeownership or investment (e.g., the rapid change in depreciation rules for real-estate investors in the late 1980s). More likely, it is from local market conditions such as unemployment, oversupply, or a change in demand because of living conditions.

Sellers often choose not to believe the market is changing, making it difficult to convince them to accept a low offer. In these cases, it is best to move on to the next deal, even if it means fewer purchases for a few months. It is also worthwhile to follow up with sellers who weren't highly motivated earlier. Sellers' attitudes and situations can change over several weeks or months of trying unsuccessfully to sell their properties. Eventually, reality may set in and these sellers will be forced to discount their prices.

When it comes time for an investor to market his or her property in a weak market, it will need to stand out in its price range. The property can still sell quickly, but buyers have a larger selection of homes to choose from, so you need to do several things to assure success. First, your budget must allow for a longer time to sell. Second, the finished product must be better than the other listings being offered, both in appearance and price. Third, the flipper must have a good marketing plan, ideally with multiple exit strategies.

Most likely, the property will sell quickly if it fits that description. If it does not sell, however, then the low purchase price allows room in the budget to carry the property for a longer period of time. Ideally, if it simply did not sell and is not showing signs that it will sell anytime soon, you would have the option of holding the property as a rental for several years, then selling it at a profit. That is a better option than being forced to "give it away."

Balanced Markets

Real-estate markets are usually closer to being balanced than they are to being at either extreme. In a balanced market, prices are rising at or just above the pace of national inflation. Houses within the median price range for the metropolitan area will go under contract, on average, between forty-five and sixty days. While markets are constantly changing due to circumstances beyond anyone's control, an equalizing effect exists in a free-market economy. Often, a market will exhibit some tendencies of the balanced, falling, or rising classifications. And within a particular market, there will always be pockets where houses are selling better or worse than in the metropolitan area as a whole.

There is profit to be made in a balanced market, following the buy-low, sell-high premise. Remember, as soon as you have the market figured out, it will change! Experienced investors may have an advantage in seeing trends, but no one can foretell the future, and the short-turnaround deals usually involve the lowest amount of risk.

EXIT STRATEGIES

More important than guessing the future of a local market is having a clear plan in mind when purchasing property. (This section expands on the lessons from chapter 5.)

Your strategy may be to take title, then wholesale the property to another investor within a few days, or perhaps rehab and sell it within a few months. Typically, flippers are in and out quickly, but there is still a spectrum of how long the entire process takes to purchase and resell a house. Usually the quickest turnaround is wholesaling to another investor. Let's take a look at some exit strategies in more detail.

The Quasi Rehab

In hot markets, you can flip properties directly to the retail market with little or no rehab work. If the property is in relatively good shape, it may only take decorating to get it ready for resale. Even if the house needs a moderate amount of work, you can take the rough edges off the project and offer it as a minor fixer-upper. A good cleanup and paint touch-up often does the trick. Usually that process takes just a few days; then you are ready to offer the property for sale.

As an investor, your choice of financing should be based on the expected time from loan initiation to loan payoff. It can make sense to use a credit line with a high interest rate and a low closing cost if you plan to flip the property in a few days or weeks. But tying up readily available funds for months can create an "opportunity cost" of turning down other deals. Plus, interest costs can get quite expensive. If possible, try to either buy the property subject to existing financing or simply tie up the property with a purchase contract that gives you the right to enter the house and start doing rehab work.

Offering Terms

Attractive financing terms have been used to move a variety of products—from cars to furniture to computers. Likewise, you can move difficult-to-sell properties by offering attractive owner-financing terms. Having alternative financing available attracts buyers who have limited choices. These terms may include helping with the down payment or financing some of the purchase price with a seller carry-back note and mortgage. Making arrangements to help buyers with financing can prove quite valuable in selling your properties. In addition, sellers who offer attractive terms can get a higher price than sellers who ask for all cash to buy a comparable house.

While it is possible to get a higher price for a property when offering terms, you cannot raise the price beyond its legitimate value. As discussed earlier, you may run into ethical issues regarding false representations of property values, loan fraud, and other questionable practices that are sometimes associated with "flipping." We do not support those practices and recommend seeking representation by legal counsel regarding the way loans are structured.

Look for advantages of flipping not only for cash, but for terms. In other words, instead of buying and flipping for all-cash profit, you accept a note for some or all of your profit. The going rate for an owner-financed note is generally much higher than what institutional lenders offer and certainly more than you could earn in a CD or money market account. For example, if the going rate for a mortgage is 5 percent, you could get 7 percent or higher on the note you finance to the buyer. And you can sell the note for cash at a later time, so you still have liquidity in your investment.

The bonus of taking "paper" (an owner-financed note) for your equity is that you can demand a higher price. Cash always buys a discount, so if you can offer a buyer a way to get into the property with less money down, you can raise the price.

The risk of taking back a note, of course, is that the payer could default. The note will generally be secured by a lien (e.g., a mortgage or deed of trust) on the property, but this lien will likely be junior to another lien, so you risk losing your position if the senior lien is in default. When you sell, require some down payment, ideally enough to recoup all the cash you invested in the deal. That way you are not reaching into your pocket if the borrower defaults.

Lease-Option: Best of Both Worlds?

Another strategy is to refinance the property after you have rehabbed it, thereby getting out all the money you invested. Then you could sell the property on a lease with an option to buy. If your tenant exercises the option after one year, you will fare better on taxes than if you had sold it quickly. You can do a 1031 exchange or just pay the capital gains rate rather than the ordinary income rate. In the meantime, you may be able to enjoy positive cash flow (You can find more information about doing lease-options at http://www.legalwiz.com/lease-option).

Keep in mind that if the tenant does not exercise his or her option to purchase, you are stuck with the property. If you are at or near the top of your real-estate market cycle, you may end up with a property you cannot sell right away and become a long-term landlord.

Rent It

While acquiring rental properties is not the foremost goal of most flippers, the subject deserves some attention. Many mainstream properties targeted by flippers (e.g., starter homes) can make excellent rental properties. If you have money tied up in the deal, you can refinance it to recoup most of your capital and lower your monthly payment. The option of holding on to a property that fails to sell in the desired time frame and renting it can be a good plan B. Then you can place the property on the market at a later date or hold it indefinitely. There are sound reasons to consider building wealth through equity as part of a flipper's long-term plan. Armed with the knowledge of multiple exit strategies, you can increase your opportunities for success.

THE GREAT DEBATE: FLIPPING VS HOLDING

This book focuses on flipping—that is, turning over properties quickly rather than keeping them long-term. In some cases, however, holding property will generate more long-term wealth for you than flipping. Therefore, you may consider flipping some properties and holding others. Or you may consider flipping for a while, then begin holding properties later. The big question is: When should you hold and when should you flip?

Flipping Pros and Cons

The main advantage of flipping is that you get your cash out now rather than later. For many people, the certainty of getting a paycheck right away is highly appealing. Flipping takes the real-estate market out of the equation; if you buy a property correctly, the market is almost irrelevant, though it does influence how long it will take to resell the property. (Of course, if you buy cheap in a soft market, you can afford to hold a property six months instead of two.)

Flipping is generally good for your cash flow, which is important in any business. If you purchase houses and acquire too much equity and not enough cash, you may get into a cash crunch if you don't have additional income.

Don't forget that you can flip houses as a part- or full-time business. You can do as much or as little as you want and can take a break from your flipping business whenever you want to. In short, once you empty your inventory, you are not tied to your business.

The main disadvantage of flipping is that it is hands-on income. Once you stop flipping, you stop making money. If you are young and like to work for a few months, then take a few months off—that's fine. But at some point, you will realize that if you don't reinvest some of your profits, you won't accumulate wealth.

Also, if you flip, you lose the benefit of market appreciation. While a risky venture, timing the market trends well can help you gain wealth in a few years by buying properties in emerging markets. In the last five years, we have seen many investors get rich simply by being in the right place at the right time. On the other hand, if you buy a property in the wrong place at the wrong time, particularly for the wrong price, you can end up with a property you cannot get rid of quickly enough. You could also get in over your head in a rehab project and have to bail, losing tens of thousands of dollars.

As we will discuss in chapter 18, you cannot take advantage of certain favorable tax laws on flipper properties. One particular loophole not available to the flipper is the 1031 tax-deferred exchange, which allows you to roll your gain into another property purchase. Also, flipping can have a negative consequence if you don't want taxable income. If you flip, you have a gain; there's not a lot you can do to hide from that income.

Finally, if you don't spend all your income on living expenses, what will you do with it? A diversified portfolio is a good idea—you could put some of your cash in bonds, money market, or mutual funds, but you might earn a better return by leaving your profits in real estate rather than taking them out.

Holding Pros and Cons

Property holders can generate true wealth over the long term. Historically, property values appreciate at a rate greater than US inflation. If you buy in the right neighborhoods, your annual appreciation may reach double digits. You can use properties with equity as collateral. They can provide rental income for your retirement years, and you can pass property down to the next generation. Once your properties are owned "free and clear," you have passive income that pays you even when you are not working.

The main disadvantage to holding is that your assets are not liquid. Unlike stocks or bonds, real estate is not easily converted to cash. When selling real estate, you have to locate a buyer, then wait for the sale to go through.

If you must sell when the market is down, you will not get the best price. If you have a tenant in your property under a lease, you cannot simply kick the tenant out. You have to wait until the lease expires, pay the tenant to leave early, or hope to find a buyer who doesn't mind having someone living in the property.

If you hold properties, you also risk running into negative cash flow. There may be times when your properties are vacant or need repairs and you have to dip into savings to feed the proverbial "alligator." And, of course, the future is always uncertain.

WHAT'S RIGHT FOR YOU?

The more important question is not whether flipping is better or worse than holding, but rather whether flipping is right for you. Ask yourself these questions:

- Do I need additional income now or in the future?
- Am I in a high income-tax bracket that would be adversely affected by more income now?
- Does my local real-estate market present an opportunity to acquire bargains, yet still command high rents that would cover my expenses if I need to hold on to the property?
- Do I have other income or savings that I could tap into in case my rental properties become vacant or need repairs?
- Do I have the time and patience to deal with tenants?
- Is the local real-estate market rising or falling at this time?

Most investors start out flipping houses, then gradually work into managing rental properties or becoming involved in larger, more complex real-estate projects. But some people don't have the temperament to deal with tenants and the headaches that come with rental properties. Some look for side income by flipping. Others want to quit their jobs and make flipping houses their full-time business.

Consider all options, including a mixture of flipping and holding properties. Be sure to reevaluate your financial goals regularly and adjust your real-estate strategies to support your goals.

WRAPPING IT UP

- Flipping works in any market.
- Keep in mind multiple exit strategies.
- Understand the difference between flipping and speculating.
- Acquire rentals along the way to build long-term wealth.

CHAPTER 17

Liability Issues

While you need not let legal issues scare you away from going gung ho into real estate, you need to be aware of these issues. Real estate is a high-risk business, particularly when dealing with motivated sellers in foreclosure and when dealing with rehab projects. We live in a litigious society in which many people seek to place blame on others. Some people believe that if you treat people right and carry sufficient insurance, you will be fine. That naive thinking can get you into a lot of trouble, and one silly lawsuit can ruin everything you've worked hard for.

KNOW THE LAW

The old expression "ignorance of the law is no defense" is surely true. You are expected to know the law as it applies to your business. If your state, county, city, or village has particular laws, codes, and regulations, you must learn them. Review your forms, agreements, and contracts to make sure the disclosures and clauses are appropriate for the particular way you do business. Although the practices described herein are generally legal and appropriate in all fifty states (and many foreign jurisdictions), you may "tweak" one little element in a contract and change everything. An investment in good legal advice and forms is an investment in protection from future legal disasters.

CARRY LOTS OF INSURANCE

We suggest insuring each property you buy with plenty of liability coverage. You may even consider a builder's-risk policy if you do a lot of rehab projects. If you are concerned about cost, get insurance with a large liability portion and a higher deductible. If you carry your property liability, personal residence, and business insurance with a single carrier, this company will offer you an umbrella policy for several million dollars of additional coverage at a reasonable price. There are certain claims, however—such as breach of contract, discrimination, and misrepresentation—that are not covered by insurance. Most insurance won't cover any intentional act. So, while insurance is helpful, it's only your first line of defense against lawsuits.

The best way to protect yourself is to avoid being sued personally—that is, you should form a legal entity to wedge between yourself and the liabilities that your business creates. This could be either a corporation or a limited liability company (LLC).

FLIP TIP

Avoid being a sole proprietor. Most people starting their own businesses do so as sole proprietors. This means they are doing business as individuals or under fictitious names or DBAs (doing business as). This scenario offers absolutely no protection, not to mention poor tax benefits (as discussed later in this chapter). If your business is sued, all your personal assets are at risk as a sole proprietor. If you are the buyer or seller on a real-estate contract, you (not your DBA) will be sued in the case of a breach of contract. If you sign a warranty deed as seller and there are any problems with title, you can be sued for breach of warranty. If workers are injured on your property while you are rehabbing it, say hello to their lawyer. The fact is, there are dozens of scenarios that can lead to liability, and you are fully exposed by doing things in your own name.

SET UP A CORPORATION OR LLC

For about one hundred dollars in most states, you can form a corporation or limited liability company (LLC) to carry out your business or trade. If properly maintained, a corporation or LLC will shield your personal assets if the business is sued or goes bankrupt. A corporation can also provide you with some tax benefits. Furthermore, a corporation or LLC gives a professional look to your business dealings. A corporation can be formed with a single owner, as can an LLC, although an LLC with just one owner (called a member) will generally be treated as a sole proprietorship for federal income-tax purposes, which can be detrimental if you are a "dealer," a tax issue discussed in the next chapter.

Both a corporation and an LLC are formed under state law by filing papers with your state's department of corporations or secretary of state. Both types of entities limit the liability of their owners, but they are taxed differently. You should discuss appropriate tax issues with your CPA or tax adviser before proceeding.

CORPORATE FORMALITIES

Many people who set up a corporation or LLC neglect to follow the corporate formalities required by the law.

For a corporation, these include, but are not limited to, the following:

- Creating bylaws
- Preparing organizational minutes
- Preparing proper corporate resolutions
- Appointing directors and officers
- Issuing stock certificates
- Annual meetings of shareholders and directors

For an LLC:

- Creating an operating agreement
- Preparing proper company resolutions
- Issuing membership certificates

As you can see, an LLC requires fewer formalities up front and less annual paperwork than a corporation. Each has its own advantages, however, which are beyond the scope of this book. While you may be tempted to try to form a corporation or LLC on your own or with a no-frills online service, you are likely better off using an attorney to file the necessary paperwork in order to make sure your company is correctly formed and maintained.

PARTNERS

Doing business with a partner can be even worse than doing business as a sole proprietor. A partnership is formed when two or more people decide to do business together for profit. It does not require a formal partnership agreement or filing any official documents, although it is often formed that way.

Here is the problem with partnerships: If your partner does something foolish, you are liable. If you commit the partnership to a contract, the partnership and its partners can be held liable for that partnership's debt. If your partner slanders someone, commits a negligent act, or incurs a debt on behalf of the partnership, you are on the hook—even if your partner files for bankruptcy. This is the doctrine of joint-and-several liability. Regardless of the percentage of fault between you and your partners, a judgment by a creditor for any tortious acts is 100 percent collectible from any one of the partners. Joint-and-several liability can be particularly disastrous if you are the silent partner with all the money.

Another problem is the accidental partnership. For instance, Harry finds a good business deal. He needs capital, so he approaches Sally. Sally agrees to invest with Harry. Sally is the silent partner. Harry deals with the public, referring to his "partner," Sally. Sally and Harry do business, make money, and part ways. A month later, Harry gets into financial trouble. Creditors come knocking on his door, but he has no money to pay them. So these creditors come after his partner Sally. Is Sally liable? In some cases, the answer is yes, if the public thought Harry and Sally were partners and Sally did nothing to stop Harry.

If you only want to do a one-shot deal with a partner, consider drafting a joint-venture agreement (see the sample joint-venture agreement on page 248 in the appendix). A joint venture is basically a partnership for a specific purpose or time period. If you intend to do business with partners for the long term, consider forming a corporation or LLC.

WRAPPING IT UP

- Protect yourself with adequate insurance.
- Avoid doing business in your own name or as a sole proprietor.
- Make certain you follow corporate formalities.
- Partners can cause liability; consider a corporate entity.

CHAPTER 18

Tax Issues Involved in Flipping Properties

You maybe be tempted to skip this chapter because you find the discussion of taxes boring. Let us put it another way: How would you like to pocket more money without working any harder and at the same time keep our government from taking what's rightfully yours? Ah, now we've got your attention!

The foolish entrepreneur is the one who waits until April 15 to file taxes, then hands a shoebox full of receipts to the accountant. Be sure to plan for your taxes at the beginning of the tax year and consult with your tax advisers throughout the year. People who say the tax system isn't fair are usually ignorant of the rules. Taxes will eat up a large percentage of your money over your lifetime, so learn how to make the rules work for you!

CAPITAL GAINS

Many people wrongly assume that flipping properties causes an investor to incur a tax "penalty" or other negative tax consequences. This assessment is not completely accurate. If you buy an investment property and hold it for twelve months or more, it is considered a "long-term capital asset." When sold, a long-term capital asset results in a long-term capital gain. The tax rate for long-term capital gains as of January 2017 is maxed out at 20 percent, depending on your income. This rate is obviously lower than regular federal personal-income-tax rates, which can currently be as high as 39.6 percent.

DEPRECIATION

Depreciation is a tax write-off you get on rental properties because, in theory, the structures "wear out." While this may be true, properties tend to appreciate, not depreciate, in value in the long run. So, the IRS lets you take a deduction for the value of the structure (not the land) over a 27.5-year period.

The drawback, however, is that the depreciation is "recaptured" at sale, resulting in taxes. The depreciation recapture is taxed at 25 percent. So, for example, if you took $20,000 of depreciation over several years, you have to pay $5,000 in recapture tax. This is in addition to capital gains tax you have to pay.

And these are just federal taxes; don't forget about state income taxes! Some states charge additional gains tax on the profit. Most states charge a documentary transfer tax based on purchase price; this is the equivalent of a "sales tax" and is generally paid by the buyer.

TAX ISSUES FOR THE WHOLESALER AND FLIPPER

The wholesaler who flips a property to another investor is getting the equivalent of a real-estate broker fee for tax purposes. This would be reported as ordinary income on Schedule C of the wholesaler's federal income-tax return. He or she could deduct expenses related to this activity on the tax return to offset the income.

Flippers who sell properties held less than one year cannot take advantage of the lower capital gains rates, but instead pay personal rates. A flipper who only sells a few properties here and there could report this income on Schedule D as a short-term capital gain. They can deduct expenses

FLIP TIP

No exchanges. Under section 1031 of the Internal Revenue Code, an investor who holds a property for "productive use" (i.e., with the intent to hold as an income-producing property or investment) can sell a property and replace it with another to defer paying gains tax. There are strict rules you must follow under the 1031 exchange section (learn more at 1031x.com). But a flipper can never exchange property, since his or her intent in buying the property is for immediate resale, thus negating the productive-use requirement. Some investors have done it, but as the saying goes, "Every tax strategy works until you get audited."

directly related to the acquisition and sale of the property. They cannot, however, deduct general business expenses on Schedule D. These must be reported on a Schedule C. This may open a Pandora's box, as discussed later in this chapter.

FILE IRS FORM 1099

If you pay a contractor or a wholesaler for a deal brought to you, and it's more than $600 in one year, you must send him or her an IRS Form 1099 by January 31 of the following tax year. You should also have gotten completed W-9 forms from your contractors. Send a copy of the forms to the IRS, along with IRS Form 1096, by February 28. Failure to file the required form could result in a penalty of fifty dollars per unfiled return or one hundred dollars if the nonfiling is proven to be intentional.

THE REAL-ESTATE DEALER ISSUE

A flipper or wholesaler is someone who buys properties with the intent of reselling them. The IRS uses a similar definition of a real-estate dealer. The capital gains and installment sales rules apply for principal residences and properties held for "productive use" (IRC §1234).

If you are actively buying and selling real estate, you may be considered a dealer in real-estate properties. A dealer is one who buys with the intent of reselling, rather than for investment. In our terms, this applies to both the dealer and the retailer. There is no magic formula for distinguishing between an investor and a dealer, but the IRS will balance a number of factors, such as the following:

- The purpose for which the property was purchased
- How long the property was held
- The number of deals (and sales) by the taxpayer in that year
- The amount of income from sales compared to the taxpayer's other income
- The amount of gain realized from the sales

If the IRS pegs you as a dealer, then you cannot report the transactions on a Schedule D; they must normally be reported on a Schedule C as inventory. Thus the gains from the sale of real estate will be subject to self-employment tax, which is currently 15.3 percent of the first $118,500 (as of 2016). If the IRS re-characterizes this income several years after the transaction, you may also be subject to additional interest and possibly a penalty.

AVOID SCHEDULE C

As you may have discerned by now, doing business on a Schedule C as a sole proprietor is not recommended. Why? Because your liability is unlimited, you are subject to self-employment tax on earnings, and your chances of being audited as a small business are higher than if you are incorporated.

As discussed previously, you should consider forming a corporation to buy and flip your properties. The discussion of whether you should have an S or C corporation is beyond the scope of this book, but suffice it to say that an LLC may not be the best choice for flipping homes. A single-member LLC is disregarded for federal income-tax purposes. This means you report your income and expenses on your personal return, subject to the same issues as stated above. The good news is that you may be able to elect to have your single-member LLC treated as a corporation for tax purposes.

FLIP TIP

Don't become a dealer. If you have been classified as or choose to represent yourself as a dealer to the Internal Revenue Service, then it should be clear that you will pay additional tax. If you do file a Schedule C, careful planning may help you avoid becoming classified as a dealer. Most tax professionals will recommend you do your flips in a different legal entity than you do your rentals. Always seek the advice of a qualified tax adviser who is familiar with real-estate transactions.

INDEPENDENT CONTRACTOR LIABILITY

The IRS and your state's department of labor are on the lookout for employers who don't collect and pay withholding taxes, unemployment, or workers' compensation insurance.

If you have employees that are "off the books," you're looking for trouble. If you get caught, you will have to pay withholding taxes and as much as a 25 percent penalty. Intentionally failing to file W-2 forms will subject you to a one-hundred-dollar fine per form. The fine for failing to complete Immigration and Naturalization Service (INS) Form I-9 is $100–$1,000 per infraction. And the corporation will not shield you from liability in this case. All officers, directors, and responsible parties are personally liable for the taxes, and this obligation cannot be discharged in bankruptcy.

If you have people who do contract work for you on a per-diem basis, they may be considered employees by the IRS. If any workers fail to pay their estimated taxes, you may still be liable for withholding. If these workers are under your control and supervision and work exclusively for you, the IRS may consider them employees, even if you don't. If this happens, you may be liable for back taxes and penalties. If you want to protect yourself, you should do the following at a minimum:

- Hire only contract workers who own their own corporations or be sure to get the business card and letterhead of any unincorporated contractors you may use in order to prove these workers are not your employees.

- Require written proof of insurance from workers (liability, unemployment, and workers' compensation).
- Have a written contract or estimate on the worker's letterhead that states that he or she will work his or her own hours and that you will have no direct supervision over the details of the work (see sample contractor agreement on page 274 in the appendix).
- Have letters of reference from other people the contractor did work for in your file to show that this person did not work solely for you.
- File IRS Form 1099 for every worker to whom you pay more than $600 per year.

In addition to possible tax implications, an independent contractor can create liability for you. For example, if your independent contractor is negligent and injures another person, the injured party can sue you directly. If facts show you exercised enough control over your contractor, a court may rule that this contractor is your employee for liability purposes. As you may know, an employer is vicariously liable for the acts of employees (i.e., liable as a matter of law, without proof of fault on the part of the employer). Make certain you follow these guidelines for hiring contractors, paying particular attention to the issue of control.

Finally, be aware of which duties are considered inherently dangerous under your state's law. These duties cannot be delegated to an independent contractor without liability on your part, regardless of whether the person you hire is considered an independent contractor or an employee.

KEEP GOOD RECORDS

It is important to maintain good records for your property dealings, particularly the rehabs. Plan ahead, so you can document everything if you are ever audited. In addition, many businesses fail due to poor accounting practices, so doing your books the right way will help you succeed.

If you are an active flipper, tracking the expenses between properties can get confusing. An off-the-shelf accounting program such as QuickBooks is good for this, particularly because of the ability to attribute expenses to specific properties. The key to keeping good records is to start by setting up simple procedures you can follow. A good CPA or bookkeeper can help you set up your accounting so your records are clean and follow generally accepted accounting principles.

WRAPPING IT UP

- Learn the basic (and not so basic) rules of real-estate taxation—it could save you a lot of dough!
- Avoid being tagged as a "dealer" in real estate.
- Beware of tax issues involved in dealing with independent contractors.
- Keep good accounting records in case of an audit.

CHAPTER 19

The Business Side of Flipping

Whether you are new to real estate or have reached a plateau, the information in this chapter will enable you to reach a higher level in your real-estate investing career. Some of this content may not apply to where you are now, but we believe it will be valuable to you in the years ahead.

CREATE YOUR PLAN

Real estate, unlike many other "investments," is more of a business than a sideline endeavor. In order to succeed, you must give it 100 percent in the beginning and have a solid written business plan. As with any business, you won't get very far if you dabble. Your business plan doesn't need to be elaborate, but working through these steps will give you a good starting point.

ESTABLISH YOUR VISION

Your vision is about what you see as possible. Where do you see yourself, your lifestyle, and your accomplishments in a year from now? Five years from now? Why do you want to do this business? Is it for the challenge, income, or lifestyle change?

Having a big dream will affect your life and the lives of those around you. We agree that the monetary rewards are nice, but to attain real success you need to discover the things in life that truly fulfill you and give your life purpose. It certainly remains true that you "can't take it with you." Contributing to those closest to us, the community, and others in need, whether it be through time, money, or both, is a powerful means to achieving personal fulfillment.

ASSESS YOUR SITUATION, STRENGTHS, AND WEAKNESSES

First, analyze your strengths and weaknesses. Ask for input from your team members, mentors, and other people you trust. Each of us has unique insight. Use your strengths to your advantage, and improve areas in which you need work.

Real estate is a people business and you must have good communication, telephone, and negotiation skills to succeed. Sales experience will be extremely helpful. In addition, an entrepreneurial mind-set and accounting, legal, construction, or other work experience will shorten your learning curve. Having computer skills and being familiar with e-mail, time management, word-processing tools, and spreadsheet software is important. Determine what you are good at and leverage your expertise in your new business.

ESTABLISH GOALS

We agree with the premise that goals are perhaps the biggest key to unlocking your success. Goals should be simple, measurable, and attainable. If your goal was to do twenty flips and net $1 million in your first year, and you have no savings or assets and few applicable skills, that goal is actually a pipe dream. Create simple weekly, monthly, and one-year goals to start.

Make x number of telephone calls a week. Spend x dollars a month on advertising. Make x number of offers a week. Pass out x number of business cards each day. Eventually, you will start to "get lucky." Successful people tackle their most difficult tasks before working on more pleasurable but less important issues.

We want you to set your standards high and strive for great results, but we also want you to be realistic. Things never go exactly as planned. Be flexible and open-minded, and make adjustments along the way. As you move forward, become adept at adjusting on the fly.

WRITE A BUSINESS PLAN

Having *any* plan is much better than nothing. You should be able to create something reasonable in a weekend. On the other hand, don't take months to create a fifty-page business plan instead of making offers on homes. Put together a plan that encompasses all the major steps needed to move the project ahead in a logical and timely manner. Create a time line for the accomplishment of the various steps. Below is an outline of key items to address in your plan:

Get your startup capital together. Be realistic in assessing your starting point. Determine your best sources of capital.

Assemble your team. Go out and get together the best team you possibly can.

Establish your workspace and hours. Your office can be simple yet functional. Decide how much time you will put into the business each week. Then create a daily work schedule.

Commit to a purchase strategy. Once you've created your brand and company, work on doing deals. Expect to spend most of your time on marketing to find flips.

Assess your competition and barriers. Your primary competition may be other investors buying deals on the MLS or advertising in your neighborhood. But there are always enough deals to go around. Look at what else is holding you back—time, money, experience, confidence—and find ways to overcome those obstacles.

Learn both by doing and through study. You will need to acquire specialized knowledge to be successful. Should you sign up for an expensive real-estate seminar? Well, maybe. If you think education is expensive, try ignorance. You can lose more money with a single mistake than you will spend by learning how to avoid one. Continuing education is an important part of your growth and long-term success as an investor. If you are just beginning, start with seminars that cost $500 or less and let the

FLIP TIP

Office details. Create a quiet workspace, even if it is a desk in the corner of one room in your home. For most investors, an outside office is unnecessary since they can meet people at coffee shops, at a title-company office, or even in prospective sellers' homes.

We are accustomed to using a desktop computer at the office. But a laptop and docking station is another good option. I'm also fond of my tablet with a wireless data connection. There are many off-site options available for backing up data, so it is no longer critical to use an external hard drive. Some combination of a printer, copier, scanner, and fax machine is an absolute must. Sometimes our online fax service simply won't connect, so we occasionally rely on our good old fax machine. There are lots of options for routing calls from multiple numbers to your smartphone. Lastly, a good headset will free your hands up while you are on the phone.

information sink in. Consider these points when determining whether to invest in any form of continuing education.

1. **Price.** Be leery of very cheap or very expensive seminars. Free seminars aren't inherently bad, but you should always expect to walk away having learned something. It costs the promoter thousands of dollars to get people into a room, so expect a hard sales pitch. As cost goes up, expect class size to go down. If the event costs $1,000 per day or more, you should expect the admission price to include follow-up training or substantial reference materials.
2. **Pitch.** Some promoters do nothing but pitch, even at $5,000 boot camps. It is insulting to hear a nonstop sales pitch when you are paying $1,000 or more a day.
3. **Refund policy.** Ask if there is an open refund policy. You should be extremely suspicious of any seminar that does not offer a refund policy.
4. **Coaching options.** Many gurus offer mentoring programs as a way to bridge the gap between theory and hands-on practice.

Be wary of paying thousands, only to find your "coach" is a fifteen-dollar-an-hour employee. You should expect some one-on-one time with the guru. If you attend seminars and have never made an offer, then a coaching or mentoring program may be an especially good fit for you. Visit http://www.legalwiz .com/business-coach/ for information on our exclusive coaching program.

No matter what the price of a book, seminar, or training program, it is only worthwhile if you actually put it to use. Study hard, apply yourself, and make offers!

Invest wisely, and build your real-estate assets. As we've mentioned earlier, real estate tends to appreciate over the long haul, at a pace equal to or greater than inflation. Use a variety of fast and long-term cash generation strategies.

Surround yourself with like-minded people. When we wrote *Flipping Properties* in 2001, "flipping" was a little-known term, even though other investors were using similar techniques to acquire and sell properties. Many of the so-called real-estate gurus have given the concept of flipping a bad name. In recent years there have been a number of television shows about flipping. These programs have increased public awareness about short-term real-estate investing, while being both entertaining and, in most cases, informative.

To find like-minded people, join a local real-estate investment association. People in these organizations will help you learn about the investment business and discover for yourself that creative real estate really does work, despite the opinions of self-proclaimed consumer advocates or well-meaning friends. If you cannot find a group nearby, form your own mastermind group that meets for breakfast once a week. If you don't know what a mastermind group is, read about it in *Think and Grow Rich* by Napoleon Hill. For a free copy, visit Flippingbizbook.com.

For your team, look for people who understand your needs, but be wary of individuals who go along with everything you say. Henry Ford would never hire yes-men; he wanted to be challenged by his employees. Many successful businesspeople readily admit they hire people smarter than themselves. Don't be afraid to work with the best mentors out there.

Below are general qualifications and traits to seek when assembling your team:

- **Experience.** You want team members who are knowledgeable about real-estate investment and who have specialized skills in the areas you are not particularly strong in. They should be up-to-date on current methods and trends as well.
- **Reputation.** Surround yourself with ethical people who have a good business reputation. They must be reliable, work well with others, and be committed to your success.
- **Organization.** Efficient team members are effective team members. When you have several team members working on a deal for you, they have to be organized to deliver great results.
- **Communication.** Demand excellent communication both from yourself and your team. A synergetic group openly shares thoughts, ideas, and even bad news. You can't make wise decisions without the facts.
- **Creativity.** Your best team members will have the ability to think creatively. They should offer alternative ways of accomplishing your goals.

Now, we'll suggest specific members you'll need on your team.

Real-estate broker. Many new investors wrongly think that they should avoid working with brokers. We've explained why it's important to work with a good broker—possibly your most important team member when you start flipping houses. Find someone who is willing to share knowledge, someone you get along well with. Chances are you'll spend lots of time together.

Real-estate attorney. Finding the right attorney is difficult because most attorneys are not investors or are unfamiliar with creative real-estate transactions. Most attorneys won't give you the advice you need to structure complex deals or maximize your profits. A good real-estate attorney advises you of the risks and suggests alternative ways of handling a transaction.

Title or escrow company. Working with a competent title or escrow company that understands your needs as a real-estate investor is extremely important. Select a title company that can not only handle conventional transactions but also double closings, seller financing, land contracts, and other types of investor closings. If issues arise in any of these areas, they are experts at solving them and clear your way to the purchase of the property. In addition, though it can be helpful to work with a larger title company with more resources, you'll still need to develop a relationship with your key contact.

Accountant. Many accountants lack experience with complex real-estate transactions. Preparing tax returns is the easy part of the tax equation. The hard (and more important) part is good planning and using aggressive strategies. Choose a CPA or tax lawyer who can expertly help you plan your business's tax strategy. Your accountant may provide bookkeeping services as well, but make sure you will be paying a reasonable fee for those services (not attorney prices).

There a lots of good books about business accounting and the tax implications of real-estate investment. Learn what you can, but work with an expert to make sure you don't make any major mistakes.

Contractors. We've discussed your need to build a complete team for the renovation side of your flipping business. You'll be relying on contractors to do quality work and pay out large sums of money. Be diligent in finding a competent general contractor and affordable workers.

Lenders. Once you start retailing, you may need a hard-money lender to provide cash to fund deals. You'll need to work with your local bank and a mortgage broker to fund longer-term projects and to help potential buyers with their financing needs.

Partners. You'll benefit from having partners and mentors to work with on your deals. After all, cookie cutter deals are rare; every situation is unique. The more you can tap into other people's knowledge and experience, the fewer mistakes you will make.

Partners may be valuable for their credit worthiness for funding a project, for their skills and expertise, for their business contacts, or for a variety of other reasons. Before you choose a partner make sure you have complementary work styles and a thorough understanding of the project or business, including return on investment, duties, communications, and other pertinent items. If your partner will be providing capital, then the funding partner should provide proof of funds.

You will have to share your profits, of course, but your partner's addition to your team may help you leverage your money and time to complete more projects. You may also lose some control. So sometimes hiring the right professional or borrowing money yourself might be a better alternative than splitting profits with a partner.

There are key differences between selecting a partner for a short-term joint venture and for a full-on business you plan to run for many years. For long-term businesses, you need to select the right partner, just like in a marriage. Ideally, work with people in a joint venture or two to confirm that they are a good match for you, then become partners in a long-term business.

Mentor or coach. We can't emphasize enough the importance of having a coach or mentor on your team. A good mentor can make the difference between moving your business forward slowly or driving it ahead quickly.

SHOULD YOU INVEST IN REAL ESTATE FULL TIME?

Many self-acclaimed real-estate gurus recommend that people quit their jobs and immediately jump into full-time real-estate investing. They often claim incredible results from students with little experience. We would like to caution that life-changing decisions are not to be taken lightly and that full-time investing is not for everyone.

PROS AND CONS OF BECOMING A FULL-TIME INVESTOR

Entering the real-estate profession as a full-time commitment offers several advantages over investing part-time. Becoming successful requires you to develop a great depth of real-estate knowledge, and the learning curve will be faster if investing is your primary work. What we call full time may be little as twenty hours a week if you are good at finding deals. And if you are retired or already established, you may not need to earn a lot to support your lifestyle.

Self-employment is not for everyone. You'll need to become a good—or ideally a great—salesperson. Being your own boss means being an accountant, bookkeeper, stock clerk, receptionist, office manager, and errand boy. You'll have to deal with customer service, bills, tax returns, office supplies, and all the other responsibilities that come with running a business. And you won't have a guaranteed salary, paid health insurance, a company car, or a guaranteed retirement plan (although you can certainly start one—see SDIRABook.com). You also take your work-related problems home with you every night.

Sound like fun? It is, once you learn how to manage your time and run your business. It is extremely rewarding to take charge of your life.

PROS AND CONS OF BEING A PART-TIME INVESTOR

One advantage of starting out part-time is that you can maintain your cash flow while learning the business. It may take months to find your first deal. That same deal may take several months to turn around, especially if you decide to fix it and sell it retail. You may also enjoy your current occupation. Many real-estate investors continue with their successful careers. Perhaps you want to experience the excitement of running a side business, or don't want to entrust your financial future to your stockbroker. If so, continue your career and invest in real estate on the side.

On the negative side, a full-time regular job leaves little free time to focus on real estate. But finding a flipping niche and being able to delegate will help compensate for lack of time. As with any education, time spent learning about real estate will require sacrifices yet eventually bring its own rewards.

Once you are making more money flipping properties than in your job, it may be time to quit that job. If you love what you do, however, flipping can be a nice way to support an underpaid but satisfying job. For example, many schoolteachers flip houses during downtime in the summer.

RUNNING YOUR REAL-ESTATE BUSINESS

Many people are intrigued by real estate because of the so-called easy money it promises. Yet becoming an "overnight sensation" in the real-estate business takes at least five years. Most people who buy business or other self-improvement books never finish reading them. More than 90 percent of the people who attend a real-estate seminar quit the real-estate business after three months. It's not easy to take on new challenges, but it is rewarding. We encourage you to be among the 10 percent who invest time and, to some degree, money to become successful real-estate entrepreneurs.

We've given you many techniques to launch your marketing machine. Pick a couple and put them to work for you. Diligence is key to success, regardless of your background. No matter how you do it, remember to follow up on potential deals.

WRAPPING IT UP

- Treat real estate like a business—follow a plan.
- Assemble a team of experts.
- Study, learn, and work with a mentor.
- Take action, and enjoy the journey!

APPENDIX

All of these items can
be downloaded at
FlippingBizBook.com

Sample Ads for Advertising to Buy Houses

Cash for Your House! We buy properties as is, almost any condition or situation. Call (555) 555-1212 or visit www.mywebsite.com.

Do You Have a Problem Property? Back taxes? Needs work? Bad tenants? Kids living rent free? We buy problem properties. Call (555) 555-1212 or visit www.mywebsite.com.

Mortgage Problem? Free advice. Call (555) 555-1212 or visit www.my website.com.

Cash for Keys! We take over house payments. Call (555) 555-1212 or visit www.mywebsite.com.

State Deed Commonly Used

Type of Deed Commonly Used	States
Warranty	Alabama, Alaska, Arizona, Arkansas, Colorado, Connecticut, Delaware, Florida, Georgia, Hawaii, Idaho, Illinois, Indiana, Iowa, Kansas, Louisiana, Maine, Massachusetts, Michigan, Minnesota, Mississippi, Missouri, Montana, Nebraska, New Hampshire, New Mexico, North Carolina, North Dakota, Ohio, Oklahoma, Oregon, Pennsylvania, Rhode Island, South Carolina, South Dakota, Tennessee, Texas, Utah, Vermont, Washington, West Virginia, Wisconsin, Wyoming
Grant	California, Maryland, Nevada
Bargain-and-Sale	District of Columbia, Kentucky, New Jersey, New York, Virginia

Real Estate Phone Script

CALL SHEET

Name _____ Phone Number _____

Spouse or other owner name _____

Source of Lead _____

Property Address _____

Do they own any other property? _____

Bedrooms/Baths _____

Garage _____ Basement _____

Updated? _____

Repairs Needed _____

What do they think it is worth? $_____ Why? _____

What did they pay for it? $_____ When? _____

What is YOUR ARV? $_____ What are the price ranges of the area? _____

(Softener—"Mr Seller is it OK if I ask you some personal questions, so I can get the complete picture of your situation and offer you the best solution possible?")

What do they owe? $_____ Is there more than one mortgage? _____

Payments on the first $ _____ Second $_____

Interest rate on the first _____% Second _____% Any other liens?_____

Current? _____ If not, arrears $_____

Foreclosure filed? _____ Sale Date? _____

Taxes and insurance $_____ Escrowed in pmt? _____

HOA dues $_____ Monthly/Annually _____

Are you flexible on price? _____ Are you open to creative offers? _____

Is the property listed? _____ When does the listing expire? _____

Appointment (use alternate days/times) _____

Should I bring a contract with me? (response) _____

Is there anyone else they could recommend who needs help? _____

PROBING QUESTIONS

How long have you been trying to sell?

What other alternative have you considered?

Have you listed it with a real-estate broker—why/why not?

If I had a magic wand, and I could give you an ideal situation, what would it be?

(If they insist on cash) What are your plans for the proceeds of the sale?

Do you think your property would be a good investment for me? In what way?

If I see the property is there anything I will see that I won't like?

TEST CLOSE QUESTIONS

Would you be interested in a scenario where you get regular monthly income and the highest price possible for your house?

By the way, when would you like me to make you a written offer?

When do you need to close by (and why)?

(If they have no equity) Are you willing to sell the property to me basically for what you owe?

(If they are behind in payments) Would you be open to me making up your back payments, taking over the property, and keep improving your credit?

Sample Promo E-mails to Real-Estate Brokers

E-MAIL TO BUYER'S BROKER:

Dear Nancy,

I want to earn you regular commissions by buying lots of houses through you. I am a seasoned real-estate investor with access to cash and can close quickly with very little hassle. I do not need you to drive me around looking at houses, I can do that on my own. What I need from you is to let me know when you see a good deal, whether on the MLS or not. Please call me at (555) 555-1212 right away so we can discuss the parameters of what kinds of deals I am looking for.

Sincerely,

William Bronchick

P.S. I may also need a broker to list the properties on the backend when I sell them!

E-MAIL TO LISTING BROKER:

Dear Bob,

I want to earn you FULL commissions on your listings. I am a seasoned real-estate investor with access to cash and can close quickly with very little hassle. I do not need you to drive me around looking at houses, I can do that on my own. What I need from you is to let me know when you see a good deal you have listed, whether on the MLS or not. Please call me at (555) 555-1212 right away so we can discuss the parameters of what kinds of deals I am looking for.

Sincerely,

Bobby Dahlstrom

P.S. I may also need a broker to list the properties on the backend when I sell them!

Sample Postcard Ad

CASH FOR YOUR HOUSE!
Any Area, Any Condition

Do you own a problem house and need to sell now?

- Does your house need repairs?
- Are you behind in mortgage or tax payments?
- Are you relocating for a new job?

- Kids living rent-free?
- No equity and can't refi?
- Estate property?

We Buy Problem Houses!

- We can pay **CASH** and close QUICKLY!
- We can evict bad tenants

- We can do necessary repairs
- We can take over **PAYMENTS**!

CALL TODAY! *All inquiries are kept strictly confidential.*
We are not real-estate agents—we don't list houses.

Call Bill Bronchick at Universal Property Holdings, LLC   Toll Free: (888) 555-1212

Sample Letters to Homeowners—Handwritten

January 14, 2017

Dear Rick,

My wife and I are looking to buy a home in Shady Acre Estates and we happened upon your property. It appears to be exactly what we are looking to buy. Should you wish to sell in the near future, please call me right away on my cell at (555) 555-1212 so we can make you an offer. We are looking to move quickly on this.

Sincerely,

Bobby Dahlstrom

P.S. — If you prefer e-mail, my address is BDahlstrom12@gmail.com.

Sample Letters to Homeowners—Typewritten

UNIVERSAL PROPERTY HOLDINGS, LLC
333 Main Street | Anytown, USA
Tel (888) 555-1212

January 15, 2017

Mr. David Parker
123 Anywhere Street
Anytown, USA

Re: Purchase Offer on 345 Elm Street

Dear Mr. Parker,

Our company is a private real-estate equity firm that purchases houses in the Anytown area, particularly in Shady Acres Estates subdivision. We came across your house at 345 Elm Street and are interested in making you a cash offer.

We can close quickly and acquire the house "as is," with no repairs required on your part. We deal honestly and fairly with all of our clients, and you can expect the same treatment on our transaction.

Please call me at (888) 555-1212 right away so we can discuss price and terms of the offer on your property.

Sincerely,
William Bronchick

P.S. I must disclose that I am a licensed real-estate broker, but not interested in listing your home. My firm is interested in buying it for ourselves.

Sample Door Hanger

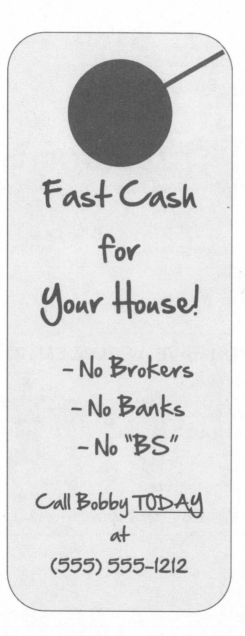

Sample Business Card

Front of Card

 Bob Smith, CEO

TruVestor, Inc.

"Truth in Real Estate...for a change"

8865 Broadway Suite 354
Highlands Ranch, CO 83721

Tel 303-336-3847
e-mail: bsmith@truvestor.com

Back of Card

DO YOU HAVE A PROBLEM HOUSE?

Needs work?
Behind in payments?
Back taxes?
Bad tenants?
Divorce?
Estate?
Kids living rent free?

We Buy Problem Houses!

Websites with Real-Estate Investing Discussion Forums

- CREOnline.com
- REIClub.com
- MrLandlord.com
- BiggerPockets.com
- Zillow.com
- DealmakersCafe.com
- MyREINspace.com

Appraisal Form

You can download and review the full version of this form here:
www.fanniemae.com/content/guide_form/1004.pdf

Uniform Residential Appraisal Report   File

The purpose of this summary appraisal report is to provide the lender/client with an accurate, and adequately supported, opinion of the market value of the subject property.

SUBJECT

Property Address		City		State	Zip Code
Borrower	Owner of Public Record		County		

Legal Description

Assessor's Parcel #		Tax Year	R.E. Taxes $

Neighborhood Name		Map Reference	Census Tract

Occupant ☐ Owner ☐ Tenant ☐ Vacant   Special Assessments $ ☐ PUD   HOA $ ☐ per year ☐ per month

Property Rights Appraised ☐ Fee Simple ☐ Leasehold ☐ Other (describe)

Assignment Type ☐ Purchase Transaction ☐ Refinance Transaction ☐ Other (describe)

Lender/Client   Address

Is the subject property currently offered for sale or has it been offered for sale in the twelve months prior to the effective date of this appraisal? ☐ Yes ☐ No

Report data source(s) used, offering price(s), and date(s).

CONTRACT

I ☐ did ☐ did not analyze the contract for sale for the subject purchase transaction. Explain the results of the analysis of the contract for sale or why the analysis was not performed.

Contract Price $ Date of Contract   Is the property seller the owner of public record? ☐ Yes ☐ No Data Source(s)

Is there any financial assistance (loan charges, sale concessions, gift or downpayment assistance, etc.) to be paid by any party on behalf of the borrower? ☐ Yes ☐ No
If Yes, report the total dollar amount and describe the items to be paid.

NEIGHBORHOOD

Note: Race and the racial composition of the neighborhood are not appraisal factors.

Neighborhood Characteristics			One-Unit Housing Trends			One-Unit Housing		Present Land Use %	
Location ☐ Urban ☐ Suburban ☐ Rural			Property Values ☐ Increasing ☐ Stable ☐ Declining			PRICE	AGE	One-Unit	%
Built-Up ☐ Over 75% ☐ 25-75% ☐ Under 25%			Demand/Supply ☐ Shortage ☐ In Balance ☐ Over Supply			$ (000)	(yrs)	2-4 Unit	%
Growth ☐ Rapid ☐ Stable ☐ Slow			Marketing Time ☐ Under 3 mths ☐ 3-6 mths ☐ Over 6 mths			Low		Multi-Family	%
Neighborhood Boundaries						High		Commercial	%
						Pred.		Other	%

Neighborhood Description

Market Conditions (including support for the above conclusions)

SITE

Dimensions		Area	Shape		View

Specific Zoning Classification   Zoning Description

Zoning Compliance ☐ Legal ☐ Legal Nonconforming (Grandfathered Use) ☐ No Zoning ☐ Illegal (describe)

Is the highest and best use of the subject property as improved (or as proposed per plans and specifications) the present use? ☐ Yes ☐ No If No, describe

Utilities	Public	Other (describe)		Public	Other (describe)	Off-site Improvements—Type	Public	Private
Electricity	☐	☐	Water	☐	☐	Street	☐	☐
Gas	☐	☐	Sanitary Sewer	☐	☐	Alley	☐	☐

FEMA Special Flood Hazard Area ☐ Yes ☐ No FEMA Flood Zone   FEMA Map #   FEMA Map Date

Are the utilities and off-site improvements typical for the market area? ☐ Yes ☐ No If No, describe

Are there any adverse site conditions or external factors (easements, encroachments, environmental conditions, land uses, etc.)? ☐ Yes ☐ No If Yes, describe

IMPROVEMENTS

General Description		Foundation		Exterior Description	materials/condition	Interior	materials/condition
Units ☐ One ☐ One with Accessory Unit		☐ Concrete Slab ☐ Crawl Space		Foundation Walls		Floors	
# of Stories		☐ Full Basement ☐ Partial Basement		Exterior Walls		Walls	
Type ☐ Det. ☐ Att. ☐ S-Det./End Unit		Basement Area sq. ft.		Roof Surface		Trim/Finish	
☐ Existing ☐ Proposed ☐ Under Const.		Basement Finish %		Gutters & Downspouts		Bath Floor	
Design (Style)		☐ Outside Entry/Exit ☐ Sump Pump		Window Type		Bath Wainscot	
Year Built		Evidence of ☐ Infestation		Storm Sash/Insulated		Car Storage ☐ None	
Effective Age (Yrs)		☐ Dampness ☐ Settlement		Screens		☐ Driveway # of Cars	
Attic ☐ None		Heating ☐ FWA ☐ HWBB ☐ Radiant	Amenities		☐ Woodstove(s) #	Driveway Surface	
☐ Drop Stair ☐ Stairs		☐ Other Fuel		☐ Fireplace(s) #	☐ Fence	☐ Garage # of Cars
☐ Floor ☐ Scuttle		Cooling ☐ Central Air Conditioning		☐ Patio/Deck	☐ Porch	☐ Carport # of Cars
☐ Finished ☐ Heated		☐ Individual ☐ Other		☐ Pool	☐ Other	☐ Att. ☐ Det. ☐ Built-in

Appliances ☐ Refrigerator ☐ Range/Oven ☐ Dishwasher ☐ Disposal ☐ Microwave ☐ Washer/Dryer ☐ Other (describe)

Finished area above grade contains: Rooms   Bedrooms   Bath(s)   Square Feet of Gross Living Area Above Grade

Additional features (special energy efficient items, etc.)

Describe the condition of the property (including needed repairs, deterioration, renovations, remodeling, etc.).

Are there any physical deficiencies or adverse conditions that affect the livability, soundness, or structural integrity of the property? ☐ Yes ☐ No If Yes, describe

Does the property generally conform to the neighborhood (functional utility, style, condition, use, construction, etc.)? ☐ Yes ☐ No If No, describe

Hard Money Loan Checklist

Submit the following information for your hard money loan:

- ☐ Fannie Mae form 1003 loan application
- ☐ Purchase contract
- ☐ Comps or appraisal (showing "as is" and after-repaired value)
- ☐ Property inspection report
- ☐ Your bio and/or resume
- ☐ A summary of your real estate experience
- ☐ Contact information of the "players"
    - a. Real estate brokers
    - b. Contractors
    - c. Closing agent
    - d. Insurance agent
    - e. Attorney
- ☐ Map to the property
- ☐ Detailed scope of work for the rehab
- ☐ Lots of pictures!
- ☐ Your corporate documents (if you are taking title in a corporate entity at closing)
- ☐ Spreadsheet showing a detailed breakdown of the transaction:
    - a. Acquisition price
    - b. Closing costs on acquisition
    - c. Loan costs
    - d. Carrying costs
    - e. Rehab costs
    - f. Misc. expenses
    - g. Resale price
    - h. Closing costs on resale
    - i. Broker's fees
    - j. Seller concessions
    - k. Net profit

Joint Venture Agreement— Fix and Flip

JOINT VENTURE AGREEMENT

AGREEMENT, made _____, 20_____, between _____ ("First Party"), having an address at _____, and _____ ("Second Party") having an address at _____ _____ collectively hereinafter referred to as "Venturers").

WITNESSETH:

WHEREAS, the first party has investment capital available for contribution to the joint venture, and

WHEREAS, The second party has a purchase contract to certain real estate located at _____ ("the Property"), and

WHEREAS each of the parties desires to own one-half undivided interest in the subject property described below and the parties have agreed to limitations upon the right and power to transfer their undivided interests and have also agreed upon the payment of expenses, delegation of responsibility and the distribution of profits and/or losses incurred with reference to the property, and

WHEREAS, it is the desires of the parties to define and set out their relationship in writing and the circumstances under which they are operating, as of the date of this Agreement.

NOW THEREFORE, in consideration oft he mutual covenants herein after contained the parties agree as follows:

1. Formation

The parties hereby enter into and form a joint venture (the "Joint Venture") for the purposes and the period and upon the terms and conditions hereinafter set forth. This Joint Venture in the real estate to be purchased by the parties shall be defined solely by this agreement, regardless of the manner in which title to property may be taken.

This agreement is not intended to create a general partnership between the parties.

The parties represent and warrant that there are no suits, judgments or liens of any kind pending or file against him/her whether individually of in conjunction with any person or entity in any jurisdiction whatsoever.

2. Purposes

The purpose of this Joint Venture is to purchase the real property located at _____ for the purpose of repairing, renovating, and selling it as expeditiously possible and to carry on any and all such other activities as may be necessary to accomplish the above described purpose of the joint venture, to incur indebtedness, secured and unsecured; to construct improvements on the Property; to mortgage, finance, refinance, encumber, lease, sell, exchange, convey, transfer or otherwise deal with or dispose of the Property; to enter into and perform contracts and agreements of any kind necessary to, in connection with or incidental to the business of the Joint Venture; and to carry on any other activities necessary to, in connection with or incidental to the foregoing, as the Venturers in their discretion may deem desirable. As used in this Agreement, the term "mortgage" includes any mortgage, deed of trust, mortgage deed or other similar instrument. Each of the parties irrevocably waives any and all right that he may have to maintain any action for partition with respect to his undivided interest in the Property or to compel any sale of the Property under any law now existing or hereafter enacted. The parties agree that title to the Property will be taken in the following manner (choose one):

_____ In trust with the Venturers as Beneficiaries and Trustees

_____ As Tenants in Common between the respective parties

_____ Solely in the name of _____.

The Venturers are hereby authorized to cause the Joint Venture to acquire the Property pursuant to that certain Contract of Sale, dated _____, 20_____, between _____ as seller and First Party as purchaser, or for a purchase price and upon such other terms and conditions as the Venturers may deem appropriate. The Venturers are authorized to execute and deliver such instruments and to take any and all actions as the Venturers may deem necessary or desirable to acquire the Property.

3. Term

The Term of the Joint Venture shall commence on the date first above written and shall continue until the purpose for which the Joint Venture was created, unless sooner terminated as hereinafter provided, but not later than 60 days after the sale of the Property and accounting and distribution of the proceeds.

4. Capital Contributions

First Party shall contribute all money needed to purchase, repair, maintain, advertise, market and incur any other expenses as well as any mortgage payments that become due during the period of ownership of the subject property as well as qualifying for any financing.

Second Party shall not be required to contribute any capital, except _____
_____
_____.

Except as specifically provided in this Agreement or required by law, no Venturer shall have the right to withdraw or reduce his contributions to the capital of the Joint Venture until the termination of the Joint Venture. No Venturer shall have the right to demand and receive any distribution from the Joint Venture in any form other than cash, regardless of the nature of such Venturer's capital contribution. No Venturer shall be paid interest on capital contributions to the Joint Venture.

A checking account will be opened before closing of the Property at _____ Bank with $_____ deposited to cover immediate needs that are reimbursing down payment costs to Second Party and to cover closing costs for acquisition of the Property. Checks under $_____ only require one signature of the parties. Checks over $_____ need both signatures of the parties. The balance of the estimated costs will be deposited when contractor has submitted his repair estimate and approved by both parties. Both parties have agreed that the estimate for all costs is approximately $_____.

5. Loans and Advances by Venturers

If any Venturer shall loan or advance any funds to the Joint Venture in excess of the capital contribution of such Venturer prescribed herein, such loan or advance shall not be deemed a capital contribution to the Joint Venture and shall not in any respect increase such Venturer's interest in the Joint Venture.

6. Allocations and Distributions

As used in this Agreement, the terms "net profits" and "net losses" shall mean the profits or losses of the Joint Venture from the conduct of the Joint Venture's business, after all expenses incurred in connection therewith have been paid or provided for, including any allowance for depreciation or amortization of the cost of the Property.

The term "cash receipts" shall mean all cash receipts of the Joint Venture from whatever source derived, including without limitation capital contributions made by the Venturers; the proceeds of any sale, exchange, condemnation or other disposition of all or any part of the Property or other assets of the Joint Venture; the proceeds of any loan to the Joint Venture; the proceeds of any mortgage or refinancing of any mortgage on all or any part of the Property or other assets of the Joint Venture; the proceeds of any insurance policy for fire or other casualty damage payable to the Joint Venture; and the proceeds from the liquidation of the Property or other assets of the Joint Venture following a termination of the Joint Venture.

The term "capital transactions" shall mean any of the following: the sale of all or any part of the Property or other assets of the Joint Venture or interests therein; the refinancing or recasting of mortgages or other liabilities of the Joint Venture; the condemnation of the Property to the extent the award is not used for restoration; the receipt of insurance proceeds; and any other similar or extraordinary receipts or proceeds which in accordance with generally accepted accounting principles are attributable to capital, including transactions in connection with the termination and dissolution of the Joint Venture.

The "capital account" for each Venturer shall mean the account established, determined and maintained for such Venturer in accordance with Section 704(b) of the Internal Revenue Code and Treasury Regulation Section 1.704-1(b)(2)(iv). The capital account for each Venturer shall be **increased by** (1) the amount of money contributed by such Venturer to the Joint Venture, (2) the fair market value of property contributed by such Venturer to the Joint Venture (net of liabilities secured by such contributed property that the Joint Venture is considered to assume or take subject to under Section 752 of the Internal Revenue Code), and (3) allocations to such Venturer of Joint Venture income and gain (or items thereof), including income and gain exempt from tax and income and gain described in Trea. Reg. Section 1.704-1(b)(2)(iv)(g), but excluding income and gain described in subsection (b)(4)(i) of said Regulation, and shall be **decreased by** (4) the amount of money distributed to such Venturer by the Joint Venture, (5) the fair market value of property distributed to such Venturer by the Joint Venture (net of liabilities secured by such distributed property that such Venturer is considered to assume or take subject to under Section 752 of the Code), (6) allocations to such Venturer of expenditures of the Joint Venture described in Section 705(a)(2)(B) of the Code, and (7) allocations of Joint Venture loss and deduction (or items thereof) including loss and deduction described in Trea. Reg. Section 1.704-1(b)(2)(iv)(g), but excluding items described in (6) above and loss or deduction described in subsections (b)(4)(i) or (b)(4)(iii) of said Regulation. Net profits and net losses of the Joint Venture from other than capital transactions, as of the end of any fiscal year or other period, shall be credited or charged to the capital accounts of the Venturers prior to any charge or credit to said capital accounts for net profits and net losses of the Joint Venture from capital transactions as of the end of such fiscal year or other period. The capital account for each Venturer shall be otherwise adjusted in accordance with the additional rules of Trea. Reg. Section 1.704-1(b)(2)(iv).

The term "Venturers' Percentage Interests" shall mean the percentages set forth opposite the name of each Venturer below:

Venturers   Percentage Interest

First Party -- 50 percent
Second Party -- 50 percent

During each fiscal year, the net profits and net losses of the Joint Venture (other than from capital transactions), and each item of income, gain, loss, deduction or credit entering into the computation thereof, shall be credited or charged, as the case may be, to the capital accounts of each Venturer in proportion to the Venturers' Percentage Interests. The net profits of the Joint Venture from capital transactions shall be allocated in the following order of priority: (a) to offset any negative balance in the capital accounts of the Venturers in proportion to the amounts of the negative balance in their respective capital accounts, until all negative balances in the capital accounts have been eliminated; then (b) to the Venturers in proportion to the Venturers' Percentage Interests. The net losses of the Joint Venture from capital transactions shall be allocated in the following order of priority: (a) to the extent that the balances in the capital accounts of any Venturers are in excess of their original contributions, to such Venturers in proportion to such excess balances in the capital accounts until all such excess balances have been reduced to zero; then (b) to the Venturers in proportion to the Venturers' Percentage Interests.

The cash receipts of the Joint Venture shall be applied in the following order of priority: (a) to the payment by the Joint Venture of interest or amortization on any mortgages on the Property, amounts due on debts and liabilities of the Joint Venture other than to any Venturer, costs of the construction of the improvements to the Property, and operating expenses of the Joint Venture; (b) to the payment of interest and amortization due on any loan made to the Joint Venture by any Venturer; (c) to the establishment of cash reserves determined by the Venturers to be necessary or appropriate, including without limitation reserves for the operation of the Joint Venture's business, construction, repairs, replacements, taxes and contingencies; and (d) to the repayment of any loans made to the Joint Venture by any Venturer. Thereafter, the cash receipts of the Joint Venture shall be distributed among the Venturers as hereafter provided.

Except as otherwise provided in this Agreement or required by law, distributions of cash receipts of the Joint Venture, other than from capital transactions, shall be allocated among the Venturers in proportion to the Venturers' Percentage Interests.

Except as otherwise provided in this Agreement or required by law, distributions of cash receipts from capital transactions shall be allocated in the following order of priority: (a) to the Venturers in proportion to their respective capital accounts until each Venturer has received cash distributions equal to any positive balance in his capital account; then (b) to the Venturers in proportion to the Venturers' Percentage Interests.

Special Allocations -- Notwithstanding the preceding provisions of this Article 8, the following special allocations shall be made in the following order:

(1) Minimum Gain Chargeback -- Except as otherwise provided in Trea. Reg. Section 1.704-2(f), if there is a net decrease in partnership minimum gain (within the meaning of Trea. Reg. Sections 1.704-2(b)(2) and 1.704-2(d)) during any fiscal year, each Venturer shall be allocated items of the Joint Venture's income and gain for such fiscal year (and, if necessary, subsequent fiscal years) in an amount equal to such Venturer's share of the net decrease in partnership minimum gain, determined in accordance with Trea. Reg. Section 1.704-2(g). Allocations made pursuant to the preceding sentence shall be made in proportion to the respective amounts required to be allocated to each Venturer pursuant thereto. The items to be so allocated shall be determined in accordance with Trea. Reg. Sections 1.704-2(f)(6) and 1.704-2(j)(2). This provision is intended to comply with the minimum gain chargeback requirement in Trea. Reg. Section 1.704-2(f) and shall be interpreted consistently therewith.

(2) Partner Minimum Gain Chargeback -- Except as otherwise provided in Trea. Reg. Section 1.704-2(i)(4), if there is a net decrease in partner nonrecourse debt minimum gain attributable to a partner nonrecourse debt during any fiscal year, each Venturer who has a share of the partner nonrecourse debt minimum gain attributable to such partner nonrecourse debt, determined in accordance with Trea. Reg. Section 1.704.2(i)(5), shall be allocated items of the Joint Venture's income and gain for such fiscal year (and, if necessary, subsequent fiscal years) in an amount equal to such Venturer's share of the net decrease in partner nonrecourse debt minimum gain attributable to such partner nonrecourse debt, determined in accordance with Trea. Reg. Section 1.704-2(i)(4). Allocations made pursuant to the preceding sentence shall be made in proportion to the respective amounts required to be allocated to each Venturer pursuant thereto. The items to be so allocated shall be determined in accordance with Trea. Reg. Sections 1.704-2(i)(4) and 1.704-2(j)(2). As used herein, "partner nonrecourse debt" has the meaning set forth in Trea. Reg. Section 1.704-2(b)(4). As used herein, "partner nonrecourse debt minimum gain" shall mean an amount, with respect to each partner nonrecourse debt, equal to the partnership minimum gain (within the meaning of Trea. Reg. Sections 1.704-2(b)(2) and 1.704-2(d)) that would result if such partner nonrecourse debt were treated as a nonrecourse liability (within the meaning of Trea. Reg. Section 1.704-2(b)(3)) determined in accordance with Trea. Reg. Section 1.704-2(i)(3). This provision is intended to comply with the minimum gain chargeback requirement in Trea. Reg. Section 1.704-2(i)(4) and shall be interpreted consistently therewith.

(3) Qualified Income Offset -- In the event any Venturer unexpectedly receives any adjustments, allocations or distributions described in Trea. Reg. Sections 1.704-1(b)(2)(ii)(d)(4), (5) or (6), items of the Joint Venture's income and gain

shall be allocated to such Venturer in an amount and manner sufficient to eliminate, to the extent required by the Regulations, any adjusted capital account deficit in such Venturer's capital account, as quickly as possible, provided that an allocation pursuant to this provision shall be made only if and to the extent that such Venturer would have an adjusted capital account deficit in such Venturer's capital account after all other allocations provided for in this Article 8 have been tentatively made as if this provision were not in this Agreement. As used herein, "adjusted capital account deficit" shall mean the deficit balance, if any, in a Venturer's capital account at the end of the relevant fiscal year after the following adjustments: (i) credit to such capital account the minimum gain chargeback which the Venturer is obligated to restore pursuant to the penultimate sentences of Trea. Reg. Sections 1.704-2(g)(1) and 1.704-2(i)(5); and (ii) debit to such capital account the items described in Trea. Reg. Sections 1.704-1(b)(2)(ii)(d)(4), (5) and (6). This provision is intended to constitute a qualified income offset within the meaning of Trea. Reg. Section 1.704-1(b)(2)(ii)(d) and shall be interpreted consistently therewith.

(4) Gross Income Allocation -- In the event any Venturer has a deficit capital account at the end of any fiscal year which is in excess of the sum of the amounts such Venturer is deemed to be obligated to restore pursuant to the penultimate sentences of Trea. Reg. Sections 1.704-2(g)(1) and 1.704-2(i)(5), each such Venturer shall be allocated items of the Joint Venture's income and gain in the amount of such excess as quickly as possible, provided that an allocation pursuant to this provision shall be made only if and to the extent that such Venturer would have a deficit in such Venturer's capital account in excess of such sum after all other allocations provided for in this Article 8 have been tentatively made as if this provision and the provisions of clause (3) above were not in this Agreement.

(5) Nonrecourse Deductions -- Nonrecourse deductions (within the meaning of Trea. Reg. Section 1.704-2(b)(1)) for any fiscal year shall be allocated among the Venturers in proportion to the Venturers' Percentage Interests.

(6) Partner Nonrecourse Deductions -- Any partner nonrecourse deductions (within the meaning of Trea. Reg. Sections 1.704-2(b)(1) and 1.704-2(b)(2)) for any fiscal year shall be allocated to the Venturer who bears the economic risk of loss with respect to the partner nonrecourse debt (within the meaning of Trea. Reg. Section 1.704-2(b)(4)) to which such partner nonrecourse deductions are attributable in accordance with Trea. Reg. Section 1.704-2(i)(1).

(7) Other Mandatory Allocations -- In the event Section 704(c) of the Internal Revenue Code or the Regulations thereunder require allocations in a manner different than that set forth above in this Article 8, the provisions of Section 704(c) and the Regulations thereunder shall control such allocations among the Venturers.

It is the intention of the Venturers that the allocations hereunder shall be deemed to have "substantial economic effect" within the meaning of Section 704 of the Internal Revenue Code and Trea. Reg. Section 1.704-1. Should the provisions of this Agreement be inconsistent with or in conflict with Section 704 of the Code or the Regulations thereunder, then Section 704 of the Code and the Regulations shall be deemed to override the contrary provisions hereof. If Section 704 or the Regulations at any time require that partnership agreements contain provisions which are not expressly set forth herein, such provisions shall be incorporated into this Agreement by reference and shall be deemed a part of this Agreement to the same extent as though they had been expressly set forth herein, and the Venturers shall amend the terms of this Agreement to add such provisions, and any such amendment shall be retroactive to whatever extent required to create allocations with a substantial economic effect.

11. Management of the Joint Venture

The business and affairs of the Joint Venture shall be conducted and managed by the Venturers in accordance with this Agreement and the laws of _____.

Except as expressly provided elsewhere in this Agreement, all decisions respecting the management, operation and control of the business and affairs of the Joint Venture and all determinations made in accordance with this Agreement shall be made by the affirmative vote or consent of Venturers holding a majority of the Venturers' Percentage Interests.

The Venturers shall devote such time and attention as the Venturers deem necessary to the conduct and management of the business and affairs of the Joint Venture.

During the existence of the joint venture the parties shall be solely responsible for performing the following duties:

(A) The first party shall contribute all monies needed to purchase, repair, maintain, advertise, market and any other expenses as well as mortgage payments that become due during the period of ownership of the subject property as well as qualifying for any necessary financing.

(B) The second party shall be solely responsible for the day-to-day management maintenance, renovation and marketing of the subject property for resale, thereby protecting the investment for both parties. The second party my make, at his sole option and expense, make alterations and improvements to the property as in her discretion are necessary and advisable.

Subject to the conditions and limitations but without limitation otherwise set forth herein and to the requirements of nay law or administrative enactment applicable here to, Second party shall:

(i) Review and research references, credentials and licenses if applicable of any contractor or repairmen which are chosen to perform repairs and renovations on the subject property.

(ii) Negotiate and contract, on behalf of the Joint Venture, with contractor and repairmen to provide services and supervise said contractor and repairmen and their work at subject property. Funds are to be allocated to contractor on a percentage of completion as deemed necessary with any initial percentage payment exceeding _____% to be approved by first party in writing.

(iii) Purchase all materials, supplies and equipment as needed for the property maintenance, repair and renovations and operation of the subject property in a cost effective manner.

(iv) Endeavor to keep monthly expenses at a minimum by pursing effective methods and procedures of cost reduction and control and advise first party on cast saving initiatives.

(v) Obtain all necessary lien releases from contractor and repairmen for payments made for work performed on the subject property.

(vi) Routinely and regularly inspect the subject property and make recommendation to the first party regarding the management, repair and marketing of the subject property

(vii) Communicate with first party on not less than a weekly basis on progress by emailing or faxing statement of expenses outlaid and general progress report.

(viii) Cause to be kept books of account in which shall be entered fully and accurately each and every transaction of the joint venture including bills paid and mortgage paid.

In the event litigation results from or arises out of this agreement or the performance thereof due to the action, inaction or default of wither party, the prevailing party shall be entitled to costs and attorneys fees which may be deducted from the profits of the other.

Each of the Venturers shall have authority to execute instruments on behalf of the Joint Venture.

The Joint Venture shall purchase insurance against loss or damage to the Property by fire or other risks embraced by extended coverage, in amounts sufficient to prevent the Joint Venture from becoming a co-insurer, and shall maintain such other hazard and liability insurance against such risks and in such amounts as customarily is maintained for similar properties in the vicinity of the Property.

The Venturers shall receive, as compensation for the services of the Venturers to the Joint Venture, such sums as may be determined from time to time by the affirmative vote or consent of Venturers holding a majority of the Venturers' Percentage Interests.

12. Assignment of Joint Venture Interests

Except as otherwise provided in this Agreement, no Venturer or other person holding any interest in the Joint Venture may assign, pledge, hypothecate, transfer or otherwise dispose of all or any part of his interest in the Joint Venture, including without limitation the capital, profits or distributions of the Joint Venture without the prior written consent of the other Venturers in each instance.

The Venturers agree that no Venturer may voluntarily withdraw from the Joint Venture without the unanimous vote or consent of the Venturers.

A Venturer may assign all or any part of such Venturer's interest in the allocations and distributions of the Joint Venture to any of the following (collectively the "permitted assignees"): any person, corporation, partnership or other entity as to which the Joint Venture has given consent to the assignment of such interest in the allocations and distributions of the Joint Venture by the affirmative vote or consent of Venturers holding a majority of the Venturers' Percentage Interests. An assignment to a permitted assignee shall only entitle the permitted assignee to the allocations and distributions to which the assigned interest is entitled, unless such permitted assignee applies for admission to the Joint Venture and is admitted to the Joint Venture as a Venturer in accordance with this Agreement.

An assignment, pledge, hypothecation, transfer or other disposition of all or any part of the interest of a Venturer in the Joint Venture in violation of the provisions hereof shall be null and void for all purposes.

No assignment, transfer or other disposition of all or any part of the interest of any Venturer permitted under this Agreement shall be binding upon the Joint Venture unless and until a duly executed and acknowledged counterpart of such assignment or instrument of transfer, in form and substance satisfactory to the Joint Venture, has been delivered to the Joint Venture.

No assignment or other disposition of any interest of any Venturer may be made if such assignment or disposition, alone or when combined with other transactions, would result in the termination of the Joint Venture within the meaning of Section 708 of the Internal Revenue Code or under any other relevant section of the Code or any successor statute. No assignment or other disposition of any interest of any Venturer may be made without an opinion of counsel satisfactory to the Joint Venture that such assignment or disposition is subject to an effective registration under, or exempt from the registration requirements of, the applicable federal and state securities laws. No interest in the Joint Venture may be assigned or given to any person below the age of 21 years or to a person who has been adjudged to be insane or incompetent.

Anything herein contained to the contrary, the Joint Venture shall be entitled to treat the record holder of the interest of a Venturer as the absolute owner thereof, and shall incur no liability by reason of distributions made in good faith to such record holder, unless and until there has been delivered to the Joint Venture the assignment or other instrument of transfer and such other evidence as may be reasonably required by the Joint Venture to establish to the satisfaction of the Joint Venture that an interest has been assigned or transferred in accordance with this Agreement.

13. Admission of New Venturers

The Venturers may admit new Venturers (or transferees of any interests of existing Venturers) into the Joint Venture by the unanimous vote or consent of the Venturers.

As a condition to the admission of a new Venturer, such Venturer shall execute and acknowledge such instruments, in form and substance satisfactory to the Joint Venture, as the Joint Venture may deem necessary or desirable to effectuate such admission and to confirm the agreement of such Venturer to be bound by all of the terms, covenants and conditions of this Agreement, as the same may have been amended. Such new Venturer shall pay all reasonable expenses in connection with such admission, including without limitation reasonable attorneys' fees and the cost of the preparation, filing or publication of any amendment to this Agreement or any registrations or filings of the Joint Venture, which the Joint Venture may deem necessary or desirable in connection with such admission.

No new Venturer shall be entitled to any retroactive allocation of income, losses, or expense deductions of the Joint Venture. The Joint Venture may make pro rata allocations of income, losses or expense deductions to a new Venturer for that portion of the tax year in which the Venturer was admitted in accordance with Section 706(d) of the Internal Revenue Code and regulations thereunder.

In no event shall a new Venturer be admitted to the Joint Venture if such admission would be in violation of applicable federal or state securities laws or would adversely affect the treatment of the Joint Venture as a partnership for income tax purposes.

14. Withdrawal Events Regarding Venturers and Election to Continue the Venture

In the event of the death, retirement, withdrawal, expulsion, or dissolution of a Venturer, or an event of bankruptcy or insolvency, as hereinafter defined, with respect to a Venturer, or the occurrence of any other event which terminates the continued membership of a Venturer in the Joint Venture pursuant to the laws of _____ (each of the foregoing being hereinafter referred to as a "Withdrawal Event"), the Joint Venture shall terminate sixty days after notice to the Venturers of such Withdrawal Event unless the business of the Joint Venture is continued as hereinafter provided.

Notwithstanding a Withdrawal Event with respect to a Venturer, the Joint Venture shall not terminate, irrespective of applicable law, if within aforesaid sixty day period the remaining Venturers, by the unanimous vote or consent of the Venturers (other than the Venturer who caused the Withdrawal Event), shall elect to continue the business of the Joint Venture.

In the event of a Withdrawal Event with respect to any Venturer, any successor in interest to such Venturer (including without limitation any executor, administrator, heir, committee, guardian, or other representative or successor) shall not become entitled to any rights or interest of such Venturer in the Joint Venture, other than the allocations and distributions to which such Venturer is entitled, unless such successor in interest is admitted as a Venturer in accordance with this Agreement.

An "event of bankruptcy or insolvency" with respect to a Venturer shall occur if such Venturer: applies for or consents to the appointment of a receiver, trustee or liquidator of all or a substantial part of his assets; or makes a general assignment for the benefit of creditors; or is adjudicated a bankrupt or an insolvent; or files a voluntary petition in bankruptcy or a petition or an answer seeking an arrangement with creditors or to take advantage of any bankruptcy, insolvency, readjustment of debt or similar law or statute, or an answer admitting the material allegations of a petition filed against him in any bankruptcy, insolvency, readjustment of debt or similar proceedings; or takes any action for the purpose of effecting any of the foregoing; or an order, judgment or decree shall be entered, with or without the application, approval or consent of such Venturer, by any court of competent jurisdiction, approving a petition for or appointing a receiver or trustee of all or a substantial part of the assets of such Venturer, and such order, judgment or decree shall continue unstayed and in effect for thirty days.

15. Dissolution and Liquidation

The Joint Venture shall terminate upon the occurrence of any of the following: the expiration of the period fixed for the duration of the Joint Venture pursuant to Article 5, as the same may be extended by the Venturers; the election by the Venturers to dissolve the Joint Venture made by the unanimous vote or consent of the Venturers; the occurrence of a Withdrawal Event with respect to a Venturer and the failure of the remaining Venturers to elect to continue the business of the Joint Venture as provided for in Article 14 above; or any other event which pursuant to this Agreement, as the same may hereafter be amended, shall cause a termination of the Joint Venture.

The liquidation of the Joint Venture shall be conducted and supervised by a person designated for such purposes by the affirmative vote or consent of Venturers holding a majority of the Venturers' Percentage Interests (the "Liquidating Agent"). The Liquidating Agent hereby is authorized and empowered to execute any and all documents and to take any and all actions necessary or desirable to effectuate the dissolution and liquidation of the Joint Venture in accordance with this Agreement.

Promptly after the termination of the Joint Venture, the Liquidating Agent shall cause to be prepared and furnished to the Venturers a statement setting forth the assets and liabilities of the Joint Venture as of the date of termination. The Liquidating Agent, to the extent practicable, shall liquidate the assets of the Joint Venture as promptly as possible, but in an orderly and businesslike manner so as not to involve undue sacrifice.

The proceeds of sale and all other assets of the Joint Venture shall be applied and distributed in the following order of priority: (a) to the payment of the expenses of liquidation and the debts and liabilities of the Joint Venture, other than debts and liabilities to Venturers; (b) to the payment of debts and liabilities to Venturers; (c) to the setting up of any reserves which the Liquidating Agent may deem necessary or desirable for any contingent or unforeseen liabilities or obligations of the Joint Venture, which reserves shall be paid over to an attorney-at-law admitted to practice in the State of _____ as escrowee, to be held for a period of two years for the purpose of payment of the aforesaid liabilities and obligations, at the expiration of which period the balance of such reserves shall be distributed as hereinafter provided; (d) to the Venturers in proportion to their respective capital accounts until each Venturer has received cash distributions equal to any positive balance in his capital account, in accordance with the rules and requirements of Trea. Reg. Section 1.704-1(b)(2)(ii)(b); and (e) to the Venturers in proportion to the Venturers' Percentage Interests.

If any Venturer has a deficit balance in his capital account following the liquidation of his interest in the Joint Venture, as determined after taking into account all capital account adjustments for the Joint Venture tax year during which such liquidation occurs, such Venturer shall restore the amount of such deficit balance to the Joint Venture by the end of such taxable year (or, if later, within ninety days after the date of such liquidation), which amount shall, upon liquidation of the Joint Venture, be paid to the creditors of the Joint Venture or distributed to the other Venturers in accordance with their positive capital account balances and the rules and requirements of Trea. Reg. Section 1.704-1(b)(2)(ii)(b).

The liquidation shall be complete within the period required by Trea. Reg. Section 1.704-1(b)(2)(ii)(b).

A taking of all or substantially all of the Property by condemnation or eminent domain shall be treated as a sale of the Property upon the dissolution of the Joint Venture. In such event any portion of the Property not so taken shall be sold, and the proceeds of such sale and the award for such taking shall be distributed in the manner provided for in this Article 15.

For purposes of allocating gain on the sale of the Property and other assets of the Joint Venture, gain shall be first allocated to the Venturers to the extent cash or other property was distributed to them pursuant to this Article 15 and the balance of such gain shall be allocated in proportion to the Venturers' Percentage Interests.

16. Representations of Venturers

Each of the Venturers represents, warrants and agrees that the Venturer is acquiring the interest in the Joint Venture for the Venturer's own account for investment purposes only and not with a view to the sale or distribution thereof; the Venturer, if an individual, is over the age of 21; if the Venturer is an organization, such organization is duly organized, validly existing and in good standing under the laws of its state of organization and that it has full power and authority to execute this Agreement and perform its obligations hereunder; the execution and performance of this Agreement by the Venturer does not conflict with, and will not result in any breach of, any law or any order, writ, injunction or decree of any court or governmental authority against or which binds the Venturer, or of any agreement or instrument to which the Venturer is a party; and the Venturer shall not dispose of such interest or any part thereof in any manner which would constitute a violation of the Securities Act of 1933, the Rules and Regulations of the Securities and Exchange Commission, or any applicable laws, rules or regulations of any state or other governmental authorities, as the same may be amended.

17. Notices

All notices, demands, requests or other communications which any of the parties to this Agreement may desire or be required to give hereunder shall be in writing and shall be deemed to have been properly given if sent by Federal Express courier or by registered or certified mail, return receipt requested, with postage prepaid, addressed as follows: (a) if to the Joint Venture, to the Joint Venture at the principal place of business of the Joint Venture heretofore stated or to such other address or addresses as may be designated by the Joint Venture by notice to the Venturers pursuant to this Article 17; and (b) if to any Venturer, to the address of said Venturer first above written, or to such other address as may be designated by said Venturer by notice to the Joint Venture and the other Venturers pursuant to this Article 17.

18. Arbitration

Any dispute, controversy or claim arising out of or in connection with this Agreement or any breach or alleged breach hereof shall, upon the request of any party involved, be submitted to, and settled by, arbitration in the city in which the principal place of business of the Joint Venture is then located, pursuant to the commercial arbitration rules then in effect of the American Arbitration Association (or at any other time or place or under any other form of arbitration mutually acceptable to the parties involved). Any award rendered shall be final and conclusive upon the parties and a judgment thereon may be entered in a court of competent jurisdiction. The expenses of the arbitration shall be borne equally by the parties to the arbitration, provided that each party shall pay for and bear the cost of its own experts, evidence and attorneys' fees, except that in the discretion of the arbitrator any award may include the attorneys' fees of a party if the arbitrator expressly determines that the party against whom such award is entered has caused the dispute, controversy or claim to be submitted to arbitration as a dilatory tactic or in bad faith.

19. Amendments

This Agreement may not be altered, amended, changed, waived or modified in any respect or particular unless the same shall be in writing and agreed to by the affirmative vote or consent of Venturers holding two-thirds of the Venturers' Percentage Interests. No amendment may be made to Articles 6, 8, 12 and 15 hereof, insofar as said Articles apply to the financial interests of the Venturers, except by the vote or consent of all of the Venturers. No amendment of any provision of this Agreement relating to the voting requirements of the Venturers on any specific subject shall be made without the affirmative vote or consent of at least the number or percentage of Venturers required to vote on such subject.

20. Miscellaneous

This Agreement and the rights and liabilities of the parties hereunder shall be governed by and determined in accordance with the laws of the State of _____.

The captions in this Agreement are for convenience only and are not to be considered in construing this Agreement. All pronouns shall be deemed to be the masculine, feminine, neuter, singular or plural as the identity of the person or persons may require. References to a person or persons shall include partnerships, corporations, limited liability companies, unincorporated associations, trusts, estates and other types of entities.

This Agreement, and any amendments hereto may be executed in counterparts all of which taken together shall constitute one agreement.

This Agreement sets forth the entire agreement of the parties hereto with respect to the subject matter hereof.

Subject to the limitations on transferability contained herein, this Agreement shall be binding upon and inure to the benefit of the parties hereto and to their respective heirs, executors, administrators, successors and assigns.

IN WITNESS WHEREOF, the parties hereto have executed this Agreement on the date first above written.

_____
First Party

_____
Second Party

Purchase Agreement– Pro Buyer

AGREEMENT FOR PURCHASE OF REAL ESTATE

AGREEMENT dated this _____day of_____, 20_____ by and between _____ hereinafter "Seller" whose address is _____ and _____ hereinafter "Buyer" (and/or assigns or nominees) whose address is _____ _____.

1. THE PROPERTY. The parties hereby agree that Seller will sell and Buyer will buy the following property, located in and situate in the County of _____, State of _____, known by street and address as _____, more particularly described as follows_____. The sale shall also include all personal property and fixtures, except _____ _____.

Unless specifically excluded, all other items will be included, whether or not affixed to the property or structures. Seller expressly warrants that property, improvements, building or structures, the appliances, roof, plumbing, heating and/or ventilation systems are in good and working order. This clause shall survive closing of title.

2. PURCHASE PRICE. The total purchase price to be paid by Buyer will be $_____ payable as follows:

Earnest money deposit (see below)	$ _____
Owner financing from seller (see below)	$ _____
New loan (see below)	$ _____
Subject to existing loans	$ _____
Cash balance due at closing	$ _____

Said price is subject to appraisal by buyer and/or agent of buyer's choice.

3. EARNEST MONEY. The buyer's earnest money shall be held in escrow by _____. Upon default of this agreement, seller shall retain earnest money as his sole remedy without further recourse between the parties.

4. NEW LOAN. This agreement is contingent upon buyer's ability to obtain a new loan in the amount of $_____. Buyer is not required to accept any loan with interest rate exceeding _____% amortized over _____years or pay any closing costs or points exceeding $_____. Buyer shall provide seller with written proof of a loan commitment on or before_____, 20_____.

5. SELLER FINANCING. Buyer shall execute a promissory note in the amount of $_____. In case of default, recourse shall be against the property

and there shall be no personal recourse against the borrower. As security for performance of the promissory note, buyer shall provide the seller a mortgage, deed of trust, or other customary security agreement which shall be subordinate to a new first mortgage not to exceed $_____.

6. <u>EXISTING LOAN</u>. In the event part of the purchase price is to be satisfied by buyer taking subject to existing financing, buyer shall not be required to show income or creditworthiness to the holder of said mortgage or deed of trust. Seller expressly agrees and understands that buyer is taking the property "subject to" such mortgages or deeds of trust, and is not expressly assuming responsibility for the underlying loans. If the actual loan balance of said loan is less than as stated herein, the purchase price shall be reduced to reflect the difference; if the actual loan balance is more than as stated herein, then buyer's required cash payment shall be reduced accordingly. Seller agrees to waives tax and insurance escrows held by said lender or its/assigns.

7. <u>CLOSING</u>. Closing will held be on or about _____, 20____, at a time and place designated by buyer. Buyer shall choose the escrow, title and/or closing agent. Seller agrees to convey title by a general warranty deed or other customary instrument of transfer.

Buyer shall pay the following closing costs: ☐ title insurance policy ☐ appraisal ☐ certificate of occupancy ☐ property transfer taxes ☐ county recording fees ☐ closing, escrow and delivery charges ☐ survey or ILC ☐ HOA transfer fee. Seller shall pay all other cost and fees.

The following items will be prorated at closing: ☐ Property taxes ☐ Homeowners' association dues ☐ Rents ☐ Other _____

The buyer may extend the closing date an additional THIRTY (30) days by paying the seller $_____in cash. Buyer reserves the right to do a final "walk through" inspection the day of closing.

8. <u>POSSESSION</u>. Seller shall surrender possession to the property in broom-clean condition, and free of all personal items and debris on or before _____, 20_____ ("possession date"). In the event possession is not delivered at closing, buyer shall withhold proceeds from the sale in the amount of $_____ as security. Seller shall be liable for damages in the amount of $_____ per day for each day the property is occupied beyond the possession date. This paragraph shall survive the closing of title.

9. <u>INSPECTION</u>. This agreement is subject to the final inspection and approval of the property by the buyer in writing on or before _____, 20_____.

10. <u>ACCESS</u>. Buyer shall be entitled a key and be entitled to access to show partners, lenders, inspectors and/or contractors prior to closing. Buyer may place an

appropriate sign on the property prior to closing for prospective tenants, contractors and/or assigns.

11. <u>ASSIGNMENT</u>. Prior to closing, purchaser may assign this contract to another party or enter into a contract with a third party to sell this property for more than the contract price offered herein. Purchaser may request a simultaneous second closing of the property with a third party, and utilize funds from said second closing to fund any or all of the purchase of the property under this contract. Purchaser may sell the property to another buyer and profit from the second closing of the property. Seller understands that Purchaser intends to sell the property at the highest price that can be obtained, regardless of the ultimate purchase price under this contract.

ADDITIONAL PROVISIONS:

STATE OF _____,
COUNTY OF _____)ss:

_____   _____
Seller   Date

On _____, 20_____, before me, _____, a notary public in and for said state personally appeared _____,

_____   _____
Seller   Date

_____
personally known to me (or proved to me based upon satisfactory evidence) to be the person(s) whose name(s) are

_____   _____
Buyer   Date

subscribed to the within instrument and acknowledged that (s)he/they executed the same in his/her/their signature on the instrument the person(s) or entity on behalf of which they acted, executed the instrument.

Witness my hand and official seal

_____
NOTARY PUBLIC
My commission expires _____

Memo of Agreement

**AFFIDAVIT AND MEMORANDUM OF
AGREEMENT CONCERNING REAL ESTATE**

State of _____)
County of _____) ss:

BEFORE ME, the undersigned authority, on this day personally appeared _____
_____, who being first duly sworn, deposes and
says that an agreement for the Purchase and Sale of the real property described as
(enter legal description below):

was entered into by and between the undersigned Affiant, as Buyer, and _____
_____, as Seller, on the _____
day of _____, 20_____.
A copy of the agreement for purchase and sale of said real property may
be obtained by contacting _____, whose
mailing address is _____
_____, and whose telephone number is _____.

Dated this _____ day of _____, 20_____.

FURTHER AFFIANT SAYETH NOT.

AFFIANT'S NAME_____

AFFIANT'S SIGNATURE_____

On _____, 20 ___, before me, _____, a notary public in and
for said state personally appeared _____, personally
known to me (or proved to me based upon satisfactory evidence) to be the person(s)
whose name(s) are subscribed to the within instrument and acknowledged that
(s)he/they executed the same in his/her/their signature on the instrument the per-
son(s) or entity on behalf of which they acted, executed the instrument.

Witness my hand and official seal

_____
NOTARY PUBLIC
My commission expires _____   [SEAL]

State Foreclosure Process

State	Process (judicial vs. non-judicial)	Foreclosure Time line (approx. days)	Redemption Period (up to _ days)
Alabama	non-judicial*	60	365
Alaska	non-judicial*	105	365
Arizona	non-judicial*	90+	180
Arkansas	both	70	365
California	non-judicial*	120	365
Colorado	non-judicial*	145	n/a
Connecticut	judicial	60	court determines
Delaware	judicial	190	n/a
Florida	judicial	135	n/a
Georgia	non-judicial*	40	n/a
Hawaii	both	220	n/a
Idaho	non-judicial*	150	365
Illinois	judicial	300	90
Indiana	judicial	260	n/a
Iowa	judicial*	160	20
Kansas	judicial	130	365
Kentucky	judicial	150	365
Louisiana	judicial	180	n/a
Maine	judicial	240	90
Maryland	non-judicial	45	court determines
Massachusetts	non-judicial	75	n/a
Michigan	non-judicial	60	365
Minnesota	non-judicial*	95	180

Mississippi	non-judicial*	90	n/a
Missouri	non-judicial*	60	365
Montana	non-judicial*	150	365
Nebraska	non-judicial	145	n/a
Nevada	non-judicial*	115	n/a
New Hampshire	non-judicial	60	n/a
New Jersey	judicial	270	180
New Mexico	judicial	150	270
New York	judicial	180	n/a
North Carolina	non-judicial*	90	10
North Dakota	judicial	150	180
Ohio	judicial	220	n/a
Oklahoma	judicial*	190	n/a
Oregon	non-judicial*	150	180
Pennsylvania	judicial	270	n/a
Rhode Island	non-judicial	65	n/a
South Carolina	judicial	150	n/a
South Dakota	non-judicial	150	365
Tennessee	non-judicial	45	730
Texas	non-judicial*	30	n/a
Utah	non-judicial	145	court determines
Vermont	judicial	95	365
Virginia	non-judicial*	45	n/a
Washington	non-judicial*	135	n/a
West Virginia	non-judicial	75	n/a
Wisconsin	judicial*	290	365
Wyoming	non-judicial*	60	365

* Indicates a state may occasionally use both processes.
Research your target state for specific guidelines.

Foreclosure Protection Laws

Created June 2006, revised August 28, 2006 and September 6, 2006, July 11, 2007, July 19, 2007, September 12, 2007, October 23, 2007, November 13, 2007, February 4, 2008, March 12, 2008, March 26, 2008, April 2, 2008, April 15, 2008, June 6, 2008, August 11, 2008, and June 24, 2009.

Links to State Legislation Websites for Information on Foreclosure Laws

The links provided below are being provided for educational purposes only and are intended to serve as a resource to assist in finding legislation which might be relevant to conducting foreclosures in states that have passed such laws or are considering enacting such legislation as of June 24, 2009.

This information is not intended to provide a complete resource of states with current or proposed foreclosure laws as such information can change on a daily basis. Nor is this information intended to provide you with any legal advice or detailed guidance on how to properly conduct foreclosure and/or pre-foreclosure activity in your state. As with any regulated activity, we strongly recommend that you consult with an attorney.

Please note that Real Market Masters Education, Inc., to include its affiliates and subsidiaries, do not maintain the sites listed below and as such has no responsibility for the accuracy, content, and current status of any information provided therein. Please note that the locations of these materials can change without notice.

States That Have Passed Legislation

Please note that states with pending legislation are on page 269.

California

California Civil Code § 1695.0-.17 regulates Equity Purchasers. To view click the link below:
http://www.leginfo.ca.gov/cgi- bin/calawquery?codesection=civ&codebody=1695

California Civil Code § 2945.0-.11 regulates Foreclosure Consultants
Effective July 1, 2009, persons acting as a "Foreclosure Consultant" will be required to register with the California Department of Justice. A Foreclosure Consultant will also be required, among other things, to obtain a surety bond in the amount of $100,000.00. The requirements were added as an amendment to the Civil Code section 2945.45. To view, click the link below:
http://www.leginfo.ca.gov/cgi- bin/calawquery?codesection=civ&codebody=1695

Colorado

Senate Bill 06-071 was signed by the governor on May 30, 2006 and went into effect immediately. The enacted Law can be found at the following website:
http://www.michie.com/colorado/lpext.dll?f=templates&fn=main-h.htm&cp=

Once at the website above, click the following folders:
1) Colorado Revised Statutes
2) Title 6 Consumer and Commercial Affairs
3) Fair Trade and Restraint of Trade
4) Article One Consumer Protection Act
5) Part 11 Colorado Foreclosure Protection Act

Delaware

Senate Bill 252 was passed in 2008. The law regulates Foreclosure Consultants and Foreclosure Purchasers who obtain property as a result of a foreclosure reconveyance. To read the law, click the link listed below:
http://delcode.delaware.gov/title6/c024b/index.shtml

District of Columbia

The District of Columbia passed a foreclosure law on January 29, 2008. To see the engrossed version of this bill, click the following link:
http://www.dccouncil.washington.dc.us/images/00001/20071016163558.pdf

Florida

On May 28, 2008, Florida passed House Bill 643. The new law went into effect on October 1, 2008. The law will regulate foreclosure rescue consultants and equity purchasers when reconveying any interest in the foreclosed home to the foreclosed upon homeowner. To view the enrolled bill, click the link below:
http://www.myfloridahouse.gov/Sections/Documents/loaddoc.aspx?FileName=_h 0643er.xml&DocumentType=Bill&BillNumber=0643&Session=2008

Georgia

Georgia Code Ann. § 10-1-393 (b)(20)(A)-(D). The law can be found at the website listed below. Once there, enter 10-1-393 in the search field. Click "Unfair or deceptive practices in consumer transactions unlawful; example," and go to the appropriate section.
http://www.lexis-nexis.com/hottopics/gacode/default.asp

Hawaii

Hawaii passed House Bill 2326 on April 25, 2008. The bill regulates distressed property purchasers and distressed property consultants. To view the bill, click the link below:
http://www.capitol.hawaii.gov/session2008/Bills/HB2326_SD1_.htm

Idaho

House Bill 1431 was signed into law on March 18, 2008. The law provides that all contracts relating to the property entered into while a residential home is in the foreclosure process must be in writing and that consumers have a five day right of rescission. The law went into effect July 1, 2008. To view the law, please click the link listed below.
http://www.legislature.idaho.gov/idstat/Title45/T45CH16.htm

Illinois

Senate Bill 2349 was passed by the Illinois Legislature and became effective January 1, 2007. The enacted statute can be found at the following website:
http://www.ilga.gov/legislation/ilcs/ilcs3.asp?ActID=2795&ChapAct=765%26nb
sp%3BILCS%26nbsp%3B940%2F&ChapterID=62&ChapterName=PROPERTY&Act
Name=Mortgage+Rescue+Fraud+Act%2E

Indiana

Senate Bill 390 was introduced in January 2007. The bill became effective on July 1, 2007. To read the law, click the website listed below:
http://www.in.gov/legislative/ic/code/title24/ar5.5/

Iowa

On April 25, 2008, Iowa passed HF 2653. The bill went into effect upon passage. It regulates foreclosure consultants and foreclosure reconveyances. To view the enrolled bill, click the link below and type "Chapter 714E" in the search field at the top of the page.
http://search.legis.state.ia.us/nxt/gateway.dll/ic?f=templates&fn=default.htm

Maine

On April 15, 2008, Maine passed LD 2189. The law regulates Foreclosure Purchasers, which is defined as a person acting as the acquirer in a foreclosure reconveyance. To view the proposed legislation, click the link below:
http://www.mainelegislature.org/legis/Statutes/32/title32ch80-Bsec0.html

Maine passed LD 503 in 2009. The law requires that a "Foreclosure Negotiator" providing debt management services as they relate to a consumer's residential mortgage loan shall be regulated as a debt management servicer. The law went into effect January 1, 2010. To view the law, click the link below:
http://www.mainelegislature.org/legis/bills/bills_124th/chappdfs/PUBLIC327.pdf

Please note the above law should be read in conjunction with the Title 32, Chapter 80-A: Debt Management Services Act, at the following link:
http://www.mainelegislature.org/legis/statutes/32/title32ch80-Asec0.html

Maryland

Maryland Real Property Code Ann. § 7-301-321
To view the statute, select Maryland Code folder. Select "Real Property" from the folder dropdown. Select Title 7 in the next folder dropdown. Finally select Subtitle 3Protection of Homeowners in Foreclosure.
http://michie.lexisnexis.com/maryland/lpext.dll?f=templates&fn=main-h.htm&cp=

On April 3, 2008, Maryland passed and placed into effect Senate Bill 218 and its companion bill House Bill 361 on an emergency basis. The law regulates Foreclosure Consultants, Foreclosure Purchasers, and Foreclosure Reconveyance. To view the law, click the following link:
http://mlis.state.md.us/2008rs/chapters_noln/Ch_6_hb0361T.pdf

Massachusetts

The Massachusetts Attorney General permanently enacted emergency regulations that will prohibit certain foreclosure transactions and create limitations on certain foreclosure related services.
http://www.mass.gov/?pageID=cagoterminal&L=3&L0=Home&L1=Government&L2=AG's+Regulations&sid=Cago&b=terminalcontent&f=government_940CMR25&csid=Cago

Minnesota

Minnesota Statutes Ann. § 325N.01-.18
http://www.revisor.leg.state.mn.us/data/revisor/statutes/2005/325N/

The Minnesota Foreclosure laws were amended on May 21, 2007. The amended laws went into effect on August 1, 2007. The amendments have not been updated into the web version of the Minnesota statutes. Please go to the following website to see the amendments.
http://www.revisor.leg.state.mn.us/bin/bldbill.php?bill=S1533.3.html&session=ls 85

Missouri

Missouri Ann. Statutes §407.935-.943
To view the statute, enter the section number separated by a dash into the Search field (i.e. 407-935). You are required to view each section separately.
http://www.moga.mo.gov/statutesearch/

Nebraska

Nebraska passed LB 123 on March 10, 2008. The law went into effect on July 18, 2008. To read the final bill, click the link listed below:
http://uniweb.legislature.ne.gov/FloorDocs/Current/PDF/Final/LB123.pdf

Nevada

Assembly Bill 440 was passed and went into effect on October 1, 2007. Go to the link listed below to read. The law pertinent portion of Title 645F is 645F.300- 645F.450.
http://www.leg.state.nv.us/NRS/NRS-645F.html#NRS645FSec300

New Hampshire

New Hampshire House Bill 365 passed and went into effect on July 16, 2007. Click the link below to read the new legislation.
http://www.gencourt.state.nh.us/rsa/html/xlviii/479-b/479-b-mrg.htm

New York

On July 26, 2006, New York enacted Senate Bill 04744-A, which went into effect February 1, 2007. The enacted law can be found by going to the website listed below. Once there, click "Laws of New York" from the "Laws" drop-down menu. Click Real Property (RPP) then Article 8 and scroll down to 265-A.
http://public.leginfo.state.ny.us/menuf.cgi

Oregon

On March 11, 2008, Oregon signed into law House Bill 3630. The law regulates Foreclosure Consultants and Equity Purchasers who reconvey the property to the foreclosed upon owner. The law went into effect upon passage.
http://www.leg.state.or.us/08ss1/measpdf/hb3600.dir/hb3630.en.pdf

Rhode Island

In July 2006, Rhode Island enacted House Bill 7650A and Senate Bill 2777A. The bills took immediate effect. Laws on Foreclosure Consultants are under Chapter 5-79-1 through 5-79-9. Laws on Foreclosure Purchasers are under Chapter 5-80-1 through 5-80-9. Both can be found at the following website:
http://www.rilin.state.ri.us/Statutes/TITLE5/INDEX.HTM

Tennessee

On April 30, 2009, House Bill 2218 was signed into law by the governor. The law went into effect at the time it was signed by the governor. The law regulates Foreclosure Rescue Consultants and foreclosure-related services. To view this law, click the link below:
http://www.capitol.tn.gov/Bills/106/Chapter/PC0198.pdf

Virginia

On March 8, 2008, Virginia enacted House Bill 408. The law amends the Virginia Consumer Protection Act to include regulation of Foreclosure Rescue activities. The law went into effect on July 1, 2008. To view the bill as passed, click the link below.
http://leg1.state.va.us/cgi-bin/legp504.exe?000+cod+59.1-200.1

Washington

On March 31, 2008, Washington passed House Bill 2791. The new law will regulate "Distressed Home Consultants" and "Distressed Home Purchasers." The law went into effect on June 12, 2008. To read the new law, click the link listed below.
http://apps.leg.wa.gov/RCW/default.aspx?cite=61.34

States With Pending Legislation

Arizona

Arizona introduced House Bill 2522 in 2009. The bill would regulate Equity Purchasers and Foreclosure Consultants. The bill would also require an "Equity Purchaser" to be licensed. The bill is pending at this time. To read the bill, click the link listed below:
HB 2522
http://www.azleg.gov/FormatDocument.asp?inDoc=/legtext/49leg/1r/bills/hb2522p
.htm

Georgia

Georgia introduced House Bill 508 in 2009. The bill would regulate Equity Purchasers and Foreclosure Rescue Consultants. To read the proposed law, click the link listed below.
HB 508
http://www.legis.ga.gov/legis/2009_10/fulltext/hb508.htm

Kansas

Kansas introduced Senate Bill 241 in 2009. The bill would regulate Distressed Property Consultants and would require that Distressed Property Consultants be licensed under the Kansas Credit Services Organization Act. To read the proposed law, click the link listed below.
SB 241
http://www.kslegislature.org/bills/2010/241.pdf

New Jersey

New Jersey introduced bills in the Assembly and Senate (Assembly Bill 281 and Senate Bill 1265) in 2008. The bills would regulate Distressed Property Purchasers and Foreclosure Consultants. To read the bills, click the link listed below and type in A281for the Assembly bill and S1265 for the Senate bill in the search field:
http://www.njleg.state.nj.us/bills/BillsByNumber.asp

In 2009, New Jersey introduced bills in the Assembly and Senate regulating Foreclosure Consultants and Distressed Property Purchasers as Debt Adjusters. To read the bills, click the link listed below and type in A3933 for the Assembly bill and S1264 for the Senate bill in the search field:

http://www.njleg.state.nj.us/bills/BillsByNumber.asp
Please note that while new laws were proposed in 2009, the 2008 bills are still eligible for passage.

North Carolina

In 2009, North Carolina proposed legislation in the House (H1060) and in the Senate (S1015). The proposed laws would prohibit certain foreclosure rescue transactions. In addition, the proposed law would regulate Land Installment Contracts. The law would prohibit the seller from placing additional liens, mortgages, or other encumbrances on the property after entering into the land installment contract with the purchaser. To view the proposed laws, click the links below:
SB 1015
http://www.ncleg.net/gascripts/BillLookUp/BillLookUp.pl?Session=2009&BillID=s1015
HB 1060
http://www.ncleg.net/gascripts/BillLookUp/BillLookUp.pl?Session=2009&BillID=H1060

Oregon

In 2009, Oregon introduced House Bill 3359 which proposes to regulate Distressed Home Consultants and Distressed Home Purchasers. To read the bill, click the link below:
HB 3359
http://www.leg.state.or.us/09reg/measpdf/hb3300.dir/hb3359.intro.pdf

Texas

In 2009, Texas proposed Senate Bill 354. The proposed law would regulate Equity Purchasers and Foreclosure Consultants if passed. To view the bill, click the link below:
http://www.capitol.state.tx.us/BillLookup/History.aspx?LegSess=81R&Bill=SB354

Repairs Checklist

Checklist of Repair/ Replacement Items for an Inexpensive Starter Home	Cost of Materials ($)	Labor Hours (rates vary with each task)	Notes
Kitchen			$6k will usually provide an all-new kitchen
Stainless-steel sink with faucet	100	3.5	Chrome
Ceiling light (use same throughout the house)	20	.5	LED nice upgrade for a little more $. Replace fluorescent fixtures if possible
Formica countertop with backsplash (per linear foot)	15	2	Granite about $70 per linear foot installed
Cabinet knobs (for 25)	35	2	Satin nickel
Basic electric range	400–600	2	White; stainless adds $100 Self-cleaning adds $100
Dishwasher (basic model new/nice model used)	350–450	3	Look for scratch & dent to save $ on appliances
Disposal Tile backsplash (per square foot) Range hood	100 10 installed 75	2 1.5	Microwave $250
Bathrooms			
Vanity with faucet	200–300	3.5	For 24 inch, wider costs more
Toilet with seat	150	2	

Towel bar set	50	.5	Satin nickel
Tub surround kit	200–800	3	Higher number is for tile
Mirror	50	1	No need for medicine cabinet
Light fixture	50	.5	For multi-light fixture Avoid bar lights
Bathtub	200	5-8	
Bedrooms			
Closet doors (4-foot unpainted)	65	3	
Ceiling fan with light	100	2	
Door (match existing style)	30	2	
Interior locksets	12	.5	Satin nickel or oil-rubbed bronze
Closet rod & shelf	50	2	
Floor Coverings (professionally installed per square foot)			
Sheet vinyl	2.50	N/A	
Tile (use 12" × 12" neutral colors)	6	N/A	
Carpet (with pad)	2.50	N/A	
Oak plank	2-7	N/A	Refinish vs new
Other Interior Items			
Molding (pre-primed per linear foot)	.50–1	.1	Colonial vs craftsman
Interior eggshell paint (per 5 gallons)	90	8	80 vs 90% efficiency
Furnace	2,500–5,000	N/A	
Water heater	300-400	2-3	
Electric Devices	1	.25	

Exterior Items			
Exterior flat paint (per 5 gallons)	100	8	
Exterior light fixture (brass)	25–50	.5	
Basic single-pane window	175	N/A	
insulated vinyl window	275	N/A	
Window screen	25	.5	
Front door	150–250	3	
Roof shingles (installed) 1,200 square foot ranch	3,000–4,000	N/A	Dimensional shingles are a nice upgrade
Front porch stoop repair (including labor)	200	N/A	
Seamless gutters (installed per linear foot)	3.50	N/A	
Siding (installed per square foot)	2–3	N/A	Masonite
Electric panel	1,200–2,000	1	Depends on code Front door is more
Exterior locksets	50–125		
Landscape Projects			
New sod (installed per square foot)	1	N/A	Overseed instead if possible
Juniper bush/small tree (3–6 feet tall)	40	1	
6-foot privacy fence (per linear foot, 8-foot lengths)	12	N/A	
Organic cedar mulch (delivered per cubic yard)	25–35	.1	Brown vs cedar

Residential Construction Contract

RESIDENTIAL CONSTRUCTION CONTRACT

CONTRACT #: _____

1. **PARTIES:** This agreement is entered into as of the _____ day of _____ 20___ between _____ (the "Owner") whose principle place of business is located at _____; and _____ (the "Contractor") whose principle place of business is located at _____ (who together will be referred to as "Parties") are entering into this Residential Construction Contract (called the "Contract"). The purpose of this Contract is to define the construction activities that the Contractor will perform, and to delineate the general obligations and responsibilities of both of the Parties.

2. **JOBSITE LOCATION:** This Contract is exclusively for work to be performed by Contractor at _____; Owner represents to the Contractor its legal right to authorize improvement work as outlined in Section 10 on the above property.

3. **THE PROJECT:** The term "Project" refers to the total construction at the location outlined in Section 2 of which the Work may be a whole or in part.

4. **THE WORK:** The term "Work" refers to the services and construction outlined in these contract documents, inclusive of all other materials, labor, and equipment needed for the successful completion of the "Project".

5. **START/COMPLETION DATES:** The Contractor shall commence work on portions of the Work which do not require a permit by _____ and shall commence work on all permit-required portions of the Work within 7 days that permits are issued by the local building department. The Contractor commits to the Project's Substantial Completion (as defined in Section 16) by _____.

6. **PROGRESS:** Both parties agree and acknowledge that time is of the essence. By executing this agreement, the Contractor agrees that the construction start and completion dates as prescribed in Section 6 of the Contract are reasonable for completing the Work as outlined in this Contract.

7. **CONTRACT AMOUNT:** The Contractor agrees to perform the Work as outlined in Section 10 and the Owner agrees to pay the Contractor the total aggregate amount of $_____, to be paid to the Contractor as prescribed in Section 9. The "Contract Price" is considered to be a total, lump sum price, and is inclusive of all labor, materials, equipment rentals, delivery fees, relative to the successful completion of the Project. If the Contractor experiences materials or labor cost increases during the prosecution of the Work, the Contractor shall seek no relief from the Owner for such costs. The Contractor shall pay for sales, consumer, use, and similar taxes for the Work provided by the Contractor associated with this Project.

8. **CONTRACTOR ENTITY:** Contractor shall utilize the same entity name which appears on this Contract when pulling permits and the Owner will make all payments as prescribed in Section 9 payable to the same.

9. **PAYMENT TERMS:** Owner affirms that the financial resources exist such that the payment terms as prescribed in this section will be met. Owner agrees to pay the Contractor a down payment, progress payments and a final payment in accordance with the following schedule:

    i. Down Payment: $_____ Due by: _____
    ii. Progress Payment of $ _____ Due upon: _____
    iii. Progress Payment of $ _____ Due upon: _____
    iv. Progress Payment of $ _____ Due upon: _____
    v. Progress Payment of $ _____ Due upon: _____
    vi. Final Payment of $ _____ Due Upon: _____

Page 1 of 6

INITIALS: _____ _____

The Contractor shall submit to the Owner an Application for Payment ("Application") upon completion of each of the stages outlined in this Section. The Owner shall have up to (5) five business days to perform a visual inspection of the work for which the Contractor has submitted the Application, upon which the Owner shall either reject the Application due to non-performance whereby the Owner must supply the Contractor with written objections to the portions of the Work for which the Application was submitted, or, present to the Contractor a Release of Lien applicable to said work. The Owner reserves the right to receive a legally executed and binding Release of Lien from the Contractor when making any and all progress or final payments.

10. **SCOPE OF WORK:** The Contractor is engaged to execute the Work as outlined herein, and the Owner reserves the right to award separate contracts to outside contractors to complete other portions of the Project. Scope of Work shall either be prescribed below, or on a separate sheet of paper attached to the Contract and signed by both Parties clearly identifying it as the Contract's Scope of Work inclusive of date and Jobsite location.

_____
_____
_____
_____
_____

11. **CHANGE ORDERS:** Any modifications, additions or deletions to the Scope of Work desired by either of the Parties must be clearly defined in a separate document and will not be considered valid unless it contains the date of the change order, any cost modifications to the Contract, any changes to the project's completion timelines, and the signatures of both Parties. Owner acknowledges that requested changes to the Scope of Work may result in a delay in Project completion, and the Contractor acknowledges that any costs associated with modifying the Scope of Work without the written approval of the Owner on a change order shall result in forfeiture of the Contractor's right to seek payment for such modifications.

12. **PLANS, DRAWINGS, BLUEPRINTS:** The Contractor shall present to the Owner any such plans, drawings, or blueprints depicting the nature of the Work, and shall obtain the Owner's signature of approval on such documents prior to (a) submitting to the building department for the purposes of securing a building permit, if applicable, and (b) prior to commencing the Work if a building permit is not required. Contractor shall prosecute the Work in strict accordance with such documents.

13. **CONCEALED CONDITIONS:** Should conditions exist at the Jobsite which are (a) subsurface or otherwise concealed physical conditions which differ from the Scope of Work outlined in Section 10 of the Contract, or, (b) unknown physical conditions which the Contractor would have no reason to believe existed, then the Contractor shall immediately notify the Owner of such conditions, and will not commence with any remediation to the discovered conditions, until such time as the Owner has authorized the Contractor to do so, and has agreed in writing to the Contractor's proposed remedy to the concealed condition, as well as any additional costs associated with such remedy should the Owner elect to do so. The Owner retains the right to solicit third party opinions as to the nature of the concealed condition and proposed remedy(s), and may elect to engage third party contractors to address and remedy the concealed condition at the Owner's sole expense. If the Contractor fails to notify the Owner of such concealed conditions, and commences with remedying the issue(s) absent the Owner's written consent, the Contractor shall forfeit any claims for compensation for work associated with same.

14. **RETENTION:** The Owner reserves the right to retain _____% of each progress and final payment until such time as the Work has been 100% completed by the Contractor. 100% completion shall mean all touch-up and cosmetic issues (as outlined in the Owner's Punch List) have been satisfactorily completed by the Contractor.

15. **ADDITIONAL WORK:** In the event that additional labor and or materials are required for completion of the Project beyond the Scope of Work prescribed in Section 10, the Contractor shall supply needed materials at its cost plus _____%, and any hourly labor shall be performed at a rate of $ _____ per man hour, however, the Contractor shall not be compensated by Owner for such extras unless the Owner agrees to the extra work in writing.

16. **SUBSTANTIAL COMPLETION:** Substantial Completion is defined as the phase in construction progress of when the Work, or a portion thereof, is sufficiently complete such that the Owner may either occupy and or utilize the space for its intended use. Cosmetic issues that do not prohibit the space from being utilized as its intended use that are yet to be remedied shall not constitute grounds for the Owner to withhold payments associated with this phase of the Work. All municipal inspections associated with the Work must have been approved by the local building department in order to achieve substantial completion of the Project.

17. **PUNCH LIST:** The Punch List is defined as a written list, created by the Owner, which identifies outstanding cosmetic and associated repairs desired post-Substantial Completion, but prior to Final Completion. The Punch List shall be submitted in writing to the Contractor within seven days upon Substantial Completion of the Work, and the Contractor has five (5) days from receipt to complete Punch List items, or will incur a penalty of $_____ for each day the Punch List is not completed beyond the five-day period. If the Contractor completes the Punch List items prior to the five-day deadline, the Owner shall extend a bonus to the Contractor of $_____ for each day ahead of the deadline. The Owner agrees that once the initial Punch List has been submitted in writing to the Contractor, additional repair items may be added, but shall not constitute grounds for Owner delaying final payment beyond completion of initial Punch List items.

18. **FINAL COMPLETION AND FINAL PAYMENT:** Final completion shall be defined as the phase of the Work where the Contractor has declared the Work and all phases of construction complete. At such time of Final Completion, the Contractor shall submit to the Owner an Application for Final Payment; however the Final Payment amount shall not include any amounts retained under Section 14, which are not considered due to the Contractor until 100% completion of the Punch List.

19. **OWNER'S RIGHT TO CARRY OUT THE WORK:** In the event that the Contractor defaults or neglects to carry out the Work in accordance with the terms of this Contract, the Owner has the right to provide written notice of said default to the Contractor, upon receipt of which the Contractor has a seven day period to correct and remedy such default. If the Contractor fails to commence to remedy the outlined default condition within the seven day period, the Owner reserves the right to engage other outside Contractors to resolve and correct the deficiency(s) and if monies still owed the Contractor are not sufficient to cover such amounts needed to remedy Contractor's deficiency, the Contractor shall pay the difference to the Owner.

20. **INDEPENDENT CONTRACTOR STATUS:** It is agreed and understood that the Contractor shall perform the Work as an Independent Contractor, maintaining his or her own business. As such, the Contractor may elect to use Subcontractors, but shall be solely responsible for supervising their work and for the quality of the work they produce.

21. **SUBCONTRACTORS:** A Subcontractor is defined as a person or entity that has a direct contract with the Contractor to perform a portion of the Work at the site. The Contractor must submit to the Owner, upon request, the names of all Subcontractors that have been engaged by the Contractor to perform a portion of the Work at the site, and the Owner reserves the right to raise a reasonable objection to the use of a particular Subcontractor(s). If the Owner declines a particular Subcontractor(s), then the Contractor shall seek a competent replacement, and the Owner shall be required to bear any additional costs incurred by the Contractor when changing Subcontractors, including price adjustments.

22. **LICENSING:** Contractor warrants possession of all necessary state and or local licensing required for the Work outlined in the Contract; also, Contractor affirms license is valid and in good standing with the entity(s) who issue said license, and that license allows for the Contractor to obtain any building permits required in the execution of the Work. Contractor's state and or local license numbers are as follows: _____ and is listed as the following license type: _____.

23. **INSURANCE REQUIREMENTS:** The Owner will be responsible for purchasing and maintaining the usual Owner's liability policy. The Contractor shall purchase and maintain insurance as will protect the Contractor from claims which may arise out of or as a result from the Contractor's operations in accordance with the execution of the Work prescribed within this Contract. The Contractor shall, at its sole expense, keep in force during all phases and up until final completion of the Work, and shall furnish to the Owner upon request, copies of insurance certificates for the following polices: (a) Statutory Worker's Compensation insurance for anyone employed by the

Contractor working at the Jobsite defined in Section 2, or, must demonstrate that the worker(s) are exempt from Worker's Compensation insurance; (b) All-Risk insurance at least in the amount for the Contract Price as defined in Section 7, naming the Owner as loss payee; (c) Comprehensive General Liability with limits of $ 3,000,000.00 per occurrence for bodily injury, personal injury and property damage. If Commercial General Liability Insurance or other form of aggregate limit is used, either the general aggregate limit shall apply separately to this Project/location or the general aggregate limit shall be twice the required occurrence limit; (d) Automobile liability of $1,000,000.00 per occurrence for bodily injury and property damage; (e) Employer's Liability of $1,000,000.00 per accident for bodily injury or disease; (f) Course of Construction for the completed value of the project with no coinsurance penalty provisions.

24. **INDEMNIFICATION:** To the fullest extent permissible by law and to the extent that losses, damages, claims, or expenses are not covered by insurance purchased by Contractor as prescribed in Section 23 of this Contract, the Contractor shall indemnify and hold harmless the Owner, Owner's employees, and Owner's agents against any claims for property damage, bodily injury, sickness disease or death arising out of or resulting from the Contractor's performance and or execution of the Work.

25. **FINES:** Any fines issued by any municipality, homeowners association, or other legally authorized entity against the jobsite location arising out of or resulting from the execution of the Work, shall be the sole responsibility of the Contractor.

26. **PENALTIES/BONUSES:** Should the Contractor fail to complete the Project in accordance with the Completion date outlined in Section 5 of the Contract, Owner reserves the right to impose a penalty of $ _____ for each day beyond the Completion date that the Project is not wholly 'Substantially Complete' as prescribed in Section 16. The penalty amounts, if any, shall be deducted from the final payment and or retention monies. Additionally, the Owner shall pay to the Contractor an early completion bonus of $ _____ per day for each day ahead of Completion date that the Contractor renders the Project 'Substantially Complete.'

27. **BUILDING PERMITS AND PERMIT FEES:** The Contractor shall apply for and secure any and all required municipal building permits required for the prosecution of the Work by the local building department which has jurisdiction over the Jobsite. The Contractor shall be solely responsible for and bear the costs of any and all building permit fees associated with the successful prosecution of the Work. In the event that the local building department levies any fines associated with failed building inspections, the Contractor shall bear the sole cost of any such fines. The Owner shall be responsible for and pay for necessary approvals, easements, and assessments associated with the Project.

28. **UTILITIES:** Unless prescribed below in the section, the Contractor will at his own expense coordinate and secure sufficient utilities for the Contractor's, and if applicable, the Subcontractor's equipment, machinery, and activities involved in the execution of the Work. The Owner shall provide the following utilities at the Jobsite:

_____

29. **INSTALLED MATERIALS:** All materials supplied and or installed by the Contractor at the Jobsite are required to be in new condition, and must conform to all applicable building codes at either time of permit issuance or installation, whichever is observed by the local building department. Owner does not assume responsibility for any delivered materials until such time of their proper installation in their final and appropriate location, which shall have been documented and signed off by the Owner.

30. **JOBSITE SUPERVISION:** The Contractor shall staff a competent construction superintendent(s) who shall be present during all phase of the Work, and who is authorized to represent the Contractor with matters pertaining to the building department, subcontractors, and the Owner. Contractor shall be exclusively responsible for scheduling any and all municipal building inspections.

31. **CODE COMPLIANCE:** The Contractor shall perform all Work on the Project in accordance with any and all applicable building codes, and any Work or portions thereof shall not be deemed complete until work has been inspected and approved by the local building department, if applicable. Additionally, the Contractor shall be aware of any changes to the standards within building codes in force at the Jobsite, and is solely responsible for any costs associated with modifying Work to conform to said codes and or changes to the codes in order to

satisfy the local building department's requirements. Ignorance of the building codes in force shall not relieve the Contractor of this responsibility.

32. **JOBSITE SAFETY:** The Contractor shall take whatever steps are deemed necessary for compliance with all applicable OSHA regulations, and will bear the entire costs associated with any fines levied by either OSHA or the local building department for any safety violations at the jobsite. The Contractor is solely responsible to ensure the safety of all workers at the Jobsite, and will immediately alert the Owner if conditions exist at the Jobsite which creates a safety hazard that requires the Owner's authorization for remedy.

33. **LEAD BASED PAINT:** In the event that the Work is being conducted on a building constructed prior to 1978, The Contractor shall be required to determine the existence of Lead Based Paint via EPA recognized testing protocols, and certify the results in accordance with EPA guidelines. If Lead Based Paint is deemed to be present, then the Contractor shall not commence with any work unless Contractor is EPA certified for work in such conditions, or the Contractor shall enlist the involvement of a Contractor who possesses such certification.

34. **SITE CONDITIONS:** The Contractor shall be responsible for keeping the Jobsite free from accumulation of debris and waste materials, and shall have all such debris and waste materials contained in a container or designated location. Contractor shall remove from the Jobsite all waste, rubbish, tools, equipment, machinery, and surplus materials associated with the Work at the Contractor's expense. Contractor shall ensure that employees and workers at the jobsite shall observe local ordinances relative to noise, vehicle parking, and shall prohibit the use or possession of illegal drugs, alcohol, and the use of profanity. The Contractor is able to access the Jobsite for the purpose of executing the Work, with the exception of any days of the week or times listed here:

_____

35. **WARRANTIES:** For a period of (1) one-year following Substantial Completion (as defined in Section 16) the Contractor shall upon written notice from the Owner correct any defects in, and if necessary replace any portion of the Work prescribed in the Contract which is found (a) to be less than the accepted industry standard; (b) not in compliance with governing building codes at the time the work was performed; (c) to render the space unusable for its intended use. Unless the Contractor can demonstrate that the work requiring remedy was not the fault of Contractor negligence, the Contractor shall bear the sole costs of all repairs and or replacements for said defects.

36. **LIENS:** The Contractor warrants that title to all Work covered by the Contractor's "Application for Payment" as defined in Section 9 of the Contract, shall pass to the Owner in full at time of payment(s). Additionally, the Contractor attests that all portions of the Work for which the Application seeks payment are, to the best of the Contractor's knowledge, free and clear of all claims and liens in favor of the Contractor, Subcontractor, materials suppliers and or other persons or entities making a claim against the Owner or jobsite for reasons of having supplied any of the following (a) materials; (b) equipment; (c) labor, relating to the Work.

37. **DISPUTE RESOLUTION:** In the event that a dispute arises under the terms of the Contract, the Parties agree to select a mutually agreeable, neutral third party to assist in mediating the dispute. If mediation is deemed unsuccessful, the Parties agree that the dispute shall be directly submitted to binding arbitration under the guidelines set forth by American Arbitration Association.

38. **ATTORNEY FEES:** If either of the Parties employs or otherwise engages an attorney in conjunction with a dispute related to the Contract, the Party who successfully defends or prosecutes such claim(s) or a portion of a claim shall be entitled to receive from the other Party such reasonable and necessary attorneys' fees, arbitration fees, court costs, and expert witness fees and expenses related to the specific claims successfully defended and or prosecuted, subject to applicable laws.

39. **NOTICES:** Any notice or demand ("Notice") given concerning the Contract shall be in writing and is considered effective upon receipt by the addressee, whether the Notice is mailed, delivered, faxed, or delivered via electronic mail. The addresses for potential Notice are defined in Section 1 of the Contract.

40. **TERMINATION OF CONTRACT BY THE CONTRACTOR**: The Contractor may terminate the Contract upon (7) seven-days written Notice to the Owner if the Owner fails to make any payments as prescribed within the Contract.

41. **TERMINATION OF THE CONTRACT BY THE OWNER**: The Owner may terminate the Contract for convenience and without cause at any phase of the Project; however the Owner is required to pay to the Contractor all sums due for portions of the Work completed up to the point of the termination of the Contract.

42. **ENTIRE AGREEMENT**: The Contract, inclusive of any addendums and attachments constitutes the entirety of this agreement between the Owner and the Contractor with respect to the Work to be performed at the Jobsite location defined in Section 2 of the Contract.

EXECUTED this _____ **day of** _____ **, 20_____.**

OWNER:

_____
COMPANY NAME

_____
PRINT NAME

_____
SIGNATURE   TITLE

_____
DATE

CONTRACTOR:

_____
COMPANY NAME

_____
PRINT NAME

_____
SIGNATURE   TITLE

_____
DATE

INITIALS: _____ _____

Scope of Work

SCOPE OF WORK		

DATE : _____ CONTRACT #:_____ CONTRACT DATE: _____

OWNER: _____

CONTRACTOR: _____

JOBSITE LOCATION: _____

Page: _____ of: _____

THE FOLLOWING IS A FINAL LISTING OF THE SCOPE OF WORK, IN ITS ENTIRETY, FOR THE CONTRACTOR TO PROVIDE AND EXECUTE AS PER THE TERMS AND CONDITIONS OF THE CONTRACT REFERENCED ABOVE:

		CONTRACTOR TO FURNISH:	
QTY	Description	LABOR	MATERIALS

By signing below, both parties agree that this Scope of Work represents the entirety of the work to be performed by Contractor and is a binding addendum to the contract as per Section 10 therein. The Contractor agrees that it is not authorized to perform or make any changes to this Scope of Work without the Owner's written and signed consent on a separate Change Order.

OWNER:_____ CONTRACTOR:_____
       PRINT NAME   PRINT NAME

_____ _____
  SIGNATURE   DATE   SIGNATURE   DATE

Stamp Lien Waiver

By endorsement hereon, the payee acknowledges receipt of the amount of this check in full payment and satisfaction for all work performed and/or materials furnished on the premises as described on the face hereof the date shown below, and waives all right to mechanic's and/or materialman's lien thereof.

SIGNATURE REQUIRED IN ONE PLACES

Date _____, 20 _____
X _____

MUST BE ENDORSED BY THE PAYEE IN PERSON, OR IF A CORPO-RATION MUST BE SIGNED BY AN OFFICER GIVING HIS TITLE.

INDEX

ACKNOWLEDGMENTS

We would like to express our gratitude to everyone who helped us take this book from an idea to a completed work. We appreciate all of you who have supported our ideas, including readers of our past publications, students, clients, and our friends and families. We also want to say thanks to our literary agent, Cynthia Zigmund, and to all the people at BenBella Books who have helped us create a text worth reading.

ABOUT THE AUTHORS

William Bronchick is an attorney, active real-estate investor, and co-author of the best-selling real-estate book *Flipping Properties*. He has appeared on many broadcast outlets, including CNBC, Fox, and NBC, and has been featured in publications such as *The Wall Street Journal*, *Investor's Business Daily*, *USA Today*, *TIME* magazine, and dozens more. He is admitted to practice law in New York and Colorado and lives in Denver, Colorado, with his family.

Robert Dahlstrom is an investor, employing broker, and co-author of *Flipping Properties*. He holds a master's degree in business administration (MBA) and a bachelor of science (BS) in accounting. He has served as a marketing consultant for many small businesses and has been mentoring students for more than twenty years. He has been interviewed by radio and print media and is a popular speaker/educator. He has been personally involved in hundreds of transactions and worked with a group that has purchased more than 4,000 foreclosures. Having built houses and duplexes from the ground up, Mr. Dahlstrom is an expert in finding and assessing potential purchases, estimating expenses, and managing the rehab process through to the sale.